THE SUNDAY EPISTLES

RICHARD T. A. MURPHY, O.P., S.T.M., S.S.D.

THE SUNDAY EPISTLES

06546

THE BRUCE PUBLISHING COMPANY
MILWAUKEE

IMPRIMI POTEST:

J. E. MARR, O.P., S.T.M.
Provincial

NIHIL OBSTAT:

JOHN A. SCHULIEN, S.T.D.
Censor librorum

IMPRIMATUR:

✠ WILLIAM E. COUSINS
Archbishop of Milwaukee
July 7, 1961

To

JACK AND KATHLEEN

Library of Congress Catalog Card Number: 61–16516

Foreword

The Church in her wisdom has prescribed that a portion of the Epistles, along with a passage from the Gospels, be read to the faithful each Sunday. This weekly procedure may appear to the puzzled listener as of somewhat dubious value, since about eighty per cent of the Epistles are selected from the writings of St. Paul.[1] The value of these writings as inspired works is not questioned; it is simply that it is often extremely difficult to understand just what St. Paul was trying to say. Nor is the difficulty a new one, for as St. Peter wrote, "In these [Paul's] epistles there are certain things difficult to understand, which the unlearned and the unstable distort, just as they do the rest of the Scriptures, to their own destruction" (2 Pt 3:16).

Paul's impact upon the Church was both great and beneficial. The Church makes extensive use of his Epistles and insists that they be read to the faithful. Her insistence is deserving of attention, because some think that only non-Catholics appreciate the Apostle to the Gentiles. A non-Catholic friend once asked me why it was that in the Catholic Church we "push Peter, but soft-pedal Paul"?

It is true that few sermons are preached upon specific texts drawn from the Pauline Epistles. Yet a ready answer to the first part of the question is the Gospels themselves; in them Peter is mentioned many more times than any other Apostle. He was not the least, nor simply an equal among equals; he was the first of them, the intimate friend of Jesus Christ, the rock upon which the Church was built, and the vicar of Christ. Into Peter's care it was that the lambs and sheep belonging to Jesus were given. Of course Peter is pushed, because Christ pushed him.

But is it true that Catholics soft-pedal Paul? If this means that Catholics choose Paul for reading in preference to the Gospels, a prayer book, or even a light novel, then it must be conceded that they soft-pedal Paul. But the concession must at once be qualified by the observation that

---

[1] Ten of the traditional fourteen Pauline Epistles are used for the Sunday Epistles. Passed over are the two letters to Timothy, the second to the Thessalonians, and Philemon. Of the other seven New Testament Epistles, only 1 Peter, 1 John, and James are used. The Acts are drawn upon only once, on Pentecost.

Catholics hear his Epistles read to them at Mass on Sunday, and can find them — indeed are urged to do so — in their Missals, or Bibles.

But if soft-pedaling Paul is taken to mean that Catholics neglect the teachings of the great Apostle of the Gentiles, then the answer must definitely be a "No!" Not a single detail of Paul's teaching has been overlooked or lost, as can be seen by comparing the ordinary teaching of the Church with the principal themes found in Paul.

Paul's theology was exclusively Christocentric. The name "Christ" appears in his epistles not less than 400 times, and he uses "Lord" 280 and "Jesus" 200 times. Paul dwells lovingly upon the theme of universal salvation; he had perceived that salvation was not an exclusive monopoly of the Chosen People, but was for all of Adam's children. The name "Adam" brings to mind the sin of Adam, the ultimate explanation of the evil found in the world of man and in the cosmos; he treats of original sin in his Epistle to the Romans, and it underlies his whole teaching on sin. An offense against the divine majesty, sin raises the question of justice; Paul takes up the matter of justification at some length. The payment of a heavy debt is not an easy thing; it is in fact impossible when the debt is infinitely above the debtor's capacity to pay it. But God had foreseen sin and had in his wisdom provided a wholly unforeseen solution to that problem — he sent a Second Adam, his only-begotten Son, to save man. Christ is our Savior. Unless the term is an empty one, which it assuredly is not, it must mean that he saved men from something evil; Jesus saved mankind from the everlasting death of sin by his suffering and death upon the cross. He was the perfect Mediator, born of a woman and yet Son of God, standing between the offended deity and the offending race of men, offering satisfaction to the one and pardon to the other. The price of his mediatorship was his death on the cross. But that death and humiliation was not final, as he arose from the dead, glorious and immortal, the pledge of our own resurrection. His resurrection placed the seal of God's approval upon the work he had come to do, and had accomplished; he is truly the Savior and the source of life and grace for all men, a new era. A new life for men has begun.

Jesus' saving work was not a mere historical fact, however important. It was the indispensable means of man's union with God by sanctifying grace. Thanks to this grace, we are no longer children of wrath, but sons of adoption, adoptive sons of God and, if faithful to our vocation, co-heirs with Christ in a blessed and unending life of bliss with God in heaven.

Jesus had said: "I am the vine, you are the branches." He is, Paul will write, the head of a mysterious organism which would later come to be spoken of by theologians as the mystical Body of Christ (note that Paul himself did not use the adjective). Members of this Body live in union with the risen Christ, as the members of a physical body live in union with their head; the same vital life animates them both. A mysterious life begins in us at baptism, when, buried as it were with Christ in the darkness of death, we arise again with him into the light of eternal life; grace is the beginning of eternal life. Incredible as it may seem (we have, however, Jesus' assurance that it is so), to all the baptized and to those living in the state of grace there is given the abiding presence, in the soul, of God himself, Father, Son, and Holy Spirit; not only a created grace, therefore, but the source of grace, the uncreated, living God himself.

During our earthly sojourn, the life of grace is maintained, strengthened, and augmented by our partaking of the Body and Blood of Christ in the Eucharist. A whole array of attractive virtues develops in those who love God, and Paul never tires of recommending these virtues.

All who live united to Christ, eating the food he has provided and imitating him in his virtue, will await with confidence the end of the world, and will face the time of Judgment, when he shall return to judge all mankind, with serenity.

These rapid glimpses of some of the highlights of Paul's teachings suffice to show that the charge of "soft-pedaling Paul" is not well grounded. The teachings of Paul, which were approved by Peter and James and Barnabas, are profound; his keen intellect and temperament made him an articulate spokesman for the new religion, but he was not himself the inventor, or founder, of Christianity. This too should be pointed out, that his letters represent only a limited period in his apostolic ministry, and do not contain the whole of his teaching; nor do they contain all the doctrines taught by that Jesus whose humble servant he was. Paul's writings contain the elements of a theology, or what we might call the ingredients of a system of Christian thought. It was, however, to take centuries before that brilliant genius appeared who first mastered the teachings of tradition and then welded them together into the systematic and all-embracing expression of faith which all the world knows as the *Summa Theologiae.*

Paul, then, is taught in every seminary, perhaps not always explicitly, but, in substance, and faithfully. Nothing he taught has been neglected. The various points of doctrine which he made find their proper place in the picture of the whole. He certainly has more to offer than the single — important though it may be — phrase: "My just man lives by faith." And even that phrase must be taken and explained in such a way as to fit in with what he teaches elsewhere in his letters.

No man can hope to read St. Paul without expending much "blood, sweat and tears." What a pity to deprive oneself, simply because the encounter will be difficult, of the thrill of meeting this colorful personality and making contact with his quick, powerful mind. The best way to read him is to begin with the first epistle he wrote, the letter to the Thessalonians. One can then read the remaining letters in chronological order. Such a procedure has many advantages. It enables the reader to become familiar with the dogmatic or doctrinal part of his epistles, so largely neglected in the selection of the Sunday epistles, and also introduces him to St. Paul's method — one rather widely neglected, one might add — of basing his moral exhortations upon doctrinal considerations.

For those bold souls who, tired of TV, magazines, and newspapers, are brave enough to take up the challenge provided by the reading of St. Paul, two appendices are added to this book, the one giving a short life of the Apostle to the Gentiles, the other arranging the epistles in their proper chronological order. The third appendix shows which chapters have been utilized in the Sunday selections.

Contents

Abbreviations

The Books as they appear in the Bible

Genesis . . . . Gn
Exodus . . . . Ex
Leviticus Lv
Numbers . . . . Nm
Deuteronomy . . . . . . Dt

Josue . . . . Jos
Judges . . . . Jgs
Ruth . . . . Ru
Samuel . . . . . . 1–2 Sm
Kings . . . . 1–2 Kgs
Paralipomenon . . . . 1–2 Par
Esdras . . . . Esd
Nehemiah . . . . . . Neh
Tobias . . . . Tb
Judith . . . . Jdt
Esther . . . . Est

Job . . . . Jb
Psalms . . . . Ps(s)
Proverbs . . . . Prv
Ecclesiastes . . . . . Eccles
 (Qoheleth) . . . . . Qoh
Canticle of Canticles . . . Ct
Wisdom . . . . Wis
Ecclesiasticus . . . . . Ecclus
 (Sirach) . . . . Sir

Isaias . . . . Is
Jeremias . . . . Jer
Lamentations . . . . . Lam
Baruch . . . . Bar
Ezechiel . . . . Ez
Daniel . . . . Dn

Osee . . . . Os
Joel . . . . Jl
Amos . . . . Am
Abdias . . . . Abd
Jonas . . . . Jon
Micheas . . . . Mi
Nahum . . . . Na
Habacuc . . . . Hb
Sophoniah . . . . . . So
Aggeus . . . . Ag
Zachariah . . . . Za
Malachias . . . . . . Mal
Maccabees . . . . . 1–2 Mac

Matthew . . . . . . Mt
Mark . . . . Mk
Luke . . . . Lk
John . . . . Jn
Acts . . . . Acts
Romans . . . . . . Rom
1–2 Corinthians . . . 1–2 Cor
Galatians . . . . . . Gal
Ephesians . . . . . . Eph
Philippians . . . . . Phil
Colossians . . . . . . Col
1–2 Thessalonians . . 1–2 Thes
1–2 Timothy . . . . 1–2 Tm
Titus . . . . Ti
Philemon . . . . . . Phlm
Hebrews . . . . . . Heb
James . . . . Jas
1–2 Peter . . . . . 1–2 Pt
1–2–3 John . . . 1–2–3 Jn
Jude . . . . Jude

Apocalypse . . . . . . Ap

The Books in Alphabetical Order

Abd . . . . Abdias
Acts . . . . Acts
Ag . . . . Aggeus
Am . . . . Amos
Ap . . . . Apocalypse

Bar . . . . Baruch

Ct . . . Canticle of Canticles
Col . . . . Colossians
1–2 Cor . . . 1–2 Corinthians

Dn . . . . Daniel	1–2 Mc . . . . . 1–2 Maccabees
Dt . . . . . . Deuteronomy	Mal . . . . Malachias
	Mk . . . . Mark
Eccles . . . . . . Ecclesiastes	Mt . . . . Matthew
Ecclus . . . . . Ecclesiasticus	Mi . . . . Micheas
Eph . . . . Ephesians	
Esd . . . . Esdras	Na . . . . Nahum
Est . . . . Esther	Neh . . . . Nehemiah
Ex . . . . Exodus	Nm . . . . Numbers
Ez . . . . Ezechiel	
	Os . . . . Osee
Gal . . . . . . Galatians	
Gn . . . . Genesis	1–2 Par . . 1–2 Paralipomenon
	1–2 Pt . . . . . 1–2 Peter
Hb . . . . Habacuc	Phlm . . . . Philemon
Heb . . . . . . Hebrews	Phil . . . . . . Philippians
	Prv . . . . Proverbs
Is . . . . Isaias	Ps(s) . . . . . . Psalms
Jas . . . . James	Qoh . . Qoheleth (Ecclesiastes)
Jb . . . . Job	
Jdt . . . . Judith	Rom . . . . . . Romans
Jer . . . . Jeremias	Ru . . . . Ruth
Jl . . . . Joel	
Jn . . . . John	1–2 Sam . . . . 1–2 Samuel
1–2–3 Jn . . . . 1–2–3 John	Sir . . . Sirach (Ecclesiasticus)
Jon . . . . Jonas	So . . . . . . Sophoniah
Jos . . . . Josue	
Jude . . . . Jude	Tb . . . . Tobias
Jgs . . . . Judges	1–2 Thes . . 1–2 Thessalonians
	1–2 Tm . . . . 1–2 Timothy
3–4 Kgs . . . . . 3–4 Kings	Ti . . . . Titus
Lam . . . . . Lamentations	Wis . . . . . . Wisdom
Lv . . . . Leviticus	
Lk . . . . Luke	Za . . . . Zachariah

THE SUNDAY EPISTLES

Exhortation to Vigilance

INTRODUCTION. The Epistle for the first Sunday in Advent is drawn from the moral or exhortatory part of Romans, and is more or less a conclusion to what might be termed the "duties of a Christian" (12:3–13:14). Having just stressed the need for fraternal charity (13:8–10) Paul enforces his appeal by reference to the End, always for him an excellent reason for loving the brethren.

THE EPISTLE: ROMANS 13:11–14

11 *And this . . . you know what time it is,*
   for now is the hour for you to wake from sleep

The text (11a) is somewhat cryptic, even telegraphic. The reader has to fill in a phrase, as if Paul had written: "And this you ought all the more to observe, because you know the time in which we live." "This" obviously refers to the charity just mentioned (v 10). In what follows Paul switches in midsentence from you to we, from the second person plural to the first. This is typically Paul; he will not be excluded from anything so important as salvation, which is common both to his readers and to himself, and from this point on will not disassociate himself from those to whom he addresses his exhortations.

The concept of "the hour" is basic to Paul's moral teaching (cf 1 Thes 5:6; 1 Cor 7:29; Col 4:5; Eph 5:16), meaning for him not so much the passage of time as an era associated with the last days. This era was inaugurated by Jesus' death and resurrection; it is a reality above and beyond time, and belongs to an order entirely different from and independent of time. It is contrasted to all that went before it less by a simple temporal succession, than by a radical difference of nature. For Paul the life of a Christian, like that of the Church, is essentially eschatological.

Paul urges the Romans to arouse themselves from spiritual sleep or 5:6; Eph 5:14; 1 Cor 7:29).
lethargy, and to be ready to live in the light of the great day (cf 1 Thes

3

11b *For salvation is nearer to us now*
     than when we became believers.

Salvation is a key word in Paul's thought. When he says that it is
nearer, he does not mean that Christ had not yet redeemed mankind,
for that eternally salvific action had already taken place. Salvation is
something both present and future; present because by it we now live
(cf Eph 2:5–8), and future because by it we shall be saved on the
last day from the wrath of God (cf Rom 5:9–10), provided, of course,
that the union with God which it made possible be maintained to the
end. St. Thomas teaches that the life of grace and that of glory are
essentially one, and of the same nature; grace is glory begun, and glory
is grace perfected. Paul uses the word here of complete and final deliverance from sin and death.

When Paul speaks of the proximity of salvation (it is *nearer* to us)
he has final and complete salvation in mind. That moment is *nearer*
for him than it was before his conversion twenty-(two) years before;
it would, however, not do Paul justice to conclude that he looked forward to the End of the World in something less than that length of
time. What he has in mind is the contrast between the period when
he did not believe in Christ, and the present, in which he possesses
the pledge of the Spirit, and salvation "in hope" (8:24); the future
sealing of his union with his savior lies only a few short years ahead.
And this is true for everyone.

12 *The night is far spent*
    the day is at hand

Having spoken of wakening from sleep, Paul gives his reasons for
vigilance and effort — the night is far gone, and one does not sleep in
the day. For a Christian the present time is no longer the night, but
the dawn of a new day in which Christ is the sun (cf Eph 6:14). As
one advances toward eternity, he is more and more bathed in the light
which comes from Christ.

12b *Let us then put off the works of darkness*
     and put on the armor of light.

Evil shuns the light of day and is oftenest done under cover of darkness. But the day turns out to be one of battle, for which one needs not simply the works of light but the arms of light as well. The armor of the Christian is one of Paul's favorite figures (1 Thes 5:8; 2 Cor 6:7; Eph 6:11–17), and by it he means especially the virtues of faith, hope, and charity. Day is not the end but the beginning of a new activity. Paul looks upon it as a time for spiritual combat, but without dwelling upon the idea of battle, he proceeds with his advice.

13 As in the day let us walk with dignity.

Paul often uses the verb *walk* to denote Christian conduct. Having a strong sense of what was proper, he felt that followers of Christ should always behave honorably and decently, and live in a manner befitting the light of day. That darkness was the preferred time for dishonorable behavior the Romans well knew; Nero himself, in disguise, used to prowl about the less respectable sections of the city at night. Christians should avoid the nocturnal adventures of pagans, and should live honorable lives.

13b Not in feastings and drunkenness
not in debauchery and wantonness
not in quarreling and jealousy.

The vices are listed in such a way that the second of each pair follows from the first (a kind of *hendiadys*, i.e., a thing is said twice using different words). At the end of many Roman banquets, which were the preliminary and excuse for drunkenness, bands of roaring drunks staggered through the streets seeking to indulge their shameless lust, and this in turn led to scenes of quarreling and jealousy. Pagan vices such as these shun the light. With its high moral code and the difficult obligations it imposes upon fallen man, Christianity replaces the sinister night of pagan immorality.

This verse is justly famous because of its connection with St. Augustine's conversion. While torn by doubts and hesitations, he heard a child crying out in the streets: "Take and read, take and read!" Opening the New Testament, his eye fell upon Paul's admonition: "Not in feastings and drunkenness, etc." As Augustine wrote, his hesitations vanished. "In that very instant, with the very ending of the sentence, it was as though a light of utter confidence shone in all my heart, and all the darkness of uncertainty vanished away" (*Confessions*, VIII, xii). He became a Christian.

14 **But put on the Lord Jesus Christ,**
    and make no provision for the flesh
    to gratify its desires.

As a robe of clothing is put on, Christ is *put on* by baptism (cf Gal 3:27). The figure of speech is not original with Paul (cf Jb 29:14; Ps 131[132]:9) but he exploits it to the full (cf Col 3:9–10; Eph 4:24; Rom 6:3–11). To put on Christ, who is the light, is to live in his spirit, yielding more and more to his influence, striving for perfection. As a result of such striving one becomes progressively detached from the flesh and its cravings.

Paul here considers the *flesh* as the seat of evil desires, as human nature dominated by sin. As a result of original sin, human nature is a wounded (but not a corrupt) nature. The intellect has been darkened, the will is attracted by evil, and the body or flesh is in almost constant rebellion against the spirit (cf 7:14–21) and clamors for attention and gratification. Paul is not opposed to a moderate care of the body, because thus the body can the better serve the spirit (cf 1 Tim. 5:23; Eph 5:29).

THE PAROUSIA

Attempts have often been made on the basis of Paul's words here (the day is at hand . . .), to prove that he thought that the end of the world, Judgment Day, was imminent, a matter of a few short weeks or years (salvation is nearer . . .). It is likewise urged that Jesus himself was in error on this point (cf Mk 13:29ff, loc. par.). Neither conclusion does justice to either man.

It is a basic rule that one passage of the Sacred Scriptures cannot contradict another, as both are equally inspired by the Holy Spirit and thus equally safeguarded from error, when rightly understood. Jesus in his parables of the kingdom had spoken of the leaven in the mass, of the seed that grows together with the cockle until the time of harvest, etc., all of which would obviously take much time. Similarly, Paul had written to the Thessalonians (1, 4:13ff) concerning the Second Coming of Jesus, but in his second letter made it clear to them that the event was far off: first would come the apostasy of many, then the appearance of the Man of Sin, and only then would Jesus come (2, 2:1–8). He had written thus in the year 51; Romans was written seven years later, in 58; and in 13:11, Paul could not have so completely forgotten what he had just written about the conversion of the nations and the return of the Jews as a body (11:25), both of which events would and still do demand a considerable length of time.

Giving Paul credit for consistency it must be said that he did not teach that the Second Coming of Christ, Presence (= Parousia) was at hand. He did *not* say that it was *close*, but that it was *closer* than before; he says that it has already begun (Eph 2:5,8), but it is also still to come in a perfect form (Rom 5:9; 2 Tim 4:18) and that Jesus himself will come (Phil 3:20; Heb 9:28).

Thus neither Paul nor his Master, Jesus (Mt 24:36), was deceived as to the end. As Jesus laid supreme emphasis on the immediate recognition of the love of the Father and was primarily concerned with preaching the coming of the Kingdom of God, and its *present* enjoyment by his children, questions of chronology were on the periphery of his attention. Paul also indicated that the final salvation which the coming of Jesus as Judge would usher in was already a glowing, wonderful reality. Christians live in the *day* of grace; there is in that kind of day no place for calendars or clocks.

Hints for Homiletics

1. In Paul's day the term *parousia* was commonly used to describe the coming or arrival of an emperor, a king, governor, or famous person, and even of the visitation of a god. *The Christian is one who awaits his king.* To have nothing to strive for or look forward to makes life sheer boredom. But there is an atmosphere of tension, of eager expectation in the Church; Christians prepare for their king by leading blameless lives, bearing wrongs patiently until he comes and rights them. There is always room for further preparation. The purple vestments at Mass remind us of penance, and of royalty.

2. The *Jehovah's Witnesses* make capital of the doctrine concerning the End, as do the *Seventh Day Adventists*. We should not leave the true doctrine concerning the End and the Coming to cranks. "This

alone the truth sometimes craves — not to be condemned unheard." Cf. St. Thomas' teaching in the *Supplement*, q. 73.

3. The life of grace is salvation begun. Salvation is something present and real, but it must be constantly maintained. Advent is a time to put off the bad habits which caused us so much grief during the past year. It is a time to practice temperance, purity, charity toward others.

Charity in Action

INTRODUCTION. Romans 14–15 should be read at one sitting, as there is no break in thought between the two chapters, and chapter 15 merely continues the exhortation begun in 14. Paul explains how the *strong* should react toward the weak. The weak were not a troublesome party or sect in the church at Rome, but timid souls assailed by doubts as to how they should act in matters of religion. Judging from the text, their scruples revolved around questions about foods, feast days (= the Sabbath?), and the use of wine (14:2,5,15,21). In dealing with this "case" Paul shows the strong but sympathetic side of his nature. The principle involved is not one of eating, but of a doubtful conscience. Paul does not believe in adopting the pagan attitude of allowing every man to lead his own life only for himself, and on a natural level; the Christian should live for the Lord (14:7), but while avoiding evil he must exercise a compassionate loving charity toward others who find it difficult to put their new faith into practice with a calm inward assurance that they are doing right. Christians cannot, should not avoid those of their brethren who have difficulties (they are the weak), but should help them, following the example of Jesus who "did not seek his own gratification" (15:3) but the good of souls. Concern for others is one of Paul's favorite themes (cf Gal 6:2; 1 Cor 13:4,7; 10:33); by it both the troubled individual and the community profit from charity in action.

In this connection, the condemnation of Baius (Denz 1201), on the strength of a literal translation of Rom 14:23, held that all the actions of pagans were sinful because they did not proceed "*ex fide*," from faith, comes to mind. But Paul speaks to Christians and of Christians, and in the context "faith" has the special nuance of "faith as regulating the decisions of conscience." For Paul, conscience is a practical guide for human acts, and it is never licit to act with a doubtful conscience.

THE EPISTLE: ROMANS 15:4–13

4 *For whatever was written in former times*
was written for our instruction

9

*that through patience and the consolation of the Scriptures
we might have hope.*

Paul has already stressed the importance of the Scriptures (4:23, cp 2 Tim 3:16) and shows how practical they are in helping the Christian maintain his equanimity and courage when confronted with the minor annoyances of life. While unpleasant, such irritations need not be an obstacle to the attainment of glory; sufferings and the trials of life help one grow in patience and hope. The Scriptures abound with examples, encouraging and comforting to us, of holy men who suffered much, but whose trials are seen to have been preludes to a great reward (cf the stories of Abraham, Jacob, Moses, Job, Jeremiah, etc; Ps 93[94]:19; 1 Pt 1:11). God's purpose in giving us the Scriptures was to sustain us *in hope.* He would not encourage us if he had no intention of fulfilling our hopes.

5 *May the God of patience and of comfort
grant you to be of one mind toward one another
according to Christ Jesus.*

The teaching of the Old Testament (v 4) and Christ's own example (v 3) should encourage all to live in perfect harmony. To be completely successful in our endeavors toward unity we need God's help. He has patience and comfort to bestow, and is the ever-flowing source of constancy and courage for those who strive to be united to him inwardly, to see things as he sees them (to have the mind of Christ — 1 Cor 2:16). In not seeking to please himself, Jesus had disposed of the chief obstacle to harmony. His followers should learn this lesson.

6 *So that together with one voice
you may glorify the God and Father
of our Lord Jesus Christ.*

The very commonness of the believers' worship and prayer should reflect and flow from a common acceptance of the truths of Christianity. This union of mind and heart results from prayer; it is a gift from above. Paul prays as the Master did at the Last Supper, asking that this union may prevail despite minor differences arising from relatively unimportant matters (cf Introduction). Paul refers to God as the God of the human nature which was united to the person of the Son, and as the Father of him who from all eternity was his own very Son (cf Jerome in loc., P.L. 26:446).

7 *Therefore welcome one another*
   even as Christ has welcomed you
   for the glory of God.

This verse develops the idea "according to Christ Jesus" (v 5). Paul has urged that oneness of mind should lead to the glory of God, and now, putting the "vegetarian controversy" (14:1–2) to one side, he urges the example of Christ as a reason for practicing charity. The Romans must co-operate with divine grace, and work at acquiring harmony of mind. To this end they should *take unto themselves* or *welcome* each other. (*Proslambanesthai* means to receive or accept someone into one's home, family, or circle; in classical Greek the term was used of an ally, a fellow worker, or a partner.) One so welcomed does not enter as a stranger in the midst of strangers, but as a member of a family into a family. Those inside the Church should welcome others as Christ (God) has welcomed them, and those who are so welcomed must be ready to work as allies and helpers in the work of Jesus, all for the glory of God.

Here as the horizon widens upon that marvelous union of opposite elements which is wrought by Christ; local controversies and vexations fade into nonexistence.

8 *For I tell you that Christ became a servant of the circumcision*
   on account of God's truth,
   to confirm the promises made unto the fathers,

Jesus came to minister to and to serve his own nation, the Jews (here named "the circumcision" by metonymy). He was sent to fulfill the promises made to the patriarchs, to Moses, and to the prophets. God's truthfulness or fidelity to his given word is therefore proved; when he makes a promise he keeps it (cf Mt 20:28; 15:24).

9 *And that the Gentiles glorify God on account of his mercy.*

In contrast to the economy of the promise, is the economy of mercy. In the case of the Jews salvation was, as it were, demanded by the covenant struck between God and his people, but the Gentiles had not been given the promise of a Messias or of any share in Israel's messianic hopes. The Gentiles are to the Jews as strangers are to sons, as ingrafted branches to the original stalk (cf 11:17ff; Eph 2:2); and yet they are called to enjoy the same glory as the chosen sons, for God's mercy — which redounds to his glory in the end — envelops them too.

Although the Jews had the promises, they had no strict *rights* upon God but were also the objects of his mercy, and although the Gentiles "came in" later, room had already been made for them in the Jewish prophecies. True Judaism was to extend a hand to all nations, and so Christ had instructed the Apostles (Go, teach all nations). The texts St. Paul now cites all convey this general idea (cf v 4 above) and indicate how deeply Paul had pondered the Old Testament in relation to his mission to the Gentiles, who are here pictured in attitudes of praise, joy, and hope, in relation to God.

9b *And it is written, Therefore I will praise thee among*
    the Gentiles and will sing to thy name (Ps 17[18]:49).

In the psalm David promises God that he will praise him amid the nations conquered by force of his arms. But David is a figure of Christ, who thus proclaims that he will praise God amid the Gentiles. This supposes that he is placed in their midst, like a cantor who intones the chant, and that all, even the Gentiles, echo his voice.

10 *And again (the Scripture) says:*
    Rejoice O Gentiles with his people (Dt 32:43),

11 *And again: Praise the Lord all you Gentiles,*
    sing his praises, all you peoples (Ps 116[117]:1).

Again the theme of praise directed toward God. This psalm is the universal *alleluia* (= Praise the Lord!), or the *alleluia* of redeemed humanity. Both Jew and Gentile are to praise the Lord; both are to share in the kingdom.

12 *And again Isaias says:*
    The root of Jesse shall come,
    he who rises to rule the Gentiles:
    in him shall the Gentiles hope (Is 11:10).

Isaias pictures the Messias, a descendant of David the son of Jesse, as rising up like a standard or banner for the peoples who make their way toward him. The nations are pictured, not as praising, but as hoping in him, which supposes that they know his plans — plans of pure mercy (cf v 8) — for their salvation. It is understood that God will satisfy the hope that he so deliberately raises.

13 *May the God of hope fill you with all the joy and peace in*
    believing, so that by the power of the Holy Spirit you
    may abound in hope.

Having used the word *hope* in the citation from Isaias, Paul begins his closing exhortation with that word. One becomes conscious of a kind of semitic rhythm here, and the words bring together the chief ideas of the letter. Belief leads to joy and peace, delicious foretastes of future happiness. There is reason then for them to hope, more — to abound in hope. God is at once the source and the object of hope; he can both arouse it, and satisfy it.

HINTS FOR HOMILETICS

1. Some people have conscience enough to rent out — to others. With admirable large-mindedness, St. Paul urges those whose religious practice knows no torturing concern, to respect the conscience of others. Putting up with others is not a very thrilling experience, but then what is pleasant to us may not be pleasing to God.

2. Patience (= *hupomone*) is a manly virtue, almost always coupled with faith, or hope, or charity and joy. The word describes the ability (of a plant) to survive in difficult circumstances. Used of men it conveys the idea of spiritual staying power, of constancy under trial. Far from being mere dumb resignation, it bespeaks the endurance of trials with a holy joy, with a song of praise for God upon one's lips. Patience is the root and guardian of all virtues (cf *Sum. Theol.* 2–2, q. 136, a. 2).

3. Advent is the season of hope. Hope concerns the motion toward a good whose attainment is difficult but possible. In the natural order hope is involved in all spheres of human activity and is especially exemplified in the world of sport: baseball, golf, etc. In the spiritual order hope is directed toward a spiritual good — God himself. Natural hope

for material things is often frustrated, but supernatural hope for spiritual and eternal goods has the best possible guarantees of success: God's infinite power, his infinite mercy, and his promises to help! Paul's hope, the very foundation of his life, was boundless; it was based on God. He never stopped to wring his hands or to lament his lot. One can almost hear him saying that a quitter never really knows whether he would have won the contest or not.

III ADVENT — GAUDETE SUNDAY

Peace and Joy in the Lord

INTRODUCTION. Philippi was a Roman colony in Macedonia, and was the first place Paul preached in Europe (Acts 16:12ff). This letter reveals the unexpectedly affectionate and tender side of Paul's nature. When the Philippians learned that he had been imprisoned, possibly somewhere near the subsequent ports of call during his second missionary journey, they hastened to send a messenger to him with money and the assurance of their prayers. Paul sends the courier, Epaphroditus, back with a letter filled with expressions of his loving gratitude and, to be sure, repeated exhortations to rejoice with him in the Lord.

THE EPISTLE: PHILIPPIANS 4:4–7

4 *Rejoice in the Lord always,*
again I will say it, rejoice!

As Paul conceived it, joy is the fundamental note of Christianity (3:1). In this short letter he ten times urges the Philippians to rejoice as he himself does, in the Lord. Paul was not a man given to incurable and exaggerated optimism, but he knew his strength; it was not founded upon a material but on a spiritual foundation. He was therefore able to sustain even imprisonment with equanimity. Startling by way of contrast to Paul's reactions to being a prisoner, chained day and night to a Roman soldier, are those of Ovid and Cicero. Paul did not whine; they filled the air, and paper, with self-pitying laments.

5 *Let your gentleness be known to all men.*

Spiritual joy does not ordinarily manifest itself publicly, but inwardly. It is normally accompanied by such likable qualities as goodness, prayer, and an abiding peace of mind, along with a vivid interest in all that is true, just, and worthy. But Paul sees beyond this to everyman's obligation to live among men, and to act as the leaven toward them; he urges the Philippians to be a good example to their world. The Vulgate translation of *epieikes* as modesty does not do the word justice. The word evokes the notions of forbearance, leniency, gentleness, kindness, obligingness, affability. Usually translated as equity, *epieikes* is a certain just (*congruous*) moderation of a particular law, in instances in which the law may be reasonably interpreted as not applying. Aristotle speaks of *epieichia* as something which is just and at times better than justice, and Paul too implies that there are greater things than the demanding exaction of one's rights. Considering the circumstances under which he wrote, this was astonishing advice, and must have impressed the Philippians deeply.

5b The Lord is nigh

It has been argued that St. Paul shared the eschatological enthusiasm of the first Christians, who looked for a speedy coming of the Lord as judge of the world. Yet the present context contains nothing about the End. It is quite possible that like *Marana tha* (1 Cor 16:22) and *Lord Jesus, come* (Ap 22:20), the phrase *The Lord is nigh* might have been a prayerful ejaculation of the early Church. The particular judgment of any man is never very far distant, and the certainty of this proximate salvation, so certain despite the delay of the Parousia, helps the Christian acquire the obliging attitude which Paul has just recommended. It is always true to say, as the Psalmist does, "The Lord is near to all who call upon him" (Ps 144[145]:18; cf 33[34]:19).

6 Have no anxiety, but in everything
by prayer and supplication with thanksgiving
let your requests be made known to God

The believer who looks upon divine Providence as much more than a mental abstraction will keep his concern for the future under control, committing it with confidence to God's capable hands. Prayer is the universal remedy for all our troubles, especially if it is confident and persevering and accompanied by a sense of deep gratitude. God has given many things to his children without their asking, but there are some things which he gives only when they ask for them in prayer.

7 And the peace of God, which surpasses all understanding,
will keep your hearts and your minds in Christ Jesus.

The peace of God is that peace in which he resides, into which his privileged friends may enter, and which he can dispense at will. It cannot be attained by mere human effort, but prayer can obtain it for us. Joy and peace are the bulwark of the mind against a wicked world. At peace with God, the believer's heart (= will) will remain fixed upon the pursuit of the good, and his mind upon what is true. — This verse is used as the conclusion of all sermons in the Missouri (Lutheran) Synod and in many if not all churches of the Wisconsin Synod.

HINTS FOR HOMILETICS

1. Coming events cast their shadows before. Advent serves to remind us that Christmas is not far off. And while Advent is a period of serious preparation (in former times it was one of penance as well), the Church thoughtfully prepares us for the joyful coming of the Savior.

2. Christian joy is the true sign of one who loves God. Its basis is not in material things, but in the awareness that one is united to God, bears witness to him and thus glorifies him. A sad saint is a sorry saint (Francis de Sales); our faces are the mirror of our souls and our silent eyes reveal the secrets of our heart (Jerome). With great perception, Leon Bloy once wrote: "Joy is the most infallible sign of the presence of God."

3. Our faces are the only books some people will ever read. Good people ought to be able to look pleasant without thereby looking vapid and fatuous. Nietzsche scoffed at the grim, sad faces of the Christians of his times: "Are these unhappy looking people your redeemed Christians?" He had a point.

IV ADVENT

What Is an Apostle?

INTRODUCTION. Paul's attempt to preach to the Athenians in words of human wisdom (cf Acts 17:22–32) had not been notably successful, and shortly thereafter he had left Athens for Corinth, where he met with a Jewish family, Aquila and Priscilla, exiled from Rome by the edict of the Emperor Claudius (A.D. 49). He stayed with these new friends for a year and a half, plying his trade as a tent-maker and preaching whenever he could (Acts 18:4,11). He had learned a lesson from his sermon on the Areopagus, however, and preached to the people of busy, wicked Corinth, not with lofty eloquence or learning, not in high-sounding or learned phrases, but "in the showing forth of the Spirit and of power" (1 Cor 2:1–4). "The Jews demand signs and the Greeks search after learning, but we preach a crucified Christ — a stumbling-block to the Jews and folly to the Gentiles. . . . But what is foolish with God is wiser than men, and what is weak with God is stronger than men" (ibid., 1:22–25).

After eighteen months in Corinth Paul made his way to Jerusalem (for the fourth time after his conversion) via Ephesus, then returned to Antioch. Shortly after he had left Corinth, an eloquent man, powerful in the Scriptures — his name was Apollo — arrived there to water the seed Paul had planted. It was not long before the Christians in that city were divided into rival camps, one favoring Paul, another Peter, a third Apollo, and a fourth, Christ. Greatly distressed at this turn of events, Paul took great pains (1 Cor 1–4) to clarify for the Corinthians the true meaning and importance of being an apostle of Christ. The Christian ministry has never been given a more glowing description as, in words of rare humility, Paul unfolds before his readers some basic truths about the men who carry on Jesus' work in this world.

THE EPISTLE: 1 COR 4:1–5

1 As ministers of Christ, then,
      and stewards of the mysteries of God,
      so let men account us.

The Apostles are hyperetas. The Greek word from which this is

18

derived refers to the rowers on the lower level of an ancient ship of war (cf trireme). From this meaning it is an easy step to that of a subordinate or servant (*minister* = one who stands at the hand of another in order to serve him). All who serve the Lord must therefore pull together, as the rowers in a galley; whatever their capabilities, it is Christ's ship that they move by their efforts, and he sits at the helm steering the ship.

Paul, Apollo, Kephas, and all Apostles are *stewards*. . . . The *oikonomos* (from which we have our word *economy*) was the administrator of his master's goods. The Apostles were all men of this sort, "in service" together. Their doctrine is not proper to themselves; they are not complete masters in its distribution, but servants co-operating with the master of God's house. While themselves working they direct others in the use of the master's goods, in this case *the mysteries of God*.

The term *mystery* is familiar to many through the fifteen mysteries of the Rosary. The word has a long history, and originally (ca first century b.c.) signified *a secret full of wisdom*. The many mystery religions flourishing among the pagans testified to man's inner longing to be united with his god. Some of the mysteries became famous, as for example, the Eleusinian mysteries, those of Ceres, Orpheus, Isis, Osiris, Mithras, etc. The mysteries consisted in a secret teaching mostly religious but sometimes political in nature, which was concealed beneath strange customs and ceremonies. The adepts or *mystae* were required to swear that they would never reveal what was revealed to them, and they have kept their promise well. It is possible however to say that these "religions" provided an outlook on life, on the origin and destiny of the human soul, an assurance of fertility, of happiness, of union with the deity, salvation (cf "Orphism and the New Testament," CBQ, VIII (1946), 36–51).

Paul took the word *mystery*, which was already known to him from Daniel 2:18–19, deepened its meaning, and applied it to God's plan of salvation. He used the word 21 times. It meant, for him, all the treasures of doctrine and of life which God had revealed to man after centuries of silence (cf Rom 16:25; 1 Cor 2:7,10; Eph 3:10; Col 2:2–3; 1:26). Now in its ultimate stage, it includes the death of Christ, the call of the Gentiles, the restoration of all things to God through Christ who is the Head; it includes also the sacraments, through which union with Christ is established and maintained.

The Council of Trent has seen in this verse an assertion of the Church's power to modify, by reason of circumstances, the accidental features of the sacraments. Thus the use of leavened or unleavened bread, reception of Communion under one species, etc. (cf Denz 931), is different in various parts of the world.

2 What is looked for in stewards, here below, is that a man prove trustworthy.

In handling his master's goods, a good steward is motivated principally by his master's best interests. He should be a dedicated man, with little thought of self. The very fact that Apostles are called upon to be dispensers of the divine mysteries makes of their calling a noble ministry; they are in truth "men of God" doing great things worthy of praise, but not for praise.

Paul here declares himself to be — not an innovator, and still less the true founder of Christianity (cf Gal 2:2; 1 Cor 11:23) but — a depositary of a doctrine which neither he nor any other has a right to modify in any of its essentials.

3 For to me it is a very small matter to be put on trial by you or by man's day.

Almost rudely, as bluntly as the situation demanded, Paul declared that he is not too deeply concerned about his own reputation among the Corinthians, whether good or bad. On the Day of the Lord he shall be judged at his proper worth by the Lord himself; in comparison with that ordeal, or moment of exaltation, the decisions handed down by man's day — the court of human opinion — mean nothing to him. He will not alter his course because of wagging tongues. But just the same, he makes it clear that he is not claiming to be perfect.

3b But I do not put myself on trial

4 For I am not conscious of anything against myself, but I am not thereby acquitted. It is the Lord who judges me.

That "no man is a good judge in his own case" is the sound view of sensible men. Paul concedes that he may not be blameless in his apostolic activities, but at least his conscience is clear. If he should have done better, the Lord will one day make that clear.

5 Therefore pass no judgments before the time,
   before the Lord comes, who will bring to light
   things hidden in darkness,
   and will disclose the motives of our hearts.
   And then each man will receive his commendation from God.

If Paul with all his apostolic graces, special revelations, and clear conscience, will not judge himself or others, the Corinthians should avoid any rash or precipitous judgment of others. The matter in hand is extremely serious, since criticism of the Apostles may have repercussions in the realm of faith. Far better to await the end-time (= kairos), when the Lord will disclose all things, and mete out the rewards or punishments which men have earned by their deeds.

HINTS FOR HOMILETICS

1. The Quartal Times (Quatre Temps) are the times set aside for ordinations to major orders, and that fact undoubtedly influenced the choice of this passage for the fourth Sunday in Advent. Priests are God's chosen instruments, selected with divine care for the particular needs of each age. Criticism of priests sets a bad tone in the parish. No priest claims to be perfect; God will judge him. Look upon the priest with the eyes of faith, and be grateful that you have this dispenser of the mysteries and riches of God in your midst.

2. No other passage in Paul's writings contains a loftier or more moving contrast between the wisdom of the world and the folly of the cross (cf 1 Cor 1:23ff). Here for the first time we have a theological expression of genuine Christian mysticism.

3. Priests should occasionally point out the loftiness and excellence of the truths of the faith which are their reason for being. Contrasts with modern substitute religions (lodges, countryclubs, etc.) will help. The laity can hardly be blamed for not appreciating the faith if they never hear the priest express his appreciation and admiration for it. Moreover, members of the laity must themselves carry the good tidings of salvation to their own little worlds.

CHRISTMAS — First Mass

In Praise of Divine Grace

INTRODUCTION. Today's Epistle might well be called the song of divine grace, or "In Praise of the Incarnation." It is remarkable that the Christian message can be so neatly summed up in these few majestic lines. In selecting this passage for the first of the Christmas Masses, the liturgy focuses attention upon the divine nature of the child who is born for us.

THE EPISTLE: TITUS 2:11-15

11 *For the grace of God has appeared,*
   bringing salvation to all men.

The important word here is "appeared" (= *epiphane*). Formerly it was used of the visible manifestation, either in person or by a show of power (i.e., healing, etc.), of a hidden divinity; in the New Testament the word is used only of Jesus' appearing upon earth (cf 2 Tim 1:10). Grace is used here in a wide sense, and includes both the "gift itself" (Christ) and "grace" as we usually understand it. Paul puts the effect for the cause; Jesus has made divine grace manifest by His incarnation. Grace is always something gratuitously given; here it stands for a truly princely largess, the coming of a Savior who shall bring about the salvation of all men, for "God wishes all men to be saved and to come to a knowledge of the truth" (1 Tim 2:4).

12 *Instructing us to renounce impiety and worldly lusts,*
   and to live temperately, justly, and piously,
   in the present world.

Although God has taken the sublime initiative by sending his Son as the Savior, salvation requires something on man's part as well. Those who profess to follow the Savior must show in their lives their desire and willingness to be saved. They will be men and women of penance, of faith, of justice (Paul mentions three of the four moral virtues here, omitting courage, but what he demands of Christians calls for a generous amount of that virtue). They must be lovers of truth, fearful of offend-

22

ing God, eager for grace and not unwilling to suffer with Jesus, their great high priest and heavenly intercessor. The present time of sin and misery will eventually come to an end; meanwhile, the Incarnation assures all men that they can be saved from all that can harm their souls in this life and in the hereafter.

13 *Awaiting the blessed hope and manifestation of the glory*
of our great God and Savior, Christ Jesus.

Christianity is characterized by a state of eager expectancy. A sort of tension prompts Jesus' followers to keep looking beyond the present life to Christ, who will inaugurate a glorious, eternal era. The text is a striking one, being a clear affirmation of the divinity of Jesus Christ, whom Paul here identifies as our great God and Savior (cp Rom 9:5). The Fathers used this text extensively in their controversies with the Arians.

14 *Who gave himself for us,*
that he might redeem us from all iniquity,
and might purify a chosen people, zealous for good works.

This verse contains three important words: to redeem (*lutroun*), to purify (*katharizein*), and chosen (*periousios*). The first word, to redeem, is used for buying back, or redemption, for the settling of a debt, and for the price paid by a slave for his freedom. Slaves sometimes acquired money and entrusted it to the priests of a temple. When they had saved up enough for their freedom, the priests paid the money to the slave's master, and the slave thus acquired his freedom. But he would then "belong to" the god. The Christian development of this idea is breathtaking. Christ has come to liberate men who are not only enslaved but are utterly incapable of doing anything about it. He is the great Liberator, the rescuer, the payer of the ransom. To whom did he pay the price — his life — of our liberation? Not to the devil, for God never delivered the world over to him, but to God the Father. The price of restoration to God's graces must have been paid to the only One who could restore man to that favor — the offended God Himself.

The second word, to cleanse or purify, is one of the richest and most complex words in the New Testament; it is used 24 times. Besides its ordinary meaning of cleansing from dirt, and healing, the word has a religious and moral signification, the general idea of which is: something clean, pure, free from guilt or pollution, unblemished, unmixed, genuine, unalloyed, true.

The third word of importance is the one translated as "chosen." Jesus came to save men (Paul includes himself here by saying "us") by his voluntary sacrifice. By that sacrifice he has delivered the redeemed from sin and has adopted them ("us") as his Chosen People. One can imagine how deeply thrilled Paul was by the work of his Master; the Church is the new Israel (cp Ex 19:5)! The people of the New Covenant are redeemed and cleansed and sealed by the blood of Christ. They shall be eager to perform works worthy of their new status. What these works are Paul has spelled out in 2:1–10.

15 *Thus speak and exhort and rebuke with all authority.*
   Let no man despise you.

Titus was bishop on the island of Crete (1:5). He had been a faithful companion to Paul on his travels, accompanying Paul and Barnabas to the Council at Jerusalem, and three times acting as Paul's envoy to Corinth. His further activities are known to us only from 3:12 and 2 Tim 4:10. Paul admonishes his protégé to teach without ceasing the sound doctrine just sketched out. And Titus should do so without fear and with authority. Possibly Titus had some misgivings as to his abilities and needed this reassurance. The Church on Crete may have been founded early, and some of the community might have resented this youthful bishop, in which case his mission there demanded a great deal of courage as well as tact.

HINTS FOR HOMILETICS

1. Only spiritual truths can insure the proper enjoyment of material things, including such things as Christmas gifts. Christ is the great Gift, wholly undeserved but utterly precious.

2. Jesus is the Savior . . . not from financial problems, or sickness, living conditions, etc., but from something infinitely more important — from spiritual death. Let us rejoice that such a Savior has chosen us to be his people, and act accordingly.

Divine Riches for Men

INTRODUCTION. St. Paul never tired of counseling his readers to strive for perfection, to practice the various virtues. Even in the short letter to Titus he recommends obedience to authority, the doing of good, tolerance, gentleness, and meekness, virtues which properly distinguish the Christian from the pagan. Before Christ's coming the world was a darksome place, wherein men were dull, foolish, disobedient, without fixed principles, slaves of various passions and pleasures, filled with malice and envy, hated by others and returning that hate with interest (Ti 3:13; cf the parallels: Rom 6:17ff; 1 Cor 6:9–11; Col 3:7–8; Eph 2:3–10). Titus is to remind his people to "be ready for every good work" (cf 3:1; 1:16); Paul gives profound, basic doctrinal reasons for so acting.

THE EPISTLE: TITUS 3:4-7

4 *But when the goodness and kindness*
    of God our Savior appeared . . .

The theme of divine mercy is resumed from 2:11–14 (1st Mass on Christmas), and the passage is well chosen for the dawn-Mass at Christmas. When the Incarnation became a reality, the dark world of paganism was suddenly illumined by astonishing evidence of God's goodness and kindness. The text reads: ". . . of our Savior God." God is the supreme cause of man's salvation. As this is an action of God which takes place outside the Trinity, it is a work common to all three divine Persons. Salvation is appropriated to the Father, Redemption to the Son, and Sanctification to the Holy Spirit.

5 *He saved us, not in virtue of works of justice performed*
    by us, but out of his mercy,
    with the bath of regeneration and renewal by the Holy Spirit.

Moved only by his mercy, God has saved us. This divine benevolence is absolutely necessary to us, for as Christ said: "Without Me you can do nothing." Without grace, no man can do anything pleasing to God

25

and deserving of supernatural reward; neither the buildings of houses or cities, nor the gaining of financial, military, or any other kind of victory, not even almsgiving, can give him any right to that first grace whereby he is justified, that is, is made "just" or holy. Only God, who dispenses his graces where he wills, can justify a man.

Regeneration or palingenesis means also a rebirth; we are spiritually reborn in the ceremonial bath of regeneration or baptism (cf Jn 3:3–8), where we put off the "old man" and are renewed inwardly. Justification is not therefore something extrinsic to us (e.g., a label) but an intrinsic change brought about by the Holy Spirit, the Sanctifier.

6   *Whom he poured out upon us richly,*
      through Jesus Christ our savior . . .

With these words, St. Paul has in three verses made mention of all three Persons of the Trinity. The imagery is vivid: the Holy Spirit is as a liquid poured out (cf Rom 5:5): Paul can seldom speak of the workings of God without using the adjective "richly," as he does here. The Holy Spirit is given richly, together with sanctifying grace, the infused virtues, and the gifts. In the early Church, various charismata sometimes accompanied baptism. The Holy Spirit is the Sanctifier (cf Col 3:10), but this Spirit is poured out upon us through Jesus Christ, whom the Father had sent as Savior.

7   *So that, justified by his grace,*
      we might become heirs, in hope,
      of everlasting life.

Neatly then, Paul summarizes the effects of baptism. They are: a new birth, justification by the grace of Christ, the giving of the Holy Spirit, and a right to the possession of eternal life. Once the Spirit enters the soul of the just man, that man is the possessor of the first fruits or pledge of an eternal life (cp 2 Cor. 1:22; 5:5; Rom 8:11; 8:23–25; Eph 2:14) which will surely be consummated. He is heir to heaven and already possesses it, in hope.

Hints for Homiletics

1. God's most attractive attribute is his mercy. It is present in all he does, and in all that Christ did while on earth. It is not, however a

false mercy. God is not moved to save us from any kind of misery — to have no trials in life can ruin us — but from the most harmful (and spiritual) kinds.

2. The Incarnation is the dawn of a new era, the great changing point in human history. The world has never been the same since God's Son walked the earth as man. Everything about Christ enriches us. Like good salesmen we should share these riches with others, without waiting to be asked about them. Many are dissatisfied with their present spiritual life, because it seems so threadbare, etc. A deeper knowledge of the great mysteries reveals the thrilling riches of God's goodness. St. Paul here tells Titus (v 8): What I say is sound. I want you to emphasize these things. Believers will thus strive the more zealously to do good.

3. The flattering attention which the Trinity lavishes upon all who are baptized should arouse a correspondingly warm response of gratitude, reverence, adoration.

The Grandeur of Christ

INTRODUCTION. The Epistle to the Hebrews does not have the usual salutation, like 1 John, but it does have the usual conclusion (13:18–25). It was written for the beleaguered Jewish-Christians in Jerusalem about A.D. 66–68. The style is unlike Paul's (124 words are used in it which are not found elsewhere in Paul's writings), and some have thought that a scribe or secretary or even Apollos used Paul's ideas in writing it.

Without introductory remarks of any kind, the author sets out to show the incomparable superiority of the New Law over the Old. One might sum up the argument of the whole letter in two words: "Quanto magis!" that is, if the Old Law, its priesthood and its sacrifices were so glorious, *how much the more* glorious is everything in the New Law.

THE EPISTLE: HEBREWS: 1:1–4

1 *God, who spoke of old to the fathers through the prophets*
in many and various ways,
2 *in these last days has spoken to us by one who is Son,*
whom he has appointed as heir of all things,
by whom also he created the ages.

The elegance of this introductory sentence is reminiscent of the first words of the Fourth Gospel. But whereas John spoke thereafter in terms of light and darkness, Paul pursues the theme of expiation, and emphasizes the imperfect nature of the former revelations. These were fragmentary (= *polumeros*) in character. Moses had his insights, David had others, Isaias lifted the veil a bit further and told of the expiatory sufferings of the Messias, while Daniel spoke of his glory. But these at best were mere scraps of knowledge, compared to what was to come.

Many and various (= *polutropos*) were the ways in which God manifested himself of old. Dreams and visions, visitations of angels, heavenly voices, prophetic utterances, the Urim and Thummim, lots for Azazel, etc., were used, but all these were incomplete and obscure. Moreover, the last prophet, Malachias, had been dead for centuries, and no voice of prophecy had been heard in the land since his time.

When the time of expectation finally came to an end, there was one single and glorious communication from God through the mouth of Jesus. With his coming the last days (= the messianic era) were inaugurated. From the moment of his Incarnation (2:8), Jesus had as a Son's right, the entire earth as his heritage. All the good things promised for the messianic era were his. In contrast to the obscure whisperings of the prophets and the mysterious language of symbols and figures, the luminous figure of Jesus stands before mankind, his rights assumed by divine favor in consequence of his divine sonship.

All the creative energies by which life and action have been or will be produced, flow from the Son. He is the creator of the ages, i.e., of the world. The text says ". . . by whom also he [God] created." The Word was not God's instrument in the creation of the world, but rather the exemplary cause of all things. The activity of God ad extra is common to all three divine Persons, inasmuch as such activity proceeds from the one divine Nature which is equally shared by all three Persons.

3 He, being the reflection of his [God's] glory
     and the very expression of his being,
     sustains all things by his powerful word.

The two brilliant metaphors used here are probably traceable to the Alexandrian teaching (Wis 7:25f) concerning Wisdom and the Logos, and are marvelously fitted to express the identity of nature existing between the two distinct Persons, the Father and the Son.

First, Christ is to the Father, who dwells in inaccessible light, as rays of light are to the sun. Inseparable from the Father, he is the faithful reflection (other synonyms for apaugasma are: flashing forth, emanation, effulgence, brilliance, éclat, and brightness) of the Father's glory. Where there is glory there is light, and light must naturally and necessarily produce rays of light. Just so, the Fathers were quick to point out, Jesus, of the same spiritual nature (= consubstantial) as the Father and equal to him in all things, is eternally generated by the Father, even before the creation of all things. The Council of Nice in A.D. 325 made use of this fine image in professing its belief in Jesus Christ, who is "light from light, true God from true God" (Denz 54).

Besides this, Jesus is the faithful image, perfect resemblance, and adequate expression of the Father. He is, therefore, equal to him. Paul declares that he, Jesus, is the very expression, imprint, stamp, seal (= charakter tes hypostaseos autou). The term "charakter" conveys the idea of an impression made by a stamp or seal upon wax. An impression thus made is the exact expression of the seal, is produced by the seal, but is distinct from it. Paul thus clarifies his opening remarks; Jesus is consubstantial and coeternal with the Father, but far from being a mere modality of his Father, is separate and distinct from him and subsistent in himself.

God's Word, then, the exemplary cause of all created beings and, with the Father and Holy Spirit the creator of the world, shares with them in his human nature in the continuous government of that world, conserves, directs, and harmonizes the universe (cf Col 1:15–18). As the Father created all things through him, so by the Father's power (a "word of power" is a "powerful word," a command capable of effecting whatsoever the speaker wills), he now upholds the universe.

**3b When he had made purification from sins,
        he took his seat at the right hand of the Majesty on high.**

These words mark a transition to the historic fact of the Incarnation, and introduce the expiatory mission of Jesus, which is the theme of the whole letter. After Jesus had effected the expiation (= rubbing out, cleansing by rubbing) of man's sins, he took his rightful place at the right hand of God ("Majesty" is another way of saying: God). The right side is the side of honor (cf Gn 48:17–19; 2 Kgs 2:19). To sit in the place of honor in God's own presence and in the heavenly court (= on high) indicates equality with God, for one does not otherwise sit in the presence of such a superior. Seated in honor close to his Father, Jesus is the channel of his authority, the fountain of his mercy, the mediator between him and his chosen people. His being seated does not mean that he is inactive.

**4 Having become so much superior to the angels
        as the name he has inherited is more excellent than theirs.**

Angels played a great part in the old dispensation, and Paul now begins a studied antithesis between the Son's position and that of the angels (1:4–2:18). Pre-existent and divine (1:3), the Son, "became superior to the angels" in his human nature, that is, he won this present exaltation and glory by his obedience to the Father (Phil 2:9). He is, therefore, superior to the angels and they recognize this fact by their homage.

A series of quotations set forth in rabbinic fashion now illustrates this general affirmation of the Son's superiority over the angels. The texts are seven in number. The first two regard Christ directly, the next two, the angels, and the remaining three, the dignity of Christ.

1. Psalm 2:7 (= Heb. 1:5a) has always been recognized as an important messianic text, but its import is not exhausted by its original reference to David. Jesus is truly God's Son.

2. 2 Sam 7:14 (= 1:5b) tells of God's promise to David that he shall have a son. That son Solomon, was a figure of the Messias to come. God would adopt Solomon as his son; Jesus is the natural Son of God.

3. Dt 32:43 (= 1:6) are the concluding words of the canticle of Moses as recorded in the LXX. The nations are urged, along with the "sons of God" (= angels), to worship the Lord. The application of these words to Christ imply his equality with God (cf Ps 96[97]: 7).

4. Psalm 103[104]:4 (= 1:7) brings out the fact that the angels are by their very nature only ministers of God, swiftly carrying out his orders. Where men see only material objects, there God is present, fulfilling his will through his servants under the forms of the wind and fire (cf 12:18–29).

5. Psalm 44[45]:6–7 (= 1:8–9) describes the Son's office: he is God, king, by nature and by virtue and, having received the festive anointing amid solemn joy, is exalted above all the elect.

6. Psalm 101[102]:25–27 (= 1:10–12) sings of the divine attributes of the Lord. Paul attributes creative power, eternity, immutability, and omnipotence to Christ.

7. Psalm 109[110]:1 (= 1:13 — not read in the Epistle of this Mass, however) is a favorite messianic text (cited 20 times in the New Testament, telling of the triumph of Christ (cp Jos 10:22–25 for the image).

HINTS FOR HOMILETICS

1. The reading of Newman's "Omnipotence in Bonds" makes an excellent preparation for the feast of Christmas.

2. The Child in the manger is not a mere baby, but one as inseparable from divinity as light is from the sun. Ordinarily men take care of babies; this one takes care of us. He is perfect God, greater even than the angels who sang at his birth.

3. Everything in the Church speaks to us of the Son of God, even the candles, whose flame reminds us that Jesus is the splendor of the Father.

SUNDAY WITHIN THE CHRISTMAS OCTAVE

The Liberty of Sons

INTRODUCTION. It was a worried Paul who wrote the letter to the Galatians in the year 57. He began it with an unusual abruptness, hurrying into the body of the letter without his usual thanksgiving for graces received. The Galatians, it seems, were beset by Judaizers who were upsetting the recently established Christian community, belittling Paul and trying to re-establish the Mosaic Law as a way of life. In his vigorous rebuttal Paul formulates the thesis that as justification (= sanctification) is by faith and not by the Law, a return to the observance of the Law would be a denial of Christ; it would also be to overlook the incomparable superiority of the New Law.

THE EPISTLE: GALATIANS 4:1-7

1 *Now I say [this]:*
   as long as the heir is a minor,
   although he is the owner of the estate,
   he is in no way better than a slave,
2   *but is under guardians and stewards,*
   until the time appointed by his father.

The Romans considered a child as an infant until he reached his seventh year, when he was taken from the care of his mother and entrusted to a slave called a pedagogue. Paul has just finished comparing the Law to a pedagogue (3:24f). The duty of a pedagogue, not a teacher in our sense of the word, was to accompany his charge to school each day, to see that he got there safely, and to superintend his conduct. He was, in short, a combination of nurse, footman, chaperone, and tutor. His relationship to his charge was that of an invalid to his health: he has to follow the disease wherever it leads, being unable to cure it, and spends his life in perpetual anxiety with no time for anything else (Republic 406a). The pedagogue had the lofty mission of making the good pleasant to the boy, so that the child would eventually be independent of his care. This independence generally coincided with the age of

33

puberty, set by law as 14–16 for boys, 12 for girls (a father, of course, might otherwise determine the time). At that time the boy for the first time put on the *toga virilis*.

Not only did the child have a pedagogue to watch over his going and coming to school, but legal guardians (= *epitropoi*) and administrators (= *oikonomoi*) also attended to his person and his goods. As long as the child remained in his minority, this situation continued. Although he was the true master of his goods, he could not dispose of them nor appear in court as long as he was a minor. He was, therefore, except for his hopes of coming into his inheritance at some future date, little better off than a slave.

The comparison is fairly obvious. The Law was a transitory thing. Under its regime, the members of the Chosen Race were for all intents and purposes nothing but slaves, and would remain so until the day appointed by God for release. For Paul, there was no question when this release took place — it was when Christ, by completing and fulfilling it, abrogated the Old Law.

3 *So we too, when we were minors,*
   were enslaved under the elements of the world.

Before the coming of Christ, the lot of the Jews was, then, the lot of mankind. They were enslaved under the elements of the world, and so were in no position to profit from the promises. By "element" (= *stoicheia* cf 4:3,9; Col. 2:8,20) the Stoics understood the four basic elements of earth, air, fire, and water. The word was also used of the letters of the *alphabet*, the abc's basic to all learning. Given a moral twist, the word indicates the most elementary kind of religious teaching, and this, in Paul's mind, described the Old Law to perfection. It was anchored to the earth in a visible, external world. Its promises were largely of a temporal order, its feasts were conditioned by the course of nature (cf 4:10), and its laws were based more on fear than upon spontaneous love. In short, notwithstanding its divine origin, the Law was imperfect and of a rudimentary character, something fitted for an earlier (younger) stage of history. The multiple prohibitions of the Scribes and Pharisees show all too well how easily that kind of teaching could become a slavery.

4 *But when the fulness of time came,*
   God sent his Son, born of a woman, born under the Law.

The fullness (= *pleroma*) of time was no matter of whim or caprice. The time which God had fixed for the termination of the minority of the human race arrived exactly as planned, not one second ahead of time nor a single second late. Paul here explicitly states that God has a Son; there is in God, therefore, at least a duality of persons. This Son pre-existed from all eternity, and is now sent forth from God (= *exapesteilen*) as a divine representative, detached, as it were, from the bosom on the Father.

The pre-existing Son of God was "made of a woman," i.e., he took upon himself our human nature. (The Greek word *genomenon* used here is practically synonymous with *gennomenon* [born]. Paul used "made" in preference to "born" because birth implies a transition from nonbeing to being. From this point of view the Son who pre-exists with the Father is more properly said to *become* man than to be born such. The later Arian and Nestorian heretics would exaggerate the meaning of "made.")

Some commentators feel that in mentioning "a woman" here, Paul discreetly alludes to the virginal conception of Christ. This is possible, but not very probable, for so stereotyped a phrase (cf Mt 11:11; Job 14:1) means here only that the pre-existent Son has invested himself with a new mode of being.

To this supreme condescension on God's part was added still another; the Son of God was also born under the yoke of the Law, a Hebrew of the Hebrews.

5 *In order that he might ransom them that were under the Law,*
   that we might receive the adoption as sons.

Two great benefits accrued to the human race as a result of Christ's incarnation and submission to the Law. The first of these was his payment of our ransom (*exagorase*), the second, our adoption as sons. Paul uses this latter expression here for the first time, but he will return to it again and again (Rom 8:15–17,23; 9:4; Eph 1:5). God has only the one natural Son, but (Paul again switches to "we" as he would not exclude himself from so marvelous a privilege) many adopted sons, another way of saying that sanctification introduces one into the intimacy of God's own life. Holiness is not a tag or label, an external declaration or act; it is a real transformation by grace which makes the adopted one like unto the natural Son of God.

6   *And because you are sons,*
  God has sent forth the Spirit of his Son into our hearts,
  crying, "Abba! Father!"

To prove the reality of our adoption God has sent the Spirit of his Son. The Father sends the Spirit, who is distinct from himself. Moreover, the Spirit is the Spirit of the Son. The Holy Spirit must then proceed from both Father and Son (cf Jn 15:26). The sending of the Holy Spirit coincides, actually, with our being adopted as sons, and cries out, earnestly and importunately (in Rom 8:15, we cry out), Father, Father! a cry which is ours also because it finds an echo in our hearts, and, by uniting us to him in the same prayer, shows that we are also sons! (Lagrange, *Ep. aux Galates*, p. 104).

Abba, Pater, are the Aramaic and Greek words for "Father," and our English word *abbot* derives from *Abba.* The people of Galatia stood, as it were, with one foot in Judaism, the other in the Greek world. The joining of two words like this in prayer (cp Mk 14:36) is therefore understandable.

7   *So through God you are no longer a slave but a son,*
  and if a son, an heir also.

Note the successive changes in the mode of address. Paul uses "we" in v 5, "you" in v 6, and now the intimate "you" (2nd pl. sing.) in v 7, where it marks the transition from a national to an individual outlook in matters of religion. Every Christian now has toward God a tenderness and intimacy which correspond to the relations existing between ordinary children and their fathers.

By Roman law all members in the family received equal shares in the inheritance. That law, then, supplies a better illustration of the privileges of the Christian than did the Jewish law, according to which the first-born acquired the lion's share of the property, etc., and the daughters received nothing unless there were no male heir.

All this wealth of the Christian comes to him through the kindness of God; accidents of birth or personal merits have nothing to do with it. God's adopted children enter into their inheritance even now without being burdened by the obligations of the Old Law. Only conduct incompatible with their dignity as God's sons can exclude them from the eternal enjoyment of that inheritance together with Christ (Rom 8:17).

HINTS FOR HOMILETICS

1. The differences between human and divine adoption help bring out the marvels of God's generosity. Cf Farrell, *Companion to the Summa,* IV, p. 125, for an excellent treatment of our adoptive sonship.

2. In the spiritual life there is a time of infancy, a time of youth, and one of maturity. Great gifts of grace can be given outright by God, others are prepared for by us through the practice of the virtues. It is a much more perfect thing, St. Thomas writes (*Sum. Theol.* 2–2, q. 157, a. 4), to attain or acquire a good, *than merely to be lacking in evil.*

3. The state has the right to impose discipline upon its subjects. Parents have also an obligation to guide, and if necessary to insist that their children develop good habits of the natural and supernatural order.

Life in the New Age

INTRODUCTION. Paul bases the moral part of his Epistle to the Romans (12:1-5) upon the doctrine he has just so laboriously exposed. The Christian is a social being. His life cannot be that of an isolated unit; he must live in constant contact with others who are sinners and saints, sharing with them both responsibilities and blessings. Unlike Luther, whose "protest" was and remained strongly individualistic, Paul desired that all who were animated by faith in Christ should be closely united one to another in a larger unity, the community, the living Church.

THE EPISTLE: ROMANS 12:1-5

1 *I exhort you, therefore, brethren,*
by the mercies of God.

"I exhort you" is neither a simple prayer nor a command, but the earnest recommendation of one who has authority but does not make a great issue of that fact. Those whom he addresses are his brethren in Christ, who had like himself benefited by the abundant mercies of God (cf 11:30–32). In words reminiscent of *Ephesians* 5:1f, Paul urges them to give themselves entirely to God, to imitate him and to do his will.

1b *To present your bodies a living sacrifice, holy,*
well-pleasing to God, your spiritual worship.

Whether involved in virtuous or sinful actions, the body is the visible expression of the soul, the sensible instrument of the will. Its various postures and gestures, folded hands pointed heavenward or bended knee, reveal the fervor of the soul and the soul's yearning for God. Paul uses the language of sacrifice to denote a spiritual reality.

In offering his body as a sacrifice, the Christian offers himself wholly to God; to be able to do so is the highest privilege of his new life. The animal sacrifices of the old regime are now things of the past; the Christian must offer himself as a living and holy victim. As the life that is in him now is a divine life, Christ's life, this sacrifice will be of infinitely greater worth than that of the dead victims of old. Moreover, only this type of sacrifice will henceforward be pleasing to God.

So to act is spiritual or reasonable service, or worship, a *logiken latreian*. There is no question here of an intellectual assent to revealed truth solely on the authority of the one revealing, but rather reference to morally good actions performed in the Lord's service. By putting his body in God's service in the performance of holy actions, and making his whole life a "liturgy," the Christian renders to God the worship his reason demands that he offer him.

2   Be not conformed to this world but be transformed by renewing of your mind.

This imperfect world is filled with evil influences and the ever-present occasions for sin. For a Christian to model himself (*schema* = a "figure," or something external, passing, and superficial) on this fleeting world and its changing fashions and tastes, its modes of thought and action, would be to renounce what is solid and eternal, to grasp at shadows rather than at the substance (cf 1 Cor 7:31).

Be transformed (from *morphe* = "form"), i.e., be truly changed, inwardly. The verb indicates a transformation that goes deep, a real changing of the inward man that will lead to a more perfect life. Growth and increase in perfection are normally to be expected in life. So too, the Christian's spiritual renovation must be a reality constantly renewed and growing. By assimilating more and more the thoughts and views of Jesus Christ (8,9ff; Eph 4:23), the believer becomes daily more and more like his Master.

2b   So that you prove what is the will of God, what is good, well-pleasing, and perfect

God's will is the supreme norm of our actions and leads us to discern and to welcome what is (note the progression from *good* to *better* and *best*) good, well-pleasing, and perfect.

The inhabitants of a particular part of a land may all speak the same language, but in voice and accent no two men are ever exactly alike. So it is with the Christian's converse with God. God will speak to him in many ways and by particular graces and inspirations (Jn 14:21). "The earnest practice of religion makes a man an ark of the covenant, containing the secrets of God, a place where God perpetuates his presence and his teaching" (Blondel). Yet however personal and intimate this contact with God may be, the Christian cannot live in isolation; as a member of Christ's Body he is united to all who are members of that Body.

These verses express a profound truth, that there can be no divorce between the believer's worship of God (*cultus*) and his moral life. The victim God asks of everyman is himself. The sacrifice consists in his following the will of God in whatsoever way it may be revealed to him. It would be a gross exaggeration of Paul's meaning to conclude that a Christian who is led by the will of God does not therefore need to obey any law or to practice his religion in his outward life. St. Paul does not here deny what he has affirmed elsewhere concerning obedience to lawful authority; rather, his words here provide mysticism with a sound foundation. He suggests that there is room for an instinctive and experimental knowledge of God, but stresses the necessity of positive law and the guidance of one's spiritual pastor.

3   For by the grace which has been given me
      I say to each one of you
      not to think more of himself than he ought to think,
      but to judge himself with moderation, each according to
      the measure of faith which God has assigned him.

On the strength of his apostolic authority and with an unusual play on words, Paul urges each of the Romans to evaluate himself and his apostolic activities properly, and to act according to his place in the community. A man's judgment of himself and his work is to be "according to the measure of faith" God has apportioned him. Paul might well have said "in accordance with the charisms, or gifts." But he wished to bring out the relations between the charisms and the faith; faith is the necessary foundation for the gifts. The faith to which Paul refers is the charismatic gift, a certain plenitude of confident faith which is capable of performing supernatural acts (cp 1 Cor 12:9; 13:2; and Rom 12:6ff). No one should become proud or arrogant because of such a gift.

4 *For as in our one body we have many members,*
  and all the members have not the same function,
5   *even so we many are one body in Christ,*
  and members each of the other.

The idea of the community as the body of Christ is introduced here because the qualities just recommended (2–3) are social in their implications (cf 1 Cor 12:12–31; Eph 4:15; Col 1:18). Just as the various members of the body need and assist one another, so too, those with different gifts should work humbly together, thus assuring the harmony and co-ordination of the whole. The idea is one of mutual dependence (cf 1 Cor 12:12–31 for a somewhat different emphasis).

HINTS FOR HOMILETICS

1. In Christian sacrifice, our will is the priest, our body the victim, our heart the altar, contrition and mortification the two-edged sword that slays the victim, charity the fire that consumes it.

2. Conformity to the world, to the Joneses? Our sense of values needs constant attention and adjustment, in proportion as we grow in perfection. But we cannot be indifferent to our neighbors either, for "No man is an island, entire of itself; everyman is a piece of the continent, a part of the main" (John Donne).

3. Paul wrote of these profound truths not to contemplatives but to people living in a "Babylon," a city of corruption. Many of his readers were to become saints and martyrs, and we can imitate them. Lot lived in Sodom, Joseph in Egypt, Tobias in Ninive, Daniel in Babylon, but just as fish taken from the sea are not salty to the taste, God's men live surrounded by wickedness without being infected by it.

II AFTER EPIPHANY

Life as a Christian

INTRODUCTION. St. Paul proceeds to apply to life his favorite metaphor. He has in the preceding verse spoken of membership in the body of Christ. In his eyes the Church was not a shapeless mass wherein men lose their individuality, but rather a system of delicately balanced and interrelated parts in which each man has a particular and a valuable role to fulfill.

THE EPISTLE: ROMANS 12:6–16
6 *Having different gifts,*
    according to the grace that has been given us.

The sentence is not well constructed, and a verb in keeping with the context must be supplied after the opening phrase; this will be "let it be used, or exercised." The gifts or *charismata* are called *gratiae gratis datae* (= graces freely given), exceptional manifestations of grace which God dispensed to whom and when he pleased. They differed from habitual or sanctifying grace in that they did not necessarily imply holiness in the one receiving them (cf Ex 22–24), but were given for the good of the Church. The primitive Church was richly endowed with these striking graces. The *charismata* are mentioned in four lists (1 Cor 12:8–10; 28–30; here, and Eph 4:11f). In all they numbered about twenty, but some of them cannot always be sharply distinguished from others. Here Paul mentions seven of the gifts. For the first four, he sets a limit, for the others he counsels the proper use.

6a *if prophecy [let it be exercised]*
    according to the proportion of faith.

In 1 Cor 14:3, prophecy (= *propheteia*) is a charism whereby one spoke words of edification for the Church; it has then to do with religious matters. As a supernatural gift, it treats of things hidden from the natural light of reason. Paul recommends that it be used "according to the 'analogy' of faith." One does not measure prophecy by his own subjective faith (how *that* could be determined is difficult to see),

42

but rather by faith in an objective sense, that is, by the common faith (Ti 1:4), the best possible way "to discern spirits" (cf 1 Cor 12:10; 14:29; Gal 1:8; 1 Thes 5:19–21).

7 *If [one has the gift of] ministry, [let him use it] in serving;*
    if teaching, in teaching;
8   *if exhortation, in exhorting;*
    he who gives, with simplicity; he who presides, with diligence;
    he who practices mercy, with cheerfulness.

Ministry (= *diakonia*) has to do with care for the practical needs of the community. Paul does not have in mind any well-defined office (priests, bishops, etc), or extraordinary gift (cf 1 Cor 16:15); nor does he mean one who dispenses alms (cf v 8). The special nature of the offices which follow seem to be the division of the general idea of ministry.

In listing the charismatic gifts, Paul puts the teacher (= *didaskon*) after the Apostles and prophets. His business was the teaching of the Christian truths. Like St. Justin, he was probably a lay catechist, whose teaching was limited to a particular church (Eph 4:11; Didache 13).

Another zealous Christian (= *parakalon*) would follow up the catechetical teaching and in private would utter words of advice and encouragement in matters of the faith to those who needed it. *Exhortation* is to prophecy as part to whole. These laymen excelled in comforting the troubled, using the only remedy they had at their command — words from the heart. But after such spiritual services, needs of the temporal order had to be attended to. From the outset the Christians had hastened to help their own poor; the almsgiver (= *metadidos*) gave not only of his earthly substance but of himself as well, for the poor were his brothers in Christ. Paul urges such generous souls to give their alms without ostentation, with simplicity, without thought of publicity or popular acclaim.

The one who presides (= *proistamenos*) directing the giving of help to the unfortunate should exhibit diligence and zeal both in acquiring alms and in distributing them. But even more perfect is the man (= *eleon*) who personally exercises mercy toward the poor and needy, in a pleasant, cheerful way. This can be more important to the poor than the deed itself.

9 *Let your love be without hypocrisy.*
   Hating what is evil, clinging to good,
10 *Be devoted to one another in brotherly love,*
    esteeming one another as more deserving [than yourselves].

A follower of Christ should be sincere and genuine, neither acting a part (cf 1 Pt 1:22) nor making empty gestures. His love for the brethren should make him hate what is bad for them. All members of the community are his "brothers." This idea originated in the Orient, the Jews having used it among themselves to indicate a community of race and of religion. The pagans sometimes called each other "brothers" (there seems to have been no place in their outlook for women), but for them the term meant little more than "pal" or "Mac." In Christian usage the term acquires a note of warmth and affection, and represents a side of religion that is equally removed from cold intellectualism and unmanly sentimentality. Each one should inwardly consider his brothers as more deserving than himself (= *en time allelous proegoumenoi*).

11 *[Be] not slothful in zeal, [be] fervent in spirit,*
    serving the Lord,
12 *rejoicing in hope,*
    be patient in affliction, persevering in prayer.
13 *Contribute to the needs of the saints, exercise hospitality.*

Paul cannot conceive of a Christian acting listlessly or indolently, as if he were a slave or time-server forced to do what he loathed doing. Paul would have him lift his feet and show an unflagging energy in the service of the Lord Jesus. To be sure, things would not always run smoothly, but the certitude of Christian hope will make him cheerful even in the painful presence of tribulation. The followers of Christ can draw upon prayer, a powerful source of help (1 Thes 5:17). One should, moreover, share what he has with those called to be saints in such a way that they will not feel that they are a burden. In the Orient hospitality, hardship's cousin, is the most fundamental of duties (cp Gen 19:1ff; Lk 24:28f), and the New Testament is filled with references to it.

14 *Bless those who persecute you; bless and do not curse them.*
15 *Rejoice with those who are joyful; weep with those who weep.*

Here is a remarkable Christian sentiment: to wish all men, even persecutors, well. The rabbis were not slow to introduce into their prayers a curse for Nazarenes, as Christians were called, but the horizon of the Christian embraces all humanity. The idea of praying for one's enemies is truly astonishing, it is Christlike. St. Paul himself provided an example of this (cf Phil 2:7), and repeatedly insisted upon the Christian's duty of sharing in another's joy and sorrows; all are members of the one body (1 Cor 12:26). St. John Chrysostom dryly notes, however (*Homil. XXII . . . ad Rom.*, P.G. 60:610), that it is much easier to weep with others than to rejoice over their good fortune. It is one thing to say, too bad, or tough luck, but quite another to cheer another's success. Envy is quick to stir to life, but the "saints" resist this temptation, because they realize that others are not, after all, *competitors* whose attainment of God would render him inaccessible to us. Moreover, behind the distribution of different talents and another's success lies the infinite goodness and wisdom of God. Quite characteristically Paul speaks first of rejoicing, and only then of weeping.

16 *Be of the same mind among yourselves,*
do not be ambitious, but adapt yourselves to the lowly.
Be not wise in your own eyes.

Paul counsels the Romans to see eye to eye on things, to share the same views, and to manifest this harmony openly. There is such a thing as the Christian mind (cf 15:5; 2 Cor 13:11; Phil 2:2; 4:2), a considerable area of common agreement, attitudes, and views which makes for peace and harmony, thus rendering the practice of charity easier. Humility is the sure sign of this Christian spirit and the best means of maintaining harmony. Men ordinarily keep their eyes upon those who have climbed the pinnacle of success, and dream only of attaining the heights themselves, but Christians are to seek out what is lowly (not in the intellectual or moral, but in the social order). Jesus came not to be served but to serve; he sought out the humble people, the poor, the scorned, the lowly ones most in need of help and encouragement. Following the example of his Master, the true Christian is more at home in attics and cellars than in palaces (Lagrange, *Ep. aux Romains*, p. 307). Far different from the Christian's interest in the "little people" of this world is that of a person who is always right. Paul seems to have Prv 3:17 in mind, and "Never be conceited" sums up his thought.

HINTS FOR HOMILETICS

1. The gifts were one of the most striking features of the early Church, and many of them designated a supernatural aptitude for governing a Christian community before the regular hierarchy was established (cf Prat, *Theology of St. Paul,* I, pp. 423–426). Once the Church was firmly established, however, they were no longer the ordinary thing, although some of them appear in the lives of the saints. Signs and wonders were more necessary in apostolic times to break the mold of paganism; the good lives of believers are now the most effective means of converting others.

2. We must love one another, not blindly condoning their faults, but with the clear eyes of faith. Rich and poor, white or blue-collar workers, professional or working-class people, all are brothers, all make up the Body of Christ, and are part of the great mystery: the Church.

3. Envy is a capital sin with many ugly daughters (cf *Sum. Theol.,* 2–2, q.36, a.4). No sin gives so little to the sinner as this green-eyed monster (cf Farrell, *A Companion to the Summa,* III, p. 102f).

III AFTER EPIPHANY

The Behavior of a Christian

INTRODUCTION. In the preceding Epistle St. Paul was intent upon the harmony which should prevail among Christians. Now he makes the point that it should not be a charity shut up within the Christian community, but should spill out from the community and embrace the whole world. Brave words from a brave man, for undoubtedly many of the Romans were of Jewish origin who had recently experienced the bitterness of expulsion and confiscation of goods under Claudius, and might understandably enough feel bitterness toward all but their own.

THE EPISTLE: ROMANS 12:16–21

16 *Be not wise in your own eyes.*
17 *To no man return evil for evil,*
acting honorably before all men.

For verse 16, cf last Sunday's epistle, p. 45, Paul's words, addressed to Christians living among suspicious and hostile Jews and pagans, are reminiscent of Mt 5:39–44. The first Christians were the victims of oft-repeated injustices, but they were to follow Jesus' example in bearing these patiently. That men have always been inclined to return evil for evil, has been consistently deplored by the best of men (cf Ps 7:5; 1 Thes 5:15; 1 Pt 3:9). Socrates declared (*Criton,* 49) that it was "Better to endure injury than to inflict it," and Cicero (*De Offic.,* I, 25, 88), voiced similar sentiments. To endure evil in a Christian spirit is the mark of a noble and honorable man, and awakens the admiration of those who witness it. A man should not look for the esteem of others, but he need not be disdainful of it, for it can be useful in advancing the good of souls and the honor of Christianity. The Christian, then, should deliberately pursue the course of honor when under duress (= pronooumenoi kala [cp Prv 3:4]).

18 *If possible, as far as this depends on you,*
be at peace with all men.

To be at peace with all is an attractive ideal but one difficult of

47

realization, for to be a lover of peace is no guarantee that one will not be attacked. Christians, however, should try to promote peace and do all that they can to be at peace. Being a last resort fraught with dreadful consequences, wars should not be started without grave cause; but if cause there be, all should fight valiantly for the cause of justice and of peace.

19 *Do not avenge yourselves, beloved,*
     but give place to the wrath [of God],
     for it is written: "Vengeance is mine, I will repay" says the Lord.

Never to seek vengeance is heroic indeed, as Paul the man knew full well. As he recommends this practice so opposed to the natural instincts of man Paul's voice becomes tender and he addresses the Romans as "Beloved." Let God handle it: Vengeance is mine, I will repay, the Lord said (Dt 32:35; Heb 10:30), and only pagans consider "getting even" a sacred duty. The Christian who has been robbed or cheated or otherwise misused has every right and an obligation (for the good of society as a whole) to have recourse to the courts in order to restore the balance of justice, but he should not take the punishment into his own hands.

20 *But if your enemy hungers, feed him;*
     if he is thirsty, give him to drink,
     for by so doing you shall heap
     coals of fire upon his head.

There is a crescendo here. It is not enough for the Christian to be passive as regards revenge; he must act positively and generously toward his enemy, helping him when he is in need. This is to "heap coals of fire upon his head" (Prv 25:21). Paul surely did not mean that one should give his enemy enough rope to hang himself, or should provide him with opportunities for greater sins and, consequently, greater punishment. That might enable a Christian to "taste the sweetness of hatred and revenge" but it would not be charity (cp St. Augustine, *Expos. ad Rom.*, P.L. 35:2083). Repeated acts of love ultimately awaken burning pangs of shame and remorse in an enemy. Conquered thus by charity and generosity, the enemy will be changed into a friend and a lover of God (cf Origen, P.G. 14:1225).

21 *Be not overcome by evil, but overcome evil by good.*

Evil can only be victorious if evil deed is answered by evil deed. To exact revenge for wrongs done to oneself and to destroy the enemy, is simply to hold a mirror up to evil and thus to multiply it. A good Christian must not permit the evil to penetrate into his soul; his true enemy is not the evildoer but evil itself. By eradicating it from his own soul, he may well gain his adversary. "He who rules his temper is a better man than he who takes a city" (Prv 16:31). St. Paul reminds us that victory over self is more glorious than one over an enemy. It is certainly a more difficult victory.

HINTS FOR HOMILETICS

1. To "heap coals of fire on another's head" is the Christian way of making friends out of one's enemies by doing good to him in return for evil. Prudence enters in here. At times one may do good to one's enemy directly, at others, it is enough to be ready to do so if there is need (*Sum. Theol.,* 2-2, q.25, a.8). But the effect may not be immediate — a wet log must first be dried out (by the fire), then it burns on the outside, and finally it becomes a glowing coal indistinguishable from the fire itself.

2. Christian virtue does not demand of a man that he become a doormat. So be a sheep, runs the Italian proverb, and a wolf will eat you up. St. Augustine, waxing eloquent on the subject of charity (*Enn. in Ps.* 47, P.L. 36:511), declared that "the world can do nothing against the violence of charity! . . . it is the virtue which no one conquers." At the same time, is should be clear that Christianity is not the passive resistance of a Ghandi.

3. Many of our troubles are of our own making. It is the people with grand larceny already in their hearts that the confidence men find easiest to handle. Cheating is never justified, of course, but is mentioned here only to show that we are often the causes of our own troubles. Those who live honorably, live virtuously.

Love and Law

INTRODUCTION. Once good citizens have discharged their civic obligations (Rom 13:1–7), there remains much to do, for there is more to life than justice. Paul here introduces his favorite theme, that of love. Our love for others is a debt that has no limits other than the love of Christ and the Father for all men (12:1).

THE EPISTLE: ROMANS 13:8–10

8a *Owe no man anything except to love one another.*

This is one of Paul's finest utterances. To pay one's taxes (13:6f) is an obligation of justice, but only one instance of it; one should try to owe no one (and not just the state) anything. There is the further obligation of exhibiting love toward others, even those who have no claims in justice for such love. The idea is remarkable and artfully put. It is good for us to have this daily debt which we can never fully liquidate (cf Origen, P.G. 14:1231).

8b *For he who loves his neighbor has fulfilled the Law.*

Neighbor is taken in the wide sense here, so as to include all men. It is impossible to love humanity, or any other abstraction. We can do good to others only in concrete, minute particulars. "The general good is the refuge of the scoundrel, hypocrite, and the flatterer" (Blake). Love, so spontaneous and full of heart, seems far-removed from the obedience due to a law, and yet the man who loves has by that fact already fulfilled the Law. The next verse indicates that Paul has the Mosaic Law especially in mind. Love of neighbor is "the royal law" (Jas 2:8).

9 *For: "You shall not commit adultery, You shall not kill,*
   You shall not steal, You shall not covet,"
   and if there is any other commandment,
   it is summed up in this sentence:
   "You shall love your neighbor as yourself."

Here is clarification of the thesis (v 8): the most important precepts of the Law are all summed up in the command to love (cf Mt 22:40). Paul singles out four commandments from the second table of the Law (6–5–7–9), omitting all mention of the love of God (cf Mk 12:28ff). But the Romans would not have forgotten Paul's lyrical outburst on this subject (Rom 8:28ff), nor fail to see that one loves his neighbor because of his own love for God. By "neighbor" is meant every member of that human family which is now unified in Christ (Gal 3:28; Mt 25:40).

10 *Love does no wrong to a neighbor.*
     Love is therefore the fulfillment of the Law.

If a man looks upon another man as his brother or neighbor, he will refrain from harming him either in his person (5), in his property (7), through his wife (6), or in his good name (9). But this is precisely what all law, including that of Moses, aims at, namely, the prevention of evil. He who loves his neighbor, therefore, fulfills the [intention of the] law. He also proves that he loves God, whom he serves in loving his neighbor.

HINTS FOR HOMILETICS

1. There are some debts a man can never pay off. He cannot, for example, honor God as God fully deserves to be honored; hence, man is always in debt to him. Moreover, love does not wear out from use, but becomes more intense.

2. For I always owe you love, the only debt which even when paid holds him who paid it a debtor still. For when it is paid it is given, but it is owed after it has been given, for there is no time when it ceases to be due. Nor is it lost when given; it is rather multiplied in the giving, for in possessing it, not in parting with it, is it given (Augustine).

3. Love of God means friendship with him. He is the primary object of the virtue of charity; our neighbor is the secondary object of that virtue. An act of charity may encounter rejection. Only if one's kindly action will be misinterpreted or be an occasion of sin (e.g., of anger) to another, should it be omitted.

V AFTER EPIPHANY AND FEAST OF THE HOLY FAMILY

Christian Family Virtues

INTRODUCTION. The morality which St. Paul teaches is not a list of prohibitions — Don't do this, don't do that. In today's Epistle he describes the normal unfolding of the life that is in the Christian by reason of his new birth (baptism). The Christian has put off the "old man" and has put on the "new" (Col 3:10; Eph 2:15), "new" expressing not merely a newness in point of time (= neos) but a new quality (= kainos) proper to the Christian. The new Christian, however, is not a superman who is above good or evil; he too must obey laws. This new life has only just begun; it is a life hidden with Christ in God (3:3) and yet it will be menaced at every step by sin. The Christian must, therefore, be a mortified man, shunning sin (cf the dismal list in vv 5–9). Paul suggests a number of virtues which all can practice, and love shines forth from each of them.

THE EPISTLE: COLOSSIANS 3:12–17

12 Put on then, as God's chosen ones, holy and beloved,
   heartfelt compassion, kindness, humility, meekness, patience.

Those whom God has out of his love chosen to be saints should clothe themselves with virtue as with a garment. First on the list of virtues is a tender compassion toward others. The Vulgate translates the Greek text (= splangchna oiktirmou) by "bowels of mercy." The "viscera" or "bowels" were the more noble viscera (the heart, lungs, kidneys), which, as they react to every human experience, are said to be the seat of the emotions of love, hatred, fear, etc. The other virtues mentioned (kindness, humility, meekness [= courtesy, considerateness],) and patience are fitting companions for a tender and compassionate heart.

13 Bear with one another and forgive one another,
   if anyone has a complaint against anyone.
   For as the Lord forgave you, you should [forgive] also.

Here is a program for Christian living. One must learn to put up

52

with others, and also how to forget and to forgive, lest irritation produce division among the brethren. Christ has given the supreme example of forgiveness which his followers ought to follow (cp Eph 4:31f).

14 But over all these [put on] love,
    which is the bond of perfection.

Continuing the figure of clothing, St. Paul urges the Colossians to put on love, for it is a bond holding the virtues together, much as a sash or belt holds the folds of a robe in place. Love brings unity to all the virtues, and gives them strength (cf the fasces); without love they are isolated, weakened, and can be easily destroyed. Men without love may, on occasion, do good to their neighbors, but such good actions are prompted less by the heart, than by the opportunity of making a grand gesture; they are not due to a habit of love but to the mood of the moment. The Christian is always a man of love.

15 And let the peace of Christ rule in your hearts,
    to which indeed you were called in the one body.
    And be thankful.

Peace is a state of calm, a freedom from agitation, a serenity, tranquillity, a companionship with justice. Peace means that a man is at one with himself and others. It is something that Christ gives (Jn 14:27), the delicious fruit of the believer's love for him. It is also a sign of unity and the preservative of the unity of the Church (Eph 4:3). As in a human body, one member cannot turn upon another, so in the Church there must be peace. A love for peace should inspire and govern all the thoughts of the Christian; the new man has not been called to enjoy this peace for himself alone, but for the good of the body (Eph 4:4), of which all are members. The Colossians have therefore many reasons for thanking God, and Paul reminds them to be grateful for their blessings.

16 Let the word of Christ dwell in you richly.
    Teach and admonish one another in all wisdom,
    singing in your hearts to God in psalms, hymns, and spiritual songs.

The word of Jesus Christ, i.e., his teaching, should be the community's most precious treasure, for it contains the answers to all the questions the new man can ask, and shows him how he shall walk. This teaching should dwell (or *indwell*) in their minds, there producing an ever more abundant fruit. Realizing how fortunate they are, they will express their gratitude in songs which praise God (see Eph 5:14; 1 Tim 3:16 for examples). The "spiritual songs" Paul mentions here may have been the charismatic improvisations suggested by the Spirit during the liturgical assemblies.

17 *And whatever you do in word or deed,*
    do everything in the name of the Lord Jesus,
    giving thanks to God the Father through him.

In conclusion, Paul stresses the Christian's basic principle of action: to sanctify every action by doing it in the name of and according to the mind of the Lord Jesus. No part of the Christian's life should be divorced from Christ but everything should be done in union with him. Characteristically, Paul ends his exhortation (cp 1:12; 2:7; 3:15) by urging gratitude.

HINTS FOR HOMILETICS

1. Great artists have vied with one another to portray with due reverence the life of the Holy Family at Nazareth. In that humble home the peace of Christ prevailed. Financial and other crises arose there too, but all such crises were met with tenderness, kindness, humility, meekness, and patience. Cf "Galilean Home" in *Integrity*, 1952.

2. Our lives are filled with insignificant happenings which, if offered and united to Christ, may be made meritorious of eternal life. A man should not limit his labors to one reward when he can have two. By making the morning offering of his work, he will receive a natural reward (wages for work done) and a supernatural one (for working in union with the Savior) as well.

3. Patience (= *makrothumia*) is an especially Christian virtue. By it a man endures delay, bears suffering, and never gives in. It is the spirit which could take revenge if it liked, but utterly refuses to do so (Chrysostom); the spirit which will never retaliate. How different from the great Greek virtue (= *megalopsuchia*) which Aristotle defined as the refusal to tolerate any insult or injury. Patience is the great characteristic of God, and the great obligation of every Christian. A true Christian, like St. Paul, will also be forever grateful for his blessings.

VI AFTER EPIPHANY

Apostolic Pride and Joy

INTRODUCTION. The letters to the Thessalonians are the first of Paul's writings, and are assigned the date of ca A.D. 50–51. Only Matthew Aramaic and possibly James were written earlier. Thessalonica was the chief city of the province of Macedonia. An excellent harbor plus its position on the Via Egnatia midway between the Adriatic and the Hellespont, made it a busy center of trade (modern Saloniki is also a flourishing city). Paul came to this city early in his second missionary journey, but after a short time was obliged to flee for his life (cf Acts 17:1ff). On reaching Athens he learned that his Thessalonian converts were undergoing severe trials. Although he desired to revisit them (cf 1 Thes 2:18), he seems never to have seen them again. Timothy was the bearer of this affectionate letter as well as of a second and later missive.

THE EPISTLE: 1 THESSALONIANS 1:2–10

2 *We give thanks to God always for you all,*
mentioning you in our prayers.

It is Paul's custom to begin his letters by thanking God for gifts received. He thereby teaches his readers that they also should trace all their graces back to God. To this one true God Paul gives genuine thanks for his beloved converts in Thessalonica.

3 *Remembering without ceasing*
in the presence of God and our Father
your work of faith and labor of love
and steadfastness of hope in our Lord Jesus Christ.

Paul's gratitude was great because his converts were openly living and professing their faith. As was to be expected, their faith issued forth in works of many kinds, for while faith is not charity, in the concrete the works of faith and those of charity coincide. Their "labor of love" does not mean "services rendered without hope of reward," but that their love for God has led them to labor to the point of weariness; in other words, their love cost them much (*kopos* conveys the notion of a difficult work). This love, *agape* and not *eros*, is one of the most brilliant ideas of the New Testament. God himself is love (1 Jn 4:8), and his active love joyously undertook the considerable task of our salvation. Christian hope, far from being mere pious optimism, is rather a solid certainty concerning some future event, in this case, the coming or return of Jesus.

Paul seems to be suggesting that in their capacity as children of God the Thessalonians should live out their lives as if in God's presence. The three theological virtues (Faith, Hope, Charity) appear together here in Paul's first letter, and were probably well known before this. It seems best to join all three (and not just "hope") to the "Lord Jesus Christ." Hope is mentioned third because the Thessalonians will have particular need of it in the days to come, and also because the letter deals with the eagerly awaited coming of Christ.

4 We know, brothers beloved of God,
that you have been chosen.

The term *brothers* has a special significance. St. Peter first used the term on Pentecost, when speaking to the crowds in Jerusalem. He was imitated in this use by Stephen, and then by Paul. Christian brotherhood is the fellowship of the redeemed. The Father loves those who have been created by love, have been adopted as sons, and redeemed by his own Son Jesus (note the connection between love and election in 2 Thes 2:13). By "choice" it is best to understand not the eternal act of God by which he chooses and predestines his elect to glory, but rather a temporal call of the chosen Thessalonians to faith. Belief normally leads to beatitude, but Paul could not have known whether all his converts would infallibly attain an eternal reward; only God knows the number of the elect.

5 For our gospel came to you not in word alone
but in power and in the Holy Spirit and perfect assurance,
as you know what kind of men we were among you, for your sakes.

The good tidings or Gospel confided to Paul was nothing less than the revelation of God's plan for saving all men. There were times when Paul would speak in weakness and timidity and much trembling (1 Cor 2:3), or was prevented from speaking at all (Acts 16:6f). Sometimes he could sense that his audience was not listening to him with an open mind, but not so at Thessalonica. While there he was aware that the Holy Spirit helped him preach "in power," that he had backed up his words with miracles and exhibitions of charismatic gifts, all of which proved the heavenly origin of his teaching. He could remember also the perfect assurance that had come over him as he preached to them. They could on their part also remember those wonderful days, and recall the kind of a life the preachers of the Gospel had led among them. Paul realized that no one can expect to win listeners over to his words unless his life shows those words in practice. Paul's constant appeals to his reading public, his reiterated "you know . . ." almost make the letters to the Thessalonians sound to us like a conversation heard from a distance.

6 And you became imitators of us and of the Lord
    receiving the word in much affliction
    with joy of the Holy Spirit.

Only in so far as he is an imitator of Christ is Paul a model for the Thessalonians, and as they had learned of Jesus from him, the word order ("of us," "of the Lord") is understandable (cf 1 Cor 4:16; 11:1). The underlying notion of "tradition" should not be overlooked (2:13; 4:1). Paul is proud of the way they had stood up under pressure, for after he had made good his escape from Thessalonica, the uproar was directed against those who had been friendly with him (cf Acts 17:5–9; 1 Thes 2:14). Suffering goes against the grain, but by sufferings all Christians are associated with the sufferings of Jesus. Sufferings are the measure of their future rest; and thus stimulate hope rather than diminish it. Those who accept the Gospel (= the "word") in affliction shall rejoice (Gal 5:22). The degree in which the believer participates in the sufferings of his Lord should then be the measure of his joy.

7 So that you became an example
    to all the believers in Macedonia and in Achaia.
8 For from you the word of the Lord has sounded forth
    not only in Macedonia and Achaia, but everywhere
    your faith in God has gone forth
    so that we need not say anything.

By their exemplary conduct under fire, the Thessalonians (here Paul exaggerates somewhat) have become a model or pattern (= *tupos*) for all true believers throughout Greece and the whole world. Granting that Thessalonica lay at the international crossroads, this was putting it rather strongly, although it could be argued that if the news were known in the capital, Corinth, everyone, everywhere, knew about it. Still, the "word of the Lord" (= the preaching of the Gospel, which has God always in view) has been noised abroad as if it were the clear, ringing note of a trumpet (or the rolling of thunder). There was nothing apologetic about it! The perfect of the verb (*exechetai*) suggests that this was no transient "ringing forth" but a continuing one. The news of conversions in Thessalonica had traveled with the speed of sound, and was followed by other conversions. Christianity did in fact spread with great rapidity throughout the Roman empire, and that at a very early date. Paul therefore has no need to add to what everyone knows. The rapidity of the growth of the Church was in part due to the excellent system of interconnecting roads built by the Romans for the speedy transportation of troops. Always maintained in good order, they served the Apostles well.

9   *For they tell concerning us how we came to you*
    and how you turned to God from idols,
    to serve a living and true God.

Instead of Paul and his companions having to broadcast this news about the Thessalonians, it was the other way around; wherever he went, people kept talking to him (present tense) about what had happened at Thessalonica. Paul's preaching had been followed by many conversions or "turnings" to God. Every conversion is dramatic; it is the reorientation of a whole life, a change in the direction of a man's will, a breaking of old ties. Their conversions had meant turning their backs upon familiar idols, that is, upon a pagan life lived against a tolerant, polytheistic background. To accept Jesus Christ was to overturn the idols of paganism.

But Christianity is not a negative religion. It involves the serving of a God whose very nature it is to be both living and true. Idols, which are not "true" gods, are not genuinely, really, gods at all. Converts now worship the true God instead of the "nothings" which had previously claimed their allegiance.

10 *And to await his Son from heaven,*
    whom he raised from the dead, Jesus,
    who delivers us from the wrath to come.

Without implying that the last day is at hand, Paul reminds his readers of the judgment which shall take place on the Last Day. Jesus will come from heaven, a triumphal return from the place to which he went after his ascension. His resurrection is "appropriated" to the Father here as elsewhere (1 Cor 6:14; 15:15; Gal 1:1; Col 2:12). Jesus will return as a deliverer from the "wrath which comes." The biblical metaphor of the "wrath which comes" has eschatological overtones, the present participle suggesting both its inevitability and its actual, present reality. God is not merely tolerant of sin, but is ever aroused to wrath by it (the anthropomorphism can be properly understood).

HINTS FOR HOMILETICS

1. The example of the Thessalonians and the life they led after their conversion were a powerful argument in favor of the new religion, and won them many companions in the faith, and in martyrdom. Good example is better than many sermons.

2. Faith, hope, and charity, active and steadfast and energetic, are the best preparation for meeting Christ the judge. One must learn to love before he can labor. Love is willing to do even little things. "I will run the way of your commandments," the Psalmist wrote, "when you give me a docile heart" (118[119]:32).

3. Paul was not afraid to urge others to imitate him. Would imitation of ourselves be imitation of Christ?

Christian Self-Control

INTRODUCTION. A lengthy interruption (1 Cor 9:1 to 10:13) prompted by the abuse some Corinthians were making (8:9–13) of their newly found liberty as Christians, occurs here, and against it Paul argues, in words which have rightly become famous, for the need of self-imposed discipline. He illustrates his thesis by an example taken from the world of sports, and by others drawn from Old Testament history.

THE EPISTLE: 1 COR. 9:24–10:5

24 *Know you not that they who run in the race*
all run indeed, but one receives the prize?
So run as to make it yours.

Everyone in Greece knew of the *Olympic* games, held every four years at Elis (one of the provinces of southern Greece), and the *Isthmian* games, held every two years near Corinth, in the spring of the year. With remarkable perspicacity, Paul translates into Christian thought the athletic ideals which so captivated the Hellenistic mind. In such athletic contests there were many contenders for a crown which only one man could win. The crown (= *brabeion*) was a wreath placed upon the head of the winner. Paul believed in playing the game of life in order to gain the prize. The idea of running toward salvation appears again and again in the epistles (Gal 2,2; 5:7; Phil 2:16; 2 Thes 3:1; Heb 12:1). Paul most probably witnessed these "games" himself at some time during his life.

25 *Every competitor restrains himself in all things,*
they to receive a perishable crown,
but we an imperishable one.

The runners chosen for the Olympic games prepared for the contest by following a strict training-program which called for constant practice and many privations in matters of food, drink, and sex. The purpose of this "asceticism" (= exercise) was to toughen and condition their bodies.

The Olympic crown was made from a wild-olive branch, the Isthmian from pine branches. The ancient Greeks thought that striving for such a prize would bring out a man's best, for thus the contest was not for the base motive of gain, but for honor won in competition by a display of courage, skill, and virtue. The crown was bestowed upon the winner along with a word of praise and amid shouts of applause that died quickly and were soon forgotten.

In the games there was only one winner in each race. In the spiritual world, however, all who run well will obtain their reward, each in his own place. With typical Semitic logic St. Paul concentrates on only one point in the comparison, the winner and his prize. He means of course to say: we must all run well, and in the right direction, like runners in the stadium, in order to win an imperishable crown of glory.

26 *I therefore run, but not aimlessly; I fight not as beating the air*
27 *but I bruise my body and bring it into bondage,*
   lest perhaps after being herald to others,
   I myself become disqualified.

Another comparison, that of the boxer not shadowboxing or punching the bag or missing the target like an unskilled fighter — but stalking a definite opponent and striking him effectively. Prudence has led Paul to mortify his own body. Because of its carnal and selfish instincts the body has to be conquered, to be reduced to its proper role of humble instrument to the soul. Paul does not waste his blows, but makes each one count. How did he do this? By fasts and vigils (2 Cor) undertaken both for himself and so as to give good example. How dreadful if the herald who has proclaimed, not the next athletic contest but the opening of heaven to mankind, should himself be disqualified as a contestant for the heavenly crown because he had neglected his training by yielding to the allurements of the flesh.

Verses 24–27 were used by the Council of Trent (Denz 804) to show that faith alone is not sufficient for salvation.

10:1 *For I do not want you to be ignorant, brethren,*
   that our fathers were all under the cloud and all passed
   through the sea,
   2 *and all were baptized into Moses in the cloud and in the sea,*
   3 *and all ate the same spiritual food,*

4 *and all drank the same spiritual drink;*
   for they drank of the spiritual rock which followed (*them*),
   and the Rock was Christ.

The miraculous cloud (Ex 13:21; Ps 105:39) which hovered over the Israelites and guided them in the desert was a sign to them of God's presence. The passage through the Red Sea (Ex 14:22) was a kind of baptism received. The manna (*ibid*. 16:13ff) and the water that gushed from the rock (*ibid*. 17:1ff; Nm 20:7–11) are called *spiritual* either because their origin was such (i.e., supernatural), or because of their spiritual meaning (i.e., as prefiguring the Eucharist). All of the Old Testament is clarified by comparison with Christ and his Church.

In saying "the spiritual rock which followed them was Christ," Paul alludes to a rabbinical legend according to which the rock which had gushed forth water when Moses struck it, followed the Israelites everywhere thereafter, thus assuring them of an adequate water supply in the desert. Paul sees this fanciful tale to be a foreshadowing of the Christian order of grace, and a revelation of the pre-existent Christ, who long before he entered history in the form of a man, was from all eternity the dispenser of the necessities of life. The rabbis tended to identify this rock with YHWH (= the Lord), who is called the "Rock of Israel" (cf Ps 17:3) and who in fact did follow the Israelites with his loving care. Paul then here makes Christ equal to YHWH who was God. One might, therefore, refer to God as *Christus Incarnandus* (Christ who must become man).

These Old Testament references with their insistent "all" are soon followed by a painful antithesis. Paul wished this antithesis in order to dispel any false confidence the Corinthians may have felt in spiritual matters because they had received so many charismatic graces. Personal and sustained effort is required of all to correspond to the divine call.

5 *Yet with most of them God was not well pleased*

Despite these striking favors, many of the Israelites perished in the desert as a punishment for their sins. The incidents mentioned were prophetic "figures" of what was to come, and the point Paul is making has now become crystal clear: even the greatest graces can terminate in the greatest of chastisements. St. Thomas tells us that divine punishment is to be feared, the cause for it should be borne in mind, and all necessary precautions taken to avoid it.

Paul's attention was focused on a comparison of gifts received, not on their quality, for he never implied that the Old Testament was on a par with the New Testament, but simply that what begins well does not always end well. Let the Corinthians bear this in mind.

HINTS FOR HOMILETICS

1. The early Christians began to prepare for Easter many days in advance, hence the strange names (Septuagesima, Sexagesima, Quinquagesima [= 70th-60th-50th]) given to these Sundays. There are now roughly that many days until Easter. The Church urges us to turn our eyes now from the Infant at Bethlehem, from the Magi, and from Nazareth, and to begin to consider Jesus under the aspect of Savior, with the shadow of Calvary already upon him.

2. The secret of victory is a well-disciplined, prayerful life. People who lead "soft" lives will be inevitably defeated in the fierce struggle against invisible and visible enemies. St. Paul would have approved the following statements. Eddie Rickenbacker, hospitalized after a racing mishap, said, after some realistic thinking: "My accident taught me to scheme. You didn't win races because you had more guts, but because you knew how to take the turns and to baby your engine. It wasn't all just shut your eyes and grit your teeth. Also, I learned never to count on the crowd to take care of you. And never to think of yesterday, because a man can go from hero to zero overnight." Once when Babe Didrickson was congratulated for being a good loser, she exploded: "I don't want to be a good loser. I never enter a contest unless I intend to win it. I always play to win." Paul said "Run!" Jesus said "Work!" Both talk the same language.

3. If Paul the Apostle felt uneasy about his own perseverance and destiny, what should the liberals of Corinth think about theirs? St. Augustine comments soberly, "His fear terrifies us. What shall the lamb do, if the ram is afraid?" Some years later (2 Tim 4:8), Paul seems to have felt more confidence in such matters, but this was perhaps the result of a private revelation he had received from God (cf Denz 826).

SEXAGESIMA

Pauline Apologia

INTRODUCTION. To refute the unflattering charges which had been made against him in his absence (cf 10:1ff), Paul felt constrained to defend himself and his dignity as a true Apostle (cf 6:4–10), something which he ordinarily would have thought a waste of time. His self-defense is a remarkable mixture of profound humility and biting sarcasm. Today's passage, which is the longest Epistle of the entire ecclesiastical year, provides us with much information about Paul not recorded elsewhere.

THE EPISTLE: 2 Cor 11:19–12:9

19 For you endure fools gladly, being wise yourselves.
20 For you let a man enslave you, devour you, exploit you,
       treat you insolently, strike you in the face.

When in Corinth, Paul concedes, he had not shown the kind of boldness the Corinthians in their "wisdom" appear to appreciate. They have allowed themselves to be reduced to religious and moral slavery after having been freed by Christ from the chains of sin and of the Law. In the name of religion they have been robbed and taken in by arrogant, violent men. Paul apologizes with heavy irony for having shown himself so lacking in this regard:

21 I admit to my shame that we have been weak . . .
       But whatever anyone may boast of,
       — I am speaking as a fool —
       I also boast [of it].

More than once Paul had found himself obliged to defend his actions and his Jewish blood (cf Gal 1:13f; Rom 11:1; Phil 3:4–6; cp Acts 22:3ff; 26:4ff). Among other things his detractors seem to have cast doubt on the purity of his blood, for Paul had been born in Tarsus, far from the Promised Land. He replies vigorously:

64

22 They are Hebrews? So am I. They are Israelites? So am I.
    They are descendants of Abraham? So am I. Servants of Christ?
    — I am going to speak like a madman — I am a better one!

Like them, Paul could speak the ancestral tongue, Hebrew (Acts 22:3). Like them, he was a member of the Chosen Race which had been the recipient of the messianic promises (Ex 19:5f; Rom 9:4; Gal 3:8). Like them, he, a true Benjamite, was consecrated to God by being circumcised on the eighth day (Phil 3:4-6). And if they claim to be descendants of Abraham, Paul matches their claims. They may proclaim themselves as true ministers of the Messias; Paul, the bit in his teeth, will outdo them here also, although they may think him mad. He is a better servant of Jesus Christ than they ever thought of being. To prove his claim, Paul proceeds to marshall the evidence, mentioning the many dangers he had encountered while preaching the Gospel. He refers to them as if they were a kind of honors course which he had passed with flying colors. Some of the details are mentioned in the Acts, but others are revealed for the first time here; it is one of the most stirring passages Paul ever wrote. He does not dwell so much upon what he has done, upon his successes, that is, but upon his sufferings and his sacrifices. The resultant pictures redounds more to Christ's glory than it does to his own, because, as he will make abundantly clear, he has provided the "weakness" and God the "strength."

23 [I surpass them] by far in [my] labors, [I was] in prisons many
        more times,
        [I suffered] from beatings far more [than they], many times I
        was near death.
24 Five times I have received from the Jews forty stripes save one.
25 Three times I have been beaten with rods; once I was stoned.
        Three times I have been shipwrecked;
        A night and a day I was adrift on the sea.

Paul traversed Asia Minor and Greece at the cost of extraordinary physical effort. He was no stranger to bodily fatigue. The Acts tell us of imprisonments in Philippi, Jerusalem, Caesarea, and Rome, but Clement of Rome declares that the Apostle was imprisoned seven times. The apocryphal Acts of Paul give Ephesus as the scene of one of these incarcerations (M. R. James, The Apocryphal New Testament, p. 292;

cf 1 Cor 15:32; 16:9; 2 Cor 1:8ff; 7:5; Rom 16:3–7). The beatings and stripes are recorded in the Acts. Dt 25:3 limited the number of stripes allowed to 40, and out of a scruple (not to break the Law by giving too many strokes), only 39 were given (13 over each shoulder, 13 on the back). The synagogues of the Diaspora exercised some jurisdiction in religious and economic matters, and as Paul's practice (at first) was to preach Christ in the synagogues, it was probably there that he was thus punished. Beatings with rods was a Roman punishment and a public one. Paul and Silas had been so treated in Philippi (Acts 16:22f). It was forbidden to subject Roman citizens to flogging, but there were inevitably illegalities in this matter. At Lystra he had been stoned by the Jews (Acts 14:19). It is not possible to determine where or when he was shipwrecked, but he must have made many other voyages by ship besides those mentioned in the Acts.

26   In journeys many times, dangers from rivers, dangers from
     robbers, dangers from my own people, dangers from Gentiles,
     dangers in the city, dangers in the desert, dangers at sea,
     dangers from false brethren.

Half of St. Paul's life was spent in traveling about on foot to preach the Gospel! One can well imagine the arduous and dangerous nature of this feat in those days when poor roads led him through badly civilized, hardly subjugated countries, infested with bands of brigands. Nor was the sea safe, as it was filled with pirates. In a move to make the coasts of Asia Minor safe for travel, Pompey once (67 B.C.) destroyed a thousand pirate ships and took 30,000 prisoners. The sea situation was so bad that Seneca could write: If the traveler does not fall into the hands of pirates it is only because he has met with shipwreck instead. One can easily imagine the difficulties awaiting those who, like Paul, traveled in the hinterlands, without either force or authority. Small wonder, then, that Mark, guessing at some of the dangers that lay ahead, turned back while on the first missionary journey with Paul.

Danger was Paul's constant companion, whether he was in the city or the wilderness. He had to be on his guard against false brethren (hypocrites, rivals, calumniators), against his own countrymen, and against superstitious pagans.

27 In labor and hardship, in many sleepless nights,
    in hunger and thirst, in fastings often, in cold and nakedness.

If nothing else, this verse brings out the great poverty of the Apostle, as contrasted with the resources of his enemies (cf 1 Thes 2:9; 2 Thes 3:8). Making his own way, working long hours but still so poor that he had to eat sparingly and had hardly any wardrobe (cf 2 Tim 4:13), he stormed heaven with his prayers.

28 Not to speak of the rest, [there is] that which presses on
    me daily, my anxiety for all the churches.

Now, leaving aside the external sufferings incidental to his apostolate (he could easily have extended the list), Paul next speaks of his inner cross, his preoccupation with and responsibility for the Churches which he has founded. He mentions this aspect of his mission only in passing, but it involved such details as worries about the instructions given after his departure, about the administration of the new communities, about keeping or restoring peace, and about his converts' progress in the faith; then too there were visitors to receive, letters to write, and a host of distracting "activities" which Paul, who wished to be all things to all men, took upon himself at the cost of time for prayer and meditation. These inner cares exacted a heavy price from him.

29 Who is weak and I am not weak?
    Who is made to stumble and I am not on fire?

In his cry of sublime beauty Paul reveals the great love he had for his converts, for by no stretch of the imagination could he be described as a Stoic! He was not unmoved at the sight of another's weakness or misery (cf 1 Cor 9:22), especially when this involved difficulties in the matter of the faith or morals of his newly won converts (cp Acts 20:31). If he detected bad example or false doctrine among them, his indignation boiled over, and he quickly took the steps necessary to mend the situation.

30 If I must boast, I will boast of my weakness.
31 The God and Father of the Lord Jesus,
    He who is blessed forever, knows that I do not lie.

32 In Damascus the governor of King Aretas guarded the city of
the Damascenes in order to arrest me,
33 but I was let down in a basket through a window in the wall,
and escaped his hands.

What seemed to Paul weakness (the ironic style prevails still), appears in quite another light to his modern readers. Prolonged and per-
sistent as they were, his trials actually proved the continual intervention
of Christ in his life. Paul realized that he was only a fragile vase (4:7)
and that the strength which filled him was not his own. In that strength
he could face the difficulties which constantly assailed him, but great
personal courage was demanded of him as well. The extent of his humility
is revealed by his deliberate reference to his escape from Damascus.
Some of his enemies may have accused him of cowardice for having fled
in this ignominious fashion (a rope basket, possibly even a fish basket!),
but Paul is ready to concede his own helplessness. God had uses for
so weak an instrument. The king mentioned here was the Nabatean
puppet king, Aretas IV, who with Roman permission ruled from 9 B.C.
to A.D. 40 and wielded power over Damascus from A.D. 37 on. The
incident mentioned here must have taken place ca A.D. 39.

12:1 One must boast! — though there is nothing to be gained by it —
but I will come to the visions and revelations of the Lord.

Paul's bodily trials (vv 23–27) had despite his precautions indicated
his great courage and endurance, and his inner trials (28f) had revealed
his deep love for his spiritual children. The flight from Damascus, suddenly remembered, had shown his absolute helplessness. Yet he seems
suddenly to notice that he is not boasting as he ought (cf 11:30), and
so, however much it went against his grain, he will boast. His extreme
reserve, bordering on timidity, leads him to multiply excuses for talking
about this next incident in his life (although there were others like it —
cf 1 Cor 14:6,18). Were his mask not so obviously a mask, one might
almost think he was describing what happened to a stranger.

2 I know a man in Christ who fourteen years ago was caught up
to the third heaven — whether in body I know not,
or out of body, I know not, God knows ...
3 And I know that this man,
— whether in the body or out of the body I know not, God knows —

4 *was caught up into Paradise, and heard ineffable words*
   which it is not permitted a man to speak.

The fourteen years are reckoned from A.D. 57, and give the year
A.D. 43. This vision then is not to be identified with the one on the
road to Damascus (ca 37). "Third heaven" and "Paradise" are inter-
changeable terms representing that portion of heaven wherein God and
the just dwell. (For the idea of "third heaven" [atmospheric, sidereal,
and empyrean] see the Book of Enoch, and the Apocalypse of Moses).
Paul had been granted the highest kind of vision, an intellectual one.
Augustine and Thomas Aquinas were of the opinion that St. Paul had
been granted a glimpse of God himself, but in a transient manner. Paul,
however, affirms only two things: the fact of an extraordinary spiritual
experience, and its date. He does not say that he saw anything, only
that he heard words which could not be repeated.

5 *For this man I shall boast, but for myself*
   I shall not boast except of my weaknesses.
6 *For if I wish to boast, I shall not be a fool,*
   as I shall be speaking the truth. But I refrain,
   so that no one may think more of me
   than he sees in me or hears from me.
7 *And so that I should not be too elated*
   over the greatness of these revelations,
   there was given to me a thorn in my flesh,
   an angel of Satan to buffet me,
   so that I should not be too elated.

The thorn or splinter in the flesh (= *skolops en sarki*) has given
rise to many explanations, such as eye trouble, epilepsy, a nervous disorder, malaria, leprosy, stammering, gout, stomach trouble, rheumatism,
sciatica, kidney stones, recurrent fever, external persecutions, mental
depression, spiritual temptations, concupiscence, etc. The Vulgate translation: "*stimulus carnis*," does not do justice to the original; it was not
something *of*, but *in*, Paul's flesh, like a splinter, something painful,
embarrassing, personal, and permanently his own; he could not boast
about it. Concupiscence is common to all men, and it seems quite unlikely that Paul was a victim of his own flesh (cf his words in Phil 3:6).
   The identification of this "thorn in the flesh" as epilepsy is quite
common. It is alleged that this disease is common to geniuses (Mo-

hammed, Augustine, St. Bernard, Savonarola, Swedenborg, Julius Caesar, Peter the Great, Napoleon, Flaubert, Dostoyevsky), but it cannot be proved with certainty in Paul's case (nor indeed in most of those mentioned as examples). There is no necessary connection between his visions and this disease. The progressive mental and physical deterioration of the true epileptic is nowhere indicated in St. Paul. Epilepsy is not continuous, nor a direct cause of death.

We know of Paul's illness that it was painful, that it came on him in violent waves, and that it deeply affected those who saw him thus afflicted. On the basis of Gal 4:14 it has been identified by some as a sort of eye trouble. The mid-East is to this day a fertile ground for eye troubles because of the dust in the air, the lack of hygiene, the intensity of the sun, etc. Paul was grateful to the Galatians because they were willing to pluck out their own eyes and give them to him. He may, then, have suffered from migraine of the eye, dreadful to endure and horrible even to look at (but for the expression, cp Rom 16:3f). A visible blemish can be most humiliating, but no blemish is as terrible as pride, toward which Paul might have been tempted by reason of his visions. Paul attributes his illness to the devil, the father of all man's evils, God so permitting.

It is quite possible that Paul's affliction was some sort of malaria, a disease quite common in the Mediterranean basin. Maltese fever produces violent headaches, racking pain, delirium, skin eruptions, loss of the hair, extreme lassitude, etc. Yet this fever is intermittent, and in between attacks Paul could have worked valiantly as any normal man. It may be that 2 Cor 1:3–8 refer to some such ailment.

8 Concerning this I three times besought the Lord
     that it should leave me.
9 But he said to me: My grace is sufficient for you,
     for [my] power is made perfect in weakness.
     Gladly then will I boast [all] the more in my infirmities
     that the power of Christ may dwell in me.

One is reminded of Jesus' thrice-repeated prayer in the Garden by this prayer of Paul. The aorist verb (parekalesa) describes an action completed in past time; the petition concerning the "angel of Satan," therefore, is no longer made, and Paul bears his affliction patiently and with resignation. The Lord's reply is in the perfect tense (*eireken*), which means that the effect (God's help) has continued from that moment to this. Paul, then, has learned his lesson — the feebler the man, the more clearly God's power shows through him and his work. As the weakness of God is stronger than men (1 Cor 1:25), Paul welcomed his own weaknesses, because through them, despite the stubborn opposition of the world and of hell itself, men were to be united to Christ. He, therefore, never felt stronger than when he was weak (cf the results, Gal 4:13ff).

HINTS FOR HOMILETICS

1. Nothing is more pleasing to God than the faithful performance, day after day, of the duties proper to our state in life. This daily heroism, with all its frustrations and annoyances, is for most men the normal way of working out their salvation. Visions are not to be desired, and if anyone has visions, he should turn away from them in mind and heart. ("No admitir" — don't admit them, is the first rule given by St. John of the Cross. It was only extenuating circumstances that prompted Paul to mention his.) On the other hand, acts of faith, hope, and charity, can never lead one astray, and are worth a dozen visions which can.

2. Life laughs at logic. As Ecclesiastes (= Qoheleth) says, the race is not always run by the swift, nor victory gained by the strong (see 9:11). The weaknesses of God's chosen ones are an invitation to them to live their faith. God's work is seldom done under the best possible conditions, or by the best possible people, but it gets done in God's way. Cf Lochet, "The Apostle in the Mystery of the Church," *Cross and Crown* V (1953), 88–98; 223–235.

3. At some time or another every man feels keenly his own absurdity, his basic deficiencies and lack of education, of special ability, of ideas, of eloquence, etc. So it was with St. Paul. But the Lord's remarkable answer to Paul applies to all: "My grace is sufficient for you." Actually God has no need of any man, but condescends to use our puny talents to bring about the ends he wishes. Not that we should hide our talents or rest on our oars, but, while recognizing our imperfections, we should all strive mightily to do God's will wherever we are. God's will for us is almost always spelled out for us by the obligations of our state in life.

QUINQUAGESIMA SUNDAY

In Praise of Love

INTRODUCTION. Writers have vied with each other in praise of the literary and rhythmical beauty of St. Paul's "hymn to charity," one of the best things he ever wrote (cp 1 Cor 15; Rom 8:31–39; 2 Cor 4:7–10; 11:19–29). Asked for a word or two about the charismatic gifts, Paul had (1 Cor 12) traced their origin to the Holy Spirit, who distributes them where he wills for the good of the body which is the Church. But there is something far better than the gifts, a far more excellent path. The Corinthians might well have asked themselves, "What other way is there?"

Here Paul paused for a moment, and then like a graceful gleaming ship of the sky, was air-borne. Or one might say that, warmed by his contemplation of the Holy Spirit, he was suddenly on fire, swept up into an entrancing vision of love. His scribe must have looked up at his master's face at the sudden change in his manner of dictation, and as the vision of divine perfection passed before Paul's eyes, have seen his countenance lighted up as if the face of an angel. Paul's heart was the heart of Christ, and never did he come closer to sounding like his Master than he does here (Mt 5:43–48).

This Song of Songs of the New Testament is a spontaneous outburst in the finest Semitic tradition, not a systematic treatise on love but a lyrical hymn based on the theme of the transcendence of love. It is noteworthy that it was the apostle of faith, Paul, and not the apostle of love, John, who so sang this magnificent song of love. By substituting the name of Jesus wherever the word love or charity appears, there emerges a good picture of Christ and of every true Christian. The *Imitation of Christ* (III, 5) drew its inspiration from this passage, and Rom 13:8–10 adds that love is the fulfillment of the law.

This chapter enjoys considerable doctrinal importance because it not only treats of love but of the other theological virtues, and of the Beatific Vision, as well.

72

THE EPISTLE: 1 COR 13:1-13

I

SUBLIMITY AND NECESSITY OF LOVE

1 *If I speak in the tongue of men and of angels, but have not love,
I am become as sounding brass or a clanging cymbal.*

In the Greek language there are many words for love.* The first of these is *eros*, used mainly for love between the sexes and for any strong passionate affection. The word is not once used in the New Testament. A second word, *philia*, includes physical love, but goes beyond it, standing for a benevolent, unselfish affection, and love. Like the Latin word *amor*, *philia* connotes domestic affection (Jesus so loved Lazarus [Jn 11:3,36] and John [*ibid*. 20:2]). Here, however, Paul uses the word *agape*, represented in Latin by *caritas* or *dilectio*, and in English by *charity* or (preferably) *love*. Agape signifies an intelligent and deliberate love, with overtones of esteem rather than affection. There is nothing emotional about it. It is, in fact, a deliberate principle, conviction, or way of living; benevolent and unselfish, it desires good for others, wishes them well, does good to them. Christians are not asked to do the impossible, to love all men in the same way they love those near and dear to them, but Paul points out that they should always love God, and be thus predisposed to love all men (*Sum. Theol.* 2-2, q.23, a.1, ad 2). In deliberately loving others they resemble God, whose creative love brought all men into existence.

The *tongues of men* (= *glossolaly*), refers to an ecstatic gift which manifested itself in strange tongues; this the Corinthians preferred, it seems, to other gifts. By *tongues of angels* Paul probably means nothing more than the most sublime language men can manage to utter. He considered it to be a kind of rhetoric, as if he were saying: "If you speak out in the loftiest of language and talk like an angel, you are only making noise if you have not love, besides." In the sound of the Greek Paul uses here (*gegona kalkos ekon kai kumbalon alaladzon*) one can almost hear the clanging of the gongs and cymbals used in pagan temple worship (glass chimes used to tinkle pleasantly but meaninglessly

---

* Cf C. S. Lewis, *The Four Loves* (New York: Harcourt, Brace & Co., 1960).

on American porches in the summer time). To speak in tongues without loving God and neighbor is to utter meaningless sound.

2   And if I have the gift of prophecy and understand
      all mysteries and all knowledge,
      And if I have all faith so as to remove mountains,
      but have not love, I am nothing.

Paul is not referring to four charisms here, but to two only: prophecy and the gift of miracles. Prophecy at its best implies a knowledge of all mysteries and of all human wisdom. It was extremely useful in the early church (cf p. 42) as it enabled the recipients to grasp the mysteries of the faith and to explain them wisely. Without love, however, the loftiest of the teaching gifts are valueless. The faith which moves mountains was the charismatic assurance that whatsoever one asked it would be done through divine power. St. Gregory Thaumaturgus is said to have moved a mountain. However, the phrase "to move mountains" was a proverb (Allo, Corinthiens, I, p. 344) and signified "to do the [humanly] impossible." From all this we can infer that Paul's converts were not uninstructed as to Jesus' moral teachings (cf Mt 17:20; 21:21). The abrupt conclusion, "I am nothing," coming after the long period (three clauses), is very dramatic.

3   And if I give away all my possessions
      and if I deliver up my body to be burned,
      but have not love, it profits me nothing.

The continued use of "all" (cf v 2) paints a vivid picture. Going now to those virtuous acts which are closely bound up with love, Paul speaks of certain heroic actions which on the surface appear to be pleasing to both God and man. To distribute all one's goods, either in one magnificent gesture or bit by bit (Paul had so much himself!), would not be a praiseworthy act if motivated by selfish interest or by a desire to gain popularity. To offer up one's life for God would indeed be true martyrdom and a sign of perfect love, but as martyrdom uselessly endured is out of the question here, Paul may have had in mind the exhausting expenditure of all one's energies in the service of the community (cf 1 Cor 12:28). Thus the sacrifice of all of one's possessions or of all one's strength may be prompted by purely natural motives, and without charity or love, is of no profit in God's sight.

The conclusions to Paul's three suppositions are interesting. Without love, he says, I am a meaningless noise, I am nothing, I gain nothing. One might possess all three of the great charismatic gifts mentioned here and be of use to the Church and still be worthless in God's sight. The gifts are not valueless, but without love the man is. By love is meant the love of neighbor, which originates in and flows from the love of God (cf Rom 13:10; Gal 5:5; 1 Tim 1:5; Jn 13:35; 1 Jn 4:8,20).

II

QUALITIES OF LOVE

Having his theme, Paul now proceeds to rhapsodize on it, contrasting the attention-drawing charisms with the silent, intimate virtues inspired by love. Love is the mother and queen of all the virtues mentioned here, and Paul effectively brings out her dynamic character by using verb forms (and not adjectives) in his description. After one positive statement he lists eight things which love is not (4b–6a), and then five qualities which it is (6b–7). As Paul writes on, Newman's definition of a gentleman, as one who never deliberately inflicts pain, comes spontaneously to mind.

4 *Love is patient, is kind,*
   is not jealous, or puffed up.

To be *patient* under grave provocation, steadfastly and deliberately bearing up under evils and suppressing the desire for revenge, is characteristic of love. To be thus *long-suffering* means also being master of resentment and irritability. Serenity and an unassuming magnanimity attend the man who is dominated by Paul's kind of love. One cannot help but think that Paul was also describing himself in this passage.

Love is *kind*, loving, merciful. St. Thomas declares that benignity is a kind of *bona igneitas*, a pleasant warmth or fire. Just as fire melts unbending things and causes them to flow, love causes a man to unbend and to share his possessions and himself with others. St. Augustine came to love St. Ambrose because of his kindness (*Confessions*, V, 13). Love, then, is passive and active. A virtuous man is good at bearing with evils and in doing good.

Paul shows his deep understanding of the human heart by placing jealousy first on the list of things which love is *not*. "Take away jealousy," said Augustine, "and what is thine is mine, and mine is thine." The sight of another's talents or good fortune does not embitter or sadden charity which sees in all things the infinite wisdom of God. Love is not boastful nor given to arrogant display; love is humble. Blessed are the meek (Mt 5:4). Paul may here be alluding obliquely to the conceits of the Gnostics.

5   [Love] *does not behave rudely, seeks not its own interests,*
    is not irritable, takes no account of evil.

In dealing with others love exercises great tact and delicacy. Refinement and politeness, decorum and propriety, go with love. Love seeks not its own interest. Being unselfish, it does not seek to acquire what belongs to others. It is a better thing to love than to be loved (*Sum. Theol.* 2-2, q.27, a.1). Love does not become easily irritated and does not harbor resentment over real or fancied injuries. Injury may sometimes have to be suffered, but love, quick to pardon, remains calm, displaying an unruffled serenity to the world. Not content with pardoning injuries, love forgets them.

6   [Love] *rejoices not at wrong,*
    but rejoices over the truth.

One who truly loves will not rejoice at the evil conduct of others even when that conduct turns to the good fortune of virtuous men, as sometimes happens, for it is an ill wind that blows no man good. It is never right to take pleasure in evil or injustice; to do so is in fact taking part in another's sin. But now Paul begins to describe love in positive terms (6b-7), and he at once associates it with truth. In biblical language, truth is synonymous with justice, that is, with moral rectitude, integrity, perfection (cf Rom 2:8; 2 Thes 2:12). Love rejoices when it sees truth and justice prevail (cf Phil 1:15-20).

7   [Love] *excuses all, believes all, hopes all, endures all things.*

Love does not really excuse all things, but love is ready to pass over in silence the faults of one's neighbors and to make allowances for them in the spirit of Christ's prayer, "Father forgive them." True Christian love is not gullible, but believing, i.e., it is quick to put a good interpretation upon another's actions, welcoming the good related of another. It is hopeful, even optimistic about the triumph of good. If one's neighbor is virtuous and good, love is confident that he will continue on in that manner; if he is a sinner, hope looks to the day of his conversion and repentance. Love's hope has tremendous staying powers, and is able to withstand disillusionment and setbacks without losing heart. One loves enemies, even, in so far as they are God's children, and love thus always attains its primary object which is God. When love has no evidence, it believes the best. When the evidence is adverse, it hopes for the best. When hopes have been repeatedly disappointed, love hangs on courageously.

III

LOVE'S EXCELLENCE

8 *Love never fails.*
   As for prophecies, they shall have an end,
   as for tongues, they shall cease,
   as for knowledge, it shall have an end.

This third section brings with it the climax of the poem, and Paul the moralist is transformed into Paul the mystic and the theologian. The love of which he speaks now is the theological virtue which has an eternal value, whereas even the most highly esteemed of the gifts, are temporal and transitory. When the day of eternity dawns there will be no further use for prophecy and knowledge, which are only lamps in the darkness of time; and tongues, which were a rapturous mode of speaking of God or to him, will no longer be necessary when one stands in the divine presence itself. Since then, the greatest of the charismatic gifts are doomed to disappear, the lesser gifts must do so as well. But love abides forever.

9 *For we know in part, and we prophesy in part.*
10 *But when the perfect comes, what is imperfect shall pass away.*

The knowledge which men acquire by their own efforts in this life goes with them into the next life, but our acquired knowledge is fragmentary at best and geared to life here below. The greatest of human intellects can catch only a tiny glimpse of God's secrets. Very solemnly Paul contrasts what is "partial" to what is "perfect" in the moral order (Rom 12:2), in the order of cognition, and in every other order as well. In the state of glory where God is seen face to face by those who have attained blessed happiness, imperfection shall not exist. A twofold comparison follows.

11 When I was a child, I spoke like a child,
     I thought like a child, I reasoned like a child.
12 When I became a man, I put away the things of a child.

A child's manner of talking, behaving, and thinking (could the Corinthians have failed to note that Paul was comparing them with children?) are suitable for a child, but not at all befitting a grown, mature man. The imperfect speech, thoughts, and arguments proper to this life shall therefore be replaced by perfection in heaven.

12 For now we see dimly, in a mirror, but then, face to face.
     Now I know in part, but then I shall know even as I am known.

Expressing the difference between this life and the next by the words now — then, Paul clearly enunciates the future reward awaiting all true followers of Christ. We cannot now see God directly and immediately, but only indirectly and as if in a mirror. Corinthian mirrors of polished metal were famous, but not even the best of them gave back a completely faithful reflection of reality. In this life we learn about God in an obscure manner, from his works (Rom 1:20); we cannot see him directly as he is. Now we have only analogical knowledge of him; as far as it goes, this is precious, but it leaves much to be desired. In heaven the blessed see God face to face (cf 1 Jn 3:2). The knowledge of God acquired on earth in a discursive manner will be replaced by direct and intuitive knowledge, when God is seen clearly, exactly, and perfectly (the creature, of course, cannot ever fully comprehend an infinite God). But one cannot know God unless he has first been known by God.

13 *Now there remain faith, hope, and love; these three.*
But the greatest of these is love.

"Now" is sometimes used in the sense of "therefore" but also (and the context demands it here) in a temporal sense. In this life, there is room for the three theological virtues, but only love remains forever, because love alone (not faith or hope) is compatible with the blessed vision, the knowledge of God (cf *Sum. Theol.*, 1–2, q.67, a.6; 2–2, q.23, a.6).

HINTS FOR HOMILETICS

1. Holiness can be accurately measured by love alone. Love is the very heart and soul of Christianity. A woman who sweeps the floor with the love of God in her heart may be far more advanced in grace than one who works wonders. The Gospels nowhere suggest that the Blessed Virgin ever worked a miracle, yet she far excels Peter, whose very shadow was known to have healed the sick (Acts 5:15).

2. The practice of loving all men does not mean that the world should be turned into a happy home for evildoers. We must always imitate the God of love, who does not allow the wicked to find lasting happiness in evil, but resists and even punishes them. Yes, love too can inflict punishment, and in this life it is for the most part medicinal or remedial.

3. I think it was Cardinal Vaughan who once said that the spokesmen for God are among the worst salesmen in the world. Perhaps the Cardinal had something, else how would the idea have gotten about among so many that God the Father is an angry God whom Jesus Christ somehow managed to placate by his sufferings and death? The Beloved Disciple has made it plain that the Father is the God who *so loved the world that he sent* his only-begotten Son into it, thereby making it possible for us to enjoy eternal life. God is love.

Ambassadors of Christ

INTRODUCTION. Paul is determined that the Corinthians shall not, through fault of his own, have the wrong notion of what an apostle is. He wants them to realize clearly that an apostle is a man driven by the love of God. He tries to rekindle their fervor by his own (5:20–6:2). His eloquence bursts forth when he resumes (6:3–10) the contrast he had begun to make (4:7–12) between death and life, which assure the efficacy of the apostolate. Nothing human can defeat it.

THE EPISTLE: 2 COR 6:1–10

1 Working together [with God], then, we entreat you
     not to receive the grace of God in vain.

The ambassadors of Christ co-operate with God, for he is the only real source of redemptive activity in their souls (1 Cor 3:9). The Corinthians must not spoil the work that has been begun in them, but are to recall and be faithful to the obligations they assumed by their conversion and baptism. Anyone who returns to his sinful ways has, in fact, rendered the divine gift of grace empty and meaningless. It is not then so much a question of receiving as of welcoming and accepting this grace; men must after all collaborate with the grace of God.

2 For [God] says,
     At a propitious time I have heard you,
     and have helped you on the day of salvation.
     Behold, now is the acceptable time,
     Now is the day of salvation.

Paul had perceived that, like the prophetic figure of the Suffering Servant of Isaias (49:4–8), he himself was an instrument of universal redemption. What was promised in Isaias (the prophetic perfect of the verbs indicates the future as already realized), is now accomplished by Christ. The time is propitious for work, with God's help. For Paul "time" had a special meaning. The period before the coming of Christ was a time of sin and of death, followed by a time of mercy and salvation which is coextensive with the messianic period. The messianic era began with the coming of Christ, and will end with his Second Coming. Now, therefore, is the day of salvation; at its very longest, it is short compared to eternity. No one knows when it will end, but while it lasts all Christians should labor diligently in the doing of good.

3 *We give no one any cause for scandal*
  that our ministry may not be blamed.

The thread of v 1, interrupted by the citation from Isaias, is taken up again. Paul's entreaty is now supplemented by a positive description of an active ambassador of Christ. His own collaboration with God had been beyond reproach, and no one had had cause for being scandalized in him, because his teaching and his manner of living were one (cf 1 Cor 9:12; 10:33). People quickly associate the shortcomings of a preacher with the doctrine he preaches, and history affords ample proof of the harm done to religion by the unreligious lives of those who announce the good tidings of the gospel. But Paul has been a true minister of the Lord.

I

4 *On the contrary, in all things*
  we show ourselves as ministers of God, in much patience

Here begins a brilliant apologia (cp 1 Cor 4:9–13; 2 Cor 4:7–10; 11:23–29; Rom 8:35f), a remarkable combination of spontaneity and art. Paul, at his best here, lets himself go in a plunging, impetuous torrent of stirring words that fall into four orderly strophes (the verse-division from 4–10 however is not good). First a contrast: *In nothing do we give cause for scandal*, but *in all things* we manifest . . . *patience.* Despite his ardent personality, Paul was a man of proved patience and constancy. He had to be to survive. His patience was tried in nine different and difficult circumstances, which he mentions in groups of three (introduced by en = in):

4b *In tribulations, necessities, difficulties,*
5 *In stripes, prisons, in riots,*
  in labors, watchings, fastings.

The first group of trials was of a general nature, and could be traced either to chance or to human malice (cf the Acts and the Epistles for details). The second and third groups are more specific to Paul's life. He had shown patience and resignation by enduring beatings, imprisonment, and the violence of excited mobs, for he made enemies as well as friends. The last group of trials were those which Paul willingly took upon himself in order to fulfill his mission: exhausting travel and preaching, sleepless nights, and anything but a balanced diet.

II

Next follows the proof that Paul works with God. He lists the virtues which were his and are every minister's inner resources in times of trial.

6   *In purity, knowledge, patience, benignity,*
      in the Holy Spirit, in love unfeigned.
7a *In the word of truth, in the power of God,*

Purity is taken here in a general sense to mean integrity and holiness of life, or purity of intention and action, unselfishness in exercising the ministry. The *knowledge* is a knowledge of the Gospel and how to apply its principles (cf 1 Cor 14:6; Rom 15:14). *Longsuffering* or *patience* refers to the patient, uncomplaining endurance of injuries, and *benignity* or *kindness* to Paul's great goodness of heart or sympathy. His ability to put others at ease was one of the reasons for the fascination he exerted over others (1 Cor 9:19–22).

From time to time Paul was greatly helped by the Holy Spirit which provided him with the light, zeal, courage he needed to think clearly and to speak out in defense of the truth. The charity which animated him was genuine (cf 2 Cor 8:8; Rom 12:9). Pretended or affected love is extremely odious in an apostle, and unthinkable in Paul's case.

The *word of truth* linked with the sincerity just mentioned aided Paul in the faithful and effective preaching of the Gospel (Eph 1:13; 2 Tim 2:15). God intervened in the affairs of men in a startling fashion when Paul preached, and as a result many blasé Corinthians had been converted. Paul knew he did not have to depend upon his human talents to do it all (1 Cor 2:4; 2 Cor 2:17).

III

7b *By means of the arms of justice for the right hand and the left,*
8a *through honor and humiliation, evil report and good report,*

The preposition *dia* (= by, with, through) replaces *en* (= in) in this strophe (7b–8a). Very fond of military metaphors, Paul uses them often (cf Rom 6:13; 13:12; Eph 6:13ff). It is not likely that any particular virtues are meant by the *arms of justice* carried in the right and the left hand. The sincere apostle is perfectly equipped for whatever he has to do, and if the arms have to be used in battle (the right hand held the offensive weapon, the left the shield), they were used only in the spirit of Jesus. Public opinion about the apostle was sometimes good, sometimes bad, but Paul, a genuine ambassador, knew that persecutions served only to bring him into contact with the "death of Christ" and his power (cf 4:7–12).

IV

8b *[Treated] as impostors and yet authentic,*
9 *as unknown and yet well-known,*
as dying, and behold, we live,
as chastised, but not killed,
10 *as sorrowful, yet always rejoicing,*
as poor, but enriching many,
as having nothing, but possessing all things.

Now the impassioned tone gives way to a note of triumph, and in a series of brilliant antitheses Paul describes the paradoxical position in which true ministers of the Gospel find themselves. He does not refer so much to the conflict raging between the inner and the outward man, as to the erroneous judgments which the world makes in regard to God's ambassadors, whose humility is foreign to the world's notion of grandeur and dignity, and does not fit into familiar, comfortable, earthly categories. The world, therefore, affects to ignore the Apostles, but it is never really unpreoccupied with those who proclaim the Gospel from the housetops, and "not in a corner" (Acts 26:26). Across the ages the Church has been pronounced by the world as dead or dying, yet she flourishes today in an age bustlingly alive to the possibilities of interplanetary travel. Her sufferings and those of her ministers are thought to be punishment inflicted by the gods (or by God), but she cannot be put to death and does not die, and each martyr produces a score of new believers. The ministers of the Gospel *should* be sad and frustrated, but are proverbially the sunniest of men, filled with an inner joy. More often than not they live in rundown slum parishes, but at their finger tips are spiritual riches which they scatter about them with prodigal hand. They have no wives, families, homes, nothing, but all homes and all doors open to them, and they never lack what is necessary for survival. Possessing God, they possess all things. Having followed the Master, they have become masters of the world (1 Cor 3:22). They stand before the world as the living fulfillment of Jesus' promise: Blessed are you when men hate you . . . and when you suffer persecution for justice' sake. He who loses his life for my sake, will find it.

HINTS FOR HOMILETICS

1. Grace knows no seasons, but some times of the year are times of special grace. Lent is always an acceptable time, given to us by God so that we can further sanctify ourselves by prayer and fasting. Fasting is not fun, but a serious obligation; it is a sign of spiritual maturity, as well, and shows we realize the need to do penance in order to foster the grace that is in us, and to obtain yet more.

2. Explain the Lenten regulations. It should be clear that fasting begins where actual necessity leaves off. But by all means let fasting begin! No food between meals, for example.

3. To be informed Catholics, able, for example, to explain to others why we fast, giving an example of patience and kindness, coming to hear the word of truth (Lenten sermons), fighting courageously for the faith in word and deed, these are worthy practices for Lent.

Holiness of Life

INTRODUCTION. Although his stay in Thessalonica had been brief, Paul had set before his converts there all the essentials of Christianity, and so in writing to them had only to remind them of what he had taught them. He does, however, single out for emphasis certain points of that teaching, particularly in regard to growth in holiness, and in uncompromising purity of life.

THE EPISTLE: 1 THESSALONIANS 4:1–8

1 *For the rest, brethren,*
   we beseech and exhort you in the Lord Jesus,
   that even as you received from us
   how you should walk to please God (and do indeed so walk),
   [that] you should abound still more.

The affection Paul felt for his converts was deep and sincere, for they were now dear friends. He begins the exhortatory part of his letter by addressing them with the specifically Christian term, *brethren*. Having instructed them to "increase and abound in love" (3:12f); he now urges them (*beseech and exhort* is like our *hope and pray*), in the name and on the authority of Christ, to abound still more. In what? The way he had taught them was one calculated to please God, not men, and they have done well thus far (Paul does not begrudge them this judicious praise). But there is more ahead of them. Thus simply does Paul sketch out the program of a steady, unspectacular progress in the way of holiness (*walk*, not *run*); the Christian life is not static, but dynamic, demanding growth. Traveler that he is, the Christian should not stray from the way but should keep moving along it, counting no act of virtue as his last until he has reached the end of his journey. Having put aside the habits of sin acquired before baptism, the Christian's life must be such as to please God in everything. The new life, then, is one of service to God. This conviction has influenced Paul's own life (Phil 3:12–14).

**2   For you know what precepts we gave you
through the Lord Jesus**

There is nothing new in any of this. The Thessalonians will remember how he instructed them when he was in their midst, and will recall that the teaching of the Gospel was not original with Paul, nor a matter of his personal likes or dislikes. Paul's precepts had been the traditional ones, and had behind them the backing of the Lord Jesus, in whose name he preached with confidence and authority.

**3   For this is the will of God, your sanctification,
that you abstain from fornication.**

Paul was a great director of souls, and his spiritual children were urged to scale the heights of sanctity. It is God's will that all men should strive after perfection and turn from what is evil. Health, pleasure, and custom, mean nothing; man's primary aim must be to advance in the love of God, which is another way of saying that they must be holy. Such sanctity demands of the follower of Christ that he shun impurity of any kind (cf 1 Cor 6:18; 7:2), especially fornication. There is no reason to suppose that the Thessalonians were particularly addicted to this vice; Paul probably warned against it to counterbalance the prevalent opinion. His recommendation of purity must have sounded novel indeed, for pagans generally looked upon continence as an unreasonable demand, and sexual experiences before and after marriage as something to be accepted with benevolent tolerance. Paul does not take his stand on the low ideals of his contemporaries, however prevalent, but on God. The Christian must respect his own body as the temple of the Holy Spirit (1 Cor 6:15ff).

**4   That each of you [should]
know how to possess his vessel in sanctification and honor**

Some translate the word for vessel (= skeuos) by wife (cf 1 Pt 3:7) and thus make of the text an exhortation to treat one's wife with respect and dignity, or an argument in favor of marriage (and thus perhaps against celibacy). But neither the context nor the verb (possess) recommend the idea of marriage. Paul nowhere taught that marriage was for all (1 Cor 7:7). The early Greek commentators, therefore, have usually taken *skeuos* to mean the vessel of one's body (cp 2 Cor 4:7: "We have this treasure [grace] in earthen vessels"). The idea that sins of impurity are a profanation of the temple of the Holy Spirit is a powerful one and Paul will take it up again in 1 Cor (5 and 6:12–20). Between Thessalonians (51) and 1 Corinthians (57–58) several years had elapsed, but Paul's teaching concerning the Holy Spirit (1 Cor 6:19) remains basically the same, the earlier writing standing to the later letter as the sketch of a master differs from his completed work. The one, however, is in the other.

5   *not in a passion of lust,*
    like the gentiles who do not know God

Christians should not yield to the almost overpowering desire (= *pathos*) of lust (= *epithumia*), which is of an imperious and aggressive nature. Ignorance often lies behind habits of impurity, and a pagan might absolutely speaking be excused for his excesses because of his ignorance of the law of God. Yet there is a deliberate ignorance which does not excuse (Rom 1:18ff). Those converted from paganism must now live as Christians. It is interesting to note that in Paul's eyes the world is now divided into Christians and Gentiles (= non-Christians) whereas formerly the division was between Jews and non-Jews.

6   *that no one transgress and take advantage of his brother*
    in this matter,
    because the Lord is avenger of all these things,
    as we told you before and testified.

Paul is not here concerned with business matters or avarice, but with the problem of purity, especially as it affects others. One cannot help admiring his delicate sensitivity here; it prompts him to use a prudent circumlocution in referring to adultery (cf Eph 5:3). In this he differs from some of our modern writers. Promiscuity or sexual license involves others (brothers in Christ or simply one's fellow man) and means that a person is ready callously to use (misuse) others for his own pleasure. A lustful man looks upon others as existing only to be exploited by him. There are many reasons for not yielding to lust; the best reason of all is that this type of sin is displeasing to God, who will one day avenge it to the full.

**7 For God has not called us unto uncleanness,
but unto sanctification.**

Once again Paul turns his attention to the grandeur of the Christian
vocation (2:12), the second reason for avoiding impurity. The divine
call demands a victory over one's lower instincts. Man was not called
for the purpose of being impure (= epi), but to live in (= en) a
holy manner. Man is, after all, only half animal; in his spirit he is made
to God's image and likeness.

**8 He therefore who disregards [this]
does not reject a man but God,
who gives unto you his Holy Spirit.**

Therefore, which introduces the third reason, makes it plain that
holiness and purity go together. If God has called men to holiness he
has also called them to purity of life. Failure to be pure is much more
than failure to keep a man-made law; it is a sin against "the" God. To
act in defiance of God's will in this matter is to sin against God who is
actually and continually here and now giving (note the present participle)
the Holy Spirit. Sins of impurity are acts committed not only against
God, but against God who is in the act of giving us the Spirit; a temple
of the Holy Spirit has the dreadful ability to eject the divine Guest
(cf Rom 5:5).

HINTS FOR HOMILETICS

1. Becoming holy is not automatic; it has to be worked at. Many
false notions concerning holiness should be clarified — it does not consist
in the ability to work miracles, to pursue lofty contemplation, to exercise
severe corporal penances, but simply in keeping the commandments and
in being faithful to the duties of one's state of life.

2. Impurity is a capital sin with some vicious and ugly "daughters"
(cf Prümmer, *Handbook of Moral Theology*, Kenedy, 1957), § 177.

3. Remedies: flee at the first sign of danger; be humble; keep busy;
pray much, especially in time of temptation (many, strange as it seems,
do not); frequently receive Holy Communion.

Imitators of God

INTRODUCTION. Ephesus lay directly to the east and across the sea from Corinth and Athens (cf. p. 217). Paul once spent three years in this famous city, and by a miracle (Acts 19) was the occasion of a tumult which was punctuated by the dramatic cry of the silversmiths: "Great is Artemis (= Diana) of the Ephesians!" The letter to the Ephesians was written during Paul's Roman Captivity (61–63), and closely resembles another letter addressed to the Colossians at about the same time. First appealing for unity (4:1ff), he begins to describe the new life led by the Christian (4:17ff) after baptism. Today's passage contains particular counsels applicable to all: the imitation of God (and of Christ), and the avoidance of carnal sins.

THE EPISTLE: EPHESIANS 5:1–9

1 *Be therefore imitators of God, as beloved children,*
2   *and walk in love, even as Christ has loved you,*
    and gave himself up for us,
    an offering and sacrifice to God of agreeable fragrance.

How startling this invitation, to be imitators of God himself! Since an imitator is as it were a carbon copy of an original, Paul means that the Christian, who by baptism has become a beloved child of God, must by the practice of certain virtues become more and more Godlike. A father loves to see his children imitating his virtuous actions. Both God and his Son Jesus are remarkable for their readiness to forgive undeserved offenses (cp 4:32) and for their unremitting love. "Be perfect, as your heavenly father is perfect," Jesus said in his inaugural address on the mountain (Mt 4:45,48), and at the end of his life, after having given his disciples the unforgettable example of his own love, he said at the Last Supper: "This is my command that you love one another as I have loved you" (Jn 15:12). Forgiveness and love are the marks of the Christian who imitates God and follows in the footsteps of Jesus Christ.

First and foremost, love. Using this word three times in two verses, St. Paul is anxious that all should direct their lives along this path, marked out for them by Christ, whose death is here represented as a voluntary oblation of himself prompted by love for "us" (Note here how as elsewhere [2:1–14 passim; Col. 1:12f; 1 Thes 5:5; Gal 3:25f; 4:4f] Paul's inclusion of himself as a beneficiary of Jesus' saving action). In stating that Jesus has offered himself as an oblation and a victim, Paul links together the two ideas of priest and sacrifice (cp Hebrews). Jesus' offering was a sacrifice of sweet savor to God; God has no nostrils, of course, but Paul likes to make use of vivid anthropomorphisms. The image was suggested to him by the memory of the many holocausts he had gazed upon in the Temple of Yahweh in Jerusalem. The smoke of these sacrifices, mounting upward toward heaven, was thought to please God (cf Gn 8:21; Ex 29:18).

3   But fornication, and all [forms of] impurity, or avarice
      must not be even mentioned among you — as befits saints —
4   Nor obscenity, or foolish talk, or scurrility
      which are not fitting, but rather [let there be] thanksgiving.

From the heights, Paul descends to reality, being always extremely practical. Many pagans considered fornication (= porneia) as ordinary a matter as food and drink, permissible, understandable, inevitable; Paul makes it clear that such behavior is not an indifferent matter for Christians, but is a serious sin. From this he goes on to condemn all other types of impurity, whether natural or unnatural (= akatharsia). Joined with these two is pleonexia, a sin repeatedly condemned in the New Testament. Translated as covetousness, avarice, or greediness, it implies the taking of an unfair advantage, a perverse desire to have what is forbidden. Jerome considered it to be greediness for sensual pleasure; Chrysostom and many moderns hold it to be a shameless desire for money, which opens the door to many vices the poor cannot afford.

The obvious meaning of "[these things] must not even be mentioned among you" is that a Christian living his new life should flee these things as he would flee the devil himself; such things should not exist in his life. Paul speaks, of course, hyperbolically. Students and teachers of moral theology have an obligation to study and discuss the sins they will later on have to deal with in the confessional, just as medical students must study and discuss aberrations and diseases which their practice will bring to them. All this study is necessary, and can be done without indulging in or approving such sins. Aside from professional necessity, however, the conversation of Christians should be such as becomes those who are consecrated to God and are called to be saints.

Unsuitable also for all who are called to sanctity is indulgence in gross and obscene speech (= aischrotes), loose, giddy chatter (= morologia), of coarse jesting (= eutrapelia [a word which can also mean an agreeable wit]). Those who imitate Christ should instead give thanks to God (= eucharistia). The saints of all ages, looking into the mirror of nature and of grace, found ample reason to thank God for the blessings his bountiful Providence had showered upon them.

5　For understand this well,
　　that no fornicator, or impure, or avaricious man
　　— he is an idolator —
　　has any inheritance in the kingdom of Christ and of God.

The gravity of the sins just condemned is now made explicit (cf Col 3:5; Phil 3:19; Mt 6:24). A man dedicated to carnal pleasures and determined to extract the maximum amount of pleasure and comfort from life, has made an idol of his own body, and to it sacrifices his soul and eternal life. The flesh has many willing victims, and slaves. Such a man does not have (note the present tense of the verb) any part in the earthly kingdom of Christ and of God (it is but one kingdom); in choosing to lead an undisciplined life, he deprives himself of his heritage, the oft-promised spiritual treasures of the messianic kingdom, available now in the Church. By preferring to live as an animal, such a man loses grace which is the principle or source of merit, and with it, all right to a heavenly reward. A more disastrous exchange cannot be imagined. As Shakespeare wrote in the *Rape of Lucrece* 212-215:

> What win I if I gain the thing I seek?
> A dream, a breath, a froth of fleeting joy.
> Who buys a moment's mirth to wail a week,
> Or sells eternity to get a toy?

6   *Let no man deceive you with empty words,*
     for because of these [vices]
     the anger of God comes upon the sons of disobedience.
7   *Do not then throw in your lot with them.*

Christians must be on their guard against those who make light of
sins of the flesh, saying that they are "natural, pleasant, etc.," and that
God will judge them leniently. Lest any doubt linger in their minds
as to how God looks upon these sins, Paul assures his readers that they
bring down (again the present tense) the wrath of God upon the "sons
of disobedience," that is, those who rebel against God (cf 2:2). God's
anger, to be manifested on Judgment day, is a *present* reality. Remembering how the Lord punished Sodom and Gomorrah (Gen 19), the clear-
eyed sons of God must not have any part with these rebels.

8   *For you were then darkness, but now you are light in the Lord;*
     walk as children of light — for the fruit of light
     is in all goodness and justice and truth.

In times past, Christians were not only in the darkness of ignorance
and sin (1 Thes 5:4–8; cp Rom 13:12), but darkness was in them. Now
that they have entered the kingdom of light and are united to (in)
the Lord (cf Ps 26:1; 118:105), they have the light in themselves, and
are the "light of the world" (Mt 5:14). But even light must, it seems,
bear fruit, so Christians should walk in the light, seeking always what
is pleasing to God. In the concrete it is not always easy to decide what
is virtuous and right; the various virtues must be ordered and blended
among themselves, like the various ingredients which enter into the
making of an exquisite perfume. It requires supernatural prudence to
judge in each case what is the right thing to do. God's children must
keep their eyes open. St. Jerome advises us (P.L. 26:524), to be like
the money-changer who before he accepts a coin not only examines
it intently, but weighs it, and finally bounces it to test its ring! The
children of God should manifest to the world a goodness, a moral rectitude, and a life that matches their shining belief.

HINTS FOR HOMILETICS

1. No more worthy project in life can be imagined than the imitation
of God and of the Savior. It entails patient forgiveness of injuries re-

ceived, and the loving avoidance of all that is offensive to God, especially sins of impurity. The words of Our Lady of Fatima concerning the number of those who go to hell because of their lustful lives, ought to be recalled to mind at decent intervals.

2. The fragrant incense used from of old in religious services symbolized the hopes of the worshipers that, just as the incense was pleasant to the nostrils of men, the sacrifice offered might be acceptable to God. The smoke of the incense rising visibly upward aptly symbolizes the inward uplifting of the worshiper's soul toward God in prayer. A life of charity in union with Jesus mounts heavenward as a sacrifice of sweet savor, and fills the whole house of the Church with its fragrance. The prayer for the feast of St. Rose of Lima runs: ". . . grant to us, thy servants, so to run in the perfume of her sweetness, that we too may deserve to become a sweet odor of Christ."

3. To discuss or to read pornographic literature, or to view sinful things in the theater without just cause can be the occasion of mortal sins. It is wrong to expose oneself needlessly to serious occasions of sin. Evil must be exposed as evil (cf 5:13): the light must dissipate the darkness.

True Liberty

INTRODUCTION. Paul evangelized the Galatians early in the second missionary journey, about 49–50 (Galatia corresponds to the territory around modern Ankara, Turkey), and found many willing listeners there. But trouble was not slow in coming under the guise of a "back to the Mosaic Law" movement. Throughout Galatians there runs, like a recurring theme in a piece of music, Paul's insistence that Christian liberty has been won by faith in Christ. Writing from Ephesus (A.D. 54–56), he urges his converts by a scriptural argument not to put themselves again under the slavery of the Law. The argument is rabbinical in style, and is based upon the spiritual (= typical) sense of Scripture. In substance, Paul argues that it is not enough to be a son of Abraham in order to inherit the promise; one must be a son such as Isaac was, that is, in virtue of something spiritual, the promise.

THE EPISTLE: GALATIANS 4:22–31

22 *It is written that Abraham had two sons,*
   one by a slave and one by a free woman.

Paul is led to make use of the Old Testament in order to turn it against those who were trying to persuade the Galatians that the practices of the Old Law should be maintained and perhaps even be preferred to Christianity. The story of Abraham and his two wives, Sarah and Hagar, is well known (Gn 16 and 21). According to the law of the times, the status of a child was determined in advance by the status of his mother. Hagar was a slave, therefore her son Ishmael was a slave; Sarah was free, so Isaac was free. In these facts Paul finds a powerful argument for adhesion to Christianity alone.

23 *But the son of the slave was born according to the flesh,*
   the son of the free woman, however, through promise.

Ishmael was born of Abraham and Hagar according to the normal course of nature, and was the type of all Israelites who could claim

94

natural descent from Abraham. Isaac, on the other hand, was born of Abraham and Sarah through divine intervention, as the result of a "promise" (Gn 17:16; 18:10), and thus was the type of all who were not carnally, but spiritually, descended from that patriarch.

24 *There is an allegory here:*
    these women are two covenants,
    one is from Mount Sinai, bearing children for slavery;
    this is Hagar.

In English, allegory is a common figure of speech, e.g., Christ is the Rock (or the Lion) of Juda, etc.; it is an imaginary identification between two wholly dissimilar things, but it sparks the imagination and stimulates thought. In the Bible there is another sense or meaning besides the literal (to which allegory belongs), and it is called by a variety of names — the spiritual, allegorical, typical, real, figurative, or prophetical sense. It does not emerge from the very words, which simply describe some event or other, but flows from the events themselves; it is the events which have a further significance. Here Paul makes use of a spiritual sense. The story of Abraham and his wives was historical, complete in itself. But somehow that story contained another story, and was therefore of prophetic importance. Abraham's wives represent the two covenants (the Old and the New) between God and man. For Paul, Hagar is proof that the Old Law is a kind of slavery which perpetuates and begets slavery.

25 *(Now Sinai is a mountain in Arabia)*

These few words constitute the most difficult text in this Epistle, if not in the whole New Testament. Some of the best manuscripts (A,B,D,E) add "Hagar" before the word "Sinai," making possible the translation: "Hagar represents the Sinai in Arabia (or: in Arabic)." Balancing the manuscript evidence are S,C,F,G, the Old Latin, all the Latin Fathers, etc., which omit the word *Hagar* (cf Lagrange, *Galates*, p. 127, for attempts made to solve this riddle by *gematria*, that is, by numerical equivalents for the letters in "Agar Sina" and "Jerusalem").

. This sentence is a parenthesis, intended to underscore the connection between the Law-given-on-Mount-Sinai (everyone subject to this Law is its slave) and Hagar-the-slave, mother of Ishmael. Paul now adds along the same lines a more modern term of comparison, the earthly city of Jerusalem.

Now she (Hagar) corresponds to the present Jerusalem,
for she is in slavery with her children.

The word *sustoichei*, translated by *corresponds*, or *answers to*, had a military significance of *line* or *file*, i.e., those who were arranged in the same category. Both Hagar and the present Jerusalem belonged together. The earthly city, then the center of Judaism, shared in a spiritual slavery because together with all her children she was subject to the Law. The servitude begun at Mount Sinai, where the Law had its solemn inauguration, continued in the modern Jerusalem, or in the Synagogue.

26   But the Jerusalem which is above is free,
and she is our mother.

Here then is the comparison. Paul sees, on the one hand, the present Jerusalem, formerly known as Mt. Sion and of old the joy of the whole nation. At present the city was more beautiful than ever, thanks to the splendor of the Herodian renaissance. The heart of every true Israelite glowed as the morning sun glittered on the gold of the Temple and the polished marble of the public buildings. On the other hand, there was Mt. Sinai, rugged and barren, its peaks and sides bleak and desolate. Now, contrary to what we might expect, Paul sees that the bleakness of Sinai and the glories of the present Jerusalem are somehow linked together and typified by Hagar, the slave woman. Mt. Sinai looks dead, Jerusalem looks very much alive; as far as salvation is concerned, they are both dead. That is the point Paul is making here.

Still, the glories of the present Jerusalem can also serve as a basis for a consideration of the glory that is to come, i.e., of that Jerusalem which is above, which is spiritual. This Jerusalem is the Church of the New Testament established by the Savior, and it is both filled with heavenly gifts and ruled over by one who sits at the right hand of the Father in heaven. Abraham's Sarah was the type or prefiguration of this Jerusalem, and just as her children were free, so shall they be who belong to this Jerusalem which is above.

In schema form, here are the things that go together.

Hagar, the slave woman	Sarah, the free woman
Ishmael, child after the flesh	Isaac, child of the promise
Slavery	Liberty
Jerusalem . . . unto bondage	Jerusalem . . . unto freedom

What Paul had in mind reduces to the following contrast:

Synagogue	Church
Old Law	New Law
Slaves under the Law	Free men under grace
Begotten on Sinai	Brought forth for heaven

27 *For it is written:*
"Rejoice, O barren one that brings not forth,
cry out and shout, you who are not in travail;
for many are the children of her that is desolate,
more than of her who has a husband."

A text from Isaias (54:1) is now introduced to show that the members of the heavenly Jerusalem (= the Church, signified by Sarah who was sterile) would one day vastly outnumber the child of Hagar, who was once blessed by Yahweh in that she was the mother of a son. Paul has his gaze fixed upon the messianic future. The marvelous fecundity of the Church is indeed a perennial cause for astonishment.

28 *So you, brethren, are children of the promise, as was Isaac.*

Resuming the argument interrupted by the citation from Isaias, Paul describes the gentile believers as those sprung from one "as good as dead." Having no right to fellowship with Christ, with no claims of race or descent, all Christians are by faith and baptism, supernaturally born into adoptive sonship.

29 *But just as then he who was born according to the flesh*
persecuted him who was according to the spirit, so also now.

The text of Genesis (21:9) simply states that Ishmael "was playing with" Isaac, but judging from Sarah's reaction this word may have been a euphemism for persecution or mockery. The hostility between the sons of Ishmael and the descendants of Isaac was perpetuated by their descendants (cf Ps 82[83]:6–8). Even at this early date Paul knew — none better — how the Christians were then persecuted.

30 But what does the Scripture say?
"Cast out the slave and her son, for the sons of the slave
shall not inherit with the son of the free woman."

Paul appeals formally to the Scripture to bear him out. Sarah's demand that Abraham drive Hagar out of the camp was forbidden by the law of the times (cf the Nuzu tablets [*Biblical Archaeologist*, 1940]), but her demand was ratified by the express command of God (Gn 21:10–12). The Law and the Gospel, then, cannot coexist, but the Law must disappear before the Gospel. This clear, incisive statement shows Paul's remarkable insight into the facts of the case. He confidently proclaimed the death of Judaism at a time when half of Christendom still clung to the Mosaic Law, and Judaizers were undermining his teaching and prestige in the very church he had founded. He was right, as it turned out, but what appears normal to us now, was almost unimaginable then.

31 So, brethren, we are not children of the slave
but of the free woman

The inescapable conclusion of this allegorical lesson is that the Galatians must make their choice once and for all. To add the Law and its burdens to Christianity would not strengthen the good points of each, but would destroy them both. Now that we (Paul again includes himself) are free from the Law, we should rejoice in that liberty or freedom which Christ has won for us (cf 5:1). Jesus alone is the source of salvation.

HINTS FOR HOMILETICS

1. Laetare Sunday comes in the middle of Lent to remind those who are doing penance in preparation for Easter that they have full reason to rejoice in Christ; coming events cast their shadows before. Jesus' coming is preceded by his light and joy, and his presence spells nothing more clearly than: liberty from sin.

2. Fundamentally the Galatian problem is our own: we are constantly urged to give up the liberty of Christ (grace, peace of mind, self-control,

true human joy) for the slavery of sin, subjection to Satan. It is the age-old conflict between true liberty and false license all over again. And the battle rages daily in each of us, and must be won every day.

3. Many generations ago this day was given over to the celebration of a feast in honor of the true cross. The Mass for the day is filled with allusions to the Holy City, once the center of Judaism, and to the new Jerusalem which is, here on earth, the Catholic Church.

On the surface there seems to be an opposition in attitudes toward Judaism between Jesus and his ardent Apostle, St. Paul. Jesus had said that he came not to destroy but to fulfill the Law, and Paul is vigorous in his denunciations of any "Back-to-Moses" movement in the Church, a seeming conflict of views. Jesus came to the Jews as the promised Messias, and those who believe in him cannot in the same breath affirm that he is the Messias and that he is not; in other words, Christianity (= Christ has come) cannot be combined with Judaism (= Christ has not come). When he came Jesus gave to the Old Law a fullness which it had never had before — the spectacle of love Incarnate in himself and including in its embrace all mankind. In his "new" teaching, Jesus retains from the Old Law all those commands which derive from the natural law, and which have always obliged mankind, even before the giving of the Old Law to Moses. But certain other commands which had as their purpose to prepare men for the coming of the messianic age, e.g., the ceremonial and judicial practices of the old Tabernacle and Temple, have all disappeared, and have no further reason for existence. St. Paul had to fight to make certain that this should be.

I SUNDAY OF THE PASSION

The Work of Christ the High Priest

INTRODUCTION. As minister of a heavenly sanctuary and mediator of a new alliance, Jesus sealed his work with the bloody sacrifice of his life. The old religious practices were incapable of purifying men or of opening the gates of heaven; by shedding his blood in sacrifice, Jesus cleansed even men's souls from guilt, and offered the perfect sacrifice to which an eternal reward is due. The argument involves a comparison (a minore ad maius) between the old and new dispensations, and demands a clear picture of the terms of comparison. In the desert, the Israelites had a tabernacle, or tent, in which they kept their religious objects (the ark, etc); replaced eventually by the temple of Solomon, the same general division was kept. The accompanying diagram will help clarify the text.

1. Veils of the Temple
2. The Seven-branched Lampstand
3. Table of the Showbread
4. Altar of Incense
5. Ark of the Covenant
6. Propitiatory (mercy-seat)
7. Altar of Holocausts
8. The Laver, or Sea
9. Bronze Pillars

EXPLANATION OF DIAGRAM

1. The two Veils of the Temple were of fine linen, blue, purple, and scarlet; one of these hid the Hekal (= the Holy Place) from profane view, the other shut off the Debir (= Holy of Holies) from the Holy Place (Ex 26:31-33). At the moment of Jesus' death the veil of the Temple was rent in two (Mt 27:51). It is not certain which of the two was torn, but the tearing of either one would have provided a significant symbolism (Heb 9:12; 10:20).

2. The Seven-branched Lampstand, now the almost universally recognized symbol of Judaism, was patterned after a weed of that shape (Ex

100

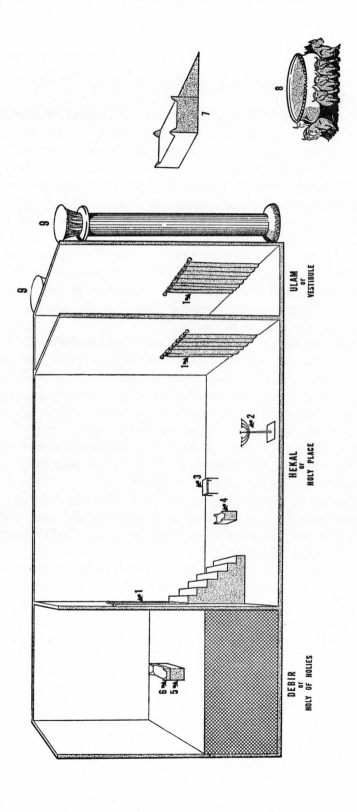

ULAM
or
VESTIBULE

HEKAL
or
HOLY PLACE

DEBIR
or
HOLY OF HOLIES

25:31–40). In this form it appeared in the Hekal only after the Exile (cf 3 Kgs 7:48–50).

3. Table of the Showbread (2 by 1 by 1½ cubits). Twelve freshly baked loaves of bread were set forth each Sabbath "in the presence of the Lord." This probably signified the grateful acknowledgment of the people of the Lord's bounty toward them (Ex 25:23; Lv 24:5–9).

4. The Incense Altar (1 by 1 by 2) stood before the inner veil and was used each morning and evening (Ex 30:1–10; 3 Kgs 6:20f). It was during his discharge of this priestly duty that Zachary was told that he would have a son (Lk 1:5ff).

5. The Ark of the Covenant (2½ by 1½ by 1½) was a small chest made of acacia wood, overlaid with gold. In it were placed the tablets of the Law (Ex 25:21, 32:15) along with some of the manna (Ex 16:32–34); Aaron's rod that sprouted (Nm 17:1–10) was placed alongside of it in the Holy of Holies.

6. The Propitiatory (or kapporeth) was a golden plaque (2½ by 1½) placed over the ark. Two golden cherubim were cast upon it, and their extended wings formed the "mercy seat" for the Lord (Ex 25:17–22). On the Day of Atonement (= Yom Kippur) the propitiatory was sprinkled with blood, and by this high-priestly action the sins of the people were deemed to be expiated, or rubbed away (cf Lv 16).

7. The Altar of Holocausts (5 by 5 by 3) was located directly in front of the entrance to the Temple (Ex 27:1–8), and apparently movable (3 Kgs 8:64; 9:25; 4 Kgs 16:14; cp 2 Par 4).

8. The Laver, or Sea, was a bronze basin (10 cu in diameter) which contained water for the purifications required of the Jews, and symbolized the holiness required for participation in God's service (Ex 30:17–21; 3 Kgs 7:23–38).

9. The Bronze Pillars, placed on either side of the entrance into the Holy Place, were named Yakin and Boaz. The exact significance of the pillars, which were probably the work of some artisan of Hiram of Tyre, is not known (cf 3 Kgs 7:15–22, 41–42).

In Israel's history there were many Temples: (1) The Tent in the Desert, Ex 25–27; (2) Solomon's, 959–952 B.C., 3 Kgs 6–7; (3) Ezechiel's 572–571 B.C., Ez 40–44; (4) The Second Temple, 520–515 B.C., Ag 1; Za 4; Esd 6; and (5) Herod the Great's greatest architectural achievement; begun in 20–19 B.C., and finished ca A.D. 64.

THE EPISTLE: HEBREWS 9:11–15

**11a   When however Christ appeared as high priest
of the good things which are come,**

We pass here from the type (Heb 9:1–10) to the antitype, from the solemn ceremonies of the Day of Expiation (Lv 16) to Christ's atoning sacrifice on Calvary. Jesus was not a priest of the order of Aaron, but he was a high priest of "the good things to come," that is, of the messianic blessings already realized and now available to succeeding generations of mankind. How Jesus deserves the title of high priest is next shown in three ways.

**11b   through the greater and more perfect tent not made by hands,
that is, not of this creation,**

The mention of the greater and more perfect *tent* recalls to mind the earthly tent for the Lord made by Moses in the desert (Ex 25:9). Some of the Fathers understood Jesus' own mortal body, which was formed directly by the Holy Spirit, to be the "greater and more perfect" one Paul mentions here. Others identified it with the Blessed Virgin, through whom Christ was born, and still others understood it to be the heavens through which — as a high priest through the tent — he passed in going to the true Holy of Holies, that is, God's presence.

**12   he entered the sanctuary once for all,
not with the blood of goats and young bulls
but with his own blood,**

The emphatic "once for all" (= ephhapax) sharply contrasts Jesus' work with that of the high priests of the Old Law, who once each year entered the Holy of Holies in observance of the ceremonies fixed for the Day of Expiation. Jesus did all that these priests did and more, for what they prefigured, he accomplished. Far more than they, then, he deserves the title of high priest, for his unique sacrifice is of eternal validity.

They carried into the Holy of Holies the blood of animals (a bullock was sacrificed for the sins of the priest, a goat for those of the people), which they sprinkled upon the propitiatory; Jesus was himself both priest and victim, thus acquiring for us an everlasting redemption.

The immediate result of his entry into the heavenly tent was ever-lasting redemption. Jesus remains in the heavenly tabernacle (the Jewish high priest stepped only briefly into the Holy of Holies). There is no need of a repetition of his sacrifice, because he has definitively and effectively secured an unending redemption (= deliverance, liberation [from sin]).

13   For if the blood of goats and bulls
        and the sprinkled ashes of a heifer
        sanctify these who have been defiled
        unto purity of the flesh,

Paul now combines two ancient ceremonies to show that he does not underestimate what the Old Law had to offer. The blood was part of the ceremony prescribed for the Day of Expiation, but the ashes of a red heifer (Nm 19) were used to make a special kind of water which cleansed those who had contracted legal impurity by coming into contact with a corpse.

14   how much the more will the blood of Christ,
        who through an eternal spirit offered himself without blemish
            to God,
        purify our conscience from dead works
        unto the service of the living God.

If the blood of goats and the ashes of the red heifer restored the faithful to an external legal cleanness, how much more will the blood of Christ, the willing and spotless victim who by a deliberate act of his own eternal will laid down his life for us, bring about an inward purity of conscience, by liberating us from our past sins (= dead works), even the remembrance of which arouses in us a sense of guilt and remorse.

We are cleansed in order to be able to offer to the living God (= the one who alone lives and gives life) the worship that is due him. The living God sees the heart, and searches out in man the inward spirit prompting his actions. Mutual confidence and love are thus restored between God and man by the blood of Christ.

The unusual expression, through an eternal spirit, refers not so much to the Holy Spirit as to an inner disposition of Christ's soul. Jesus' earthly actions all had a mark of eternity about them, and his sacrificial death on Calvary had an eternal and infinite value, an unending efficacy, for he has never revoked the intention which led him to Calvary. The redemption achieved there is an eternal one which shall never be canceled out or changed. He therefore constantly maintains in God's presence the spirit which led him to offer to his Father the infinitely meritorious and satisfactory sacrifice of his life.

15 *And therefore he is mediator of a new covenant, that —*
 since a death has occurred to redeem the transgressions
 committed under the first covenant —
 those who are called may receive the promised eternal inheritance.

The new alliance has a twofold effect, one *negative* — atonement, leading to the remission of sins committed against a Law powerless to undo them, and the other *positive* — a new covenant for those who have been liberated from sin and established in possession of supernatural goods, here called a promise (recall Abraham) and a heritage (the lot granted by God). Once attained, an eternal inheritance cannot be lost. Jesus was and is the mediator who brought about the new covenant, combining in himself the offices of Moses and Aaron. A mediator stands between conflicting parties, representing them both and able to dispose of the goods proper to both; Jesus alone is the mediator who has successfully established the new covenant between God and man. Only through him do we have any supernatural life at all.

Antitheses between

Old Law	New Law
	as regards
	SACRIFICES
Blood of sheep, goats, bulls	Blood of Christ
Victims violently slain	Christ died a voluntary victim
Offered up by others	Christ offered himself
Victims without corporal blemish	Utter holiness

THEIR EFFECTS

External cleanness	Cleanness of conscience
Participation in divine cult, social life	Sin destroyed, men enabled to serve the living God
Basic incapacity to produce grace	Inward sanctification, men made sons of God

THE TWO PRIESTHOODS

Aaron, high priest of the Old Law	Christ, high priest of the New Law
Annual sacrifice, offered year after year	One sacrificial act at the end of the ages
Reminder of sin	Destroying sin, reconciling us to God
With a blood not his own	Through bloody immolation of self
Sin typically destroyed	Sin really destroyed, and forever
In the darkness of the Holy of Holies	Christ appears for us before the God of Light
Then returned to people	He shall appear on Judgment Day

N.B.: The type is not well understood
except in the antitype. Reality
cannot be reconstructed by
starting with shadows. . . .

HINTS FOR HOMILETICS

1. From Passion Sunday until Easter the Church is preoccupied with Christ's Passion and Death. The images of Christ and the saints are veiled in somber colors, to help us enter into the spirit of Passiontide. Christ also hid himself on occasion (Jn 11:53f) until the coming of his "hour."

2. *The wounds of Christ plead more eloquently for pardon than our sins do for vengeance.* Let us hide ourselves in these precious wounds of Christ, our Mediator. At Mass He is the priest and the victim, and offers honor and thanks to the Father obtaining for us both grace and pardon. Let us often attend Holy Mass: "On the days we hear Mass devoutly we receive the divine blessing on all we do" (Chrysostom).

3. Certain terms need explaining. *Expiation* means to rub out, to erase; the sins of mankind no longer exist as a source of irritation and enmity between God and man. By his sacrificial death, Jesus offered an acceptable sacrifice for sin; as a result God is rendered *propitious,* that is, is made favorable toward man. *Satisfaction* meets the requirements of the law and results in God's being reconciled to the offending sinner. A *covenant* (= con+venire) indicates a coming together of minds, an agreement. Jesus is surety of this covenant of God with man.

II SUNDAY OF THE PASSION — PALM SUNDAY

Jesus Is Lord

INTRODUCTION. In his charming and very personal letter to the Philippians, St. Paul makes much of that unity and forgetfulness of self which should reign among the followers of Christ, and climaxes his plea by quoting a very ancient liturgical hymn. Modern translators set this hymn off as poetry. Called by some the pearl of the whole letter, it is a brilliant and highly concentrated expression of orthodox Christology, and for richness of content and profundity of phrase is equaled (and in some respects even surpassed) only by Colossians 1:15–23 and 2:9–15. That Paul should have inserted such a hymn in his letter without bothering to explain the terms he thus endorses, indicates that its sublime doctrine formed a part of ordinary Christian belief, and belonged to the common apostolic teaching. In other words, he takes for granted that no one should be ignorant of these facts; it is enough simply to recall them that all may profit from them.

THE EPISTLE: PHILIPPIANS 2:5–11

5 *Have this mind among you*
   which was in Christ Jesus.

Like human beings everywhere, the Philippians were plagued by two very common failings: a spirit of contention, and a tendency to vain glory. St. Paul was opposed to these forces so destructive of unity. Basing his plea for unity on a personal basis — "If you would comfort me . . ." (vv 1–2) — he then urges them to model their lives on the example of Christ. The sentence is clipped and terse and very difficult to translate, but the above translation fits the context very well; Jesus is their model, and they are to imitate *his* sentiments. What those sentiments were is set forth in the following verses. The hymn now begins.

107

CHRIST'S PRE-EXISTENCE

6 *He, being in the condition of God,*
   did not cling jealously
   to his equality of rank with God,

The text is unusually difficult. A literal translation would be: "Who, being in the form of (or, by nature) God, did not consider being equal to God something to be clung to (or, robbery; or, a prize to be attained). The general meaning is clear, and the traditional view of Christ emerges without distortion from a critical examination of the text. Although pre-existing as God, Jesus renounced his divine honors and abased himself, becoming mortal man. Obediently he suffered the horrible death of crucifixion, and as a reward the Father exalted him, conferring upon him the title and dignity of LORD, whereby he has the right to the explicit homage of all creation.

"Being in the condition of God" (= en morphe theou huparchon). We must remind ourselves that St. Paul used the language of the man-in-the-street, and not the categorical terms of Aristotle, the Greek philosopher. In philosophy the word *morphe* (= form [i.e., the active principle] has as its correlative the word *hule* (= matter, or potency). Paul obviously does not mean that the divinity was the vivifying and activating power in Jesus Christ, and his humanity its mere material receptacle, for that would logically imply that Christ did not have a human soul. Actually *morphe* signifies "that aspect of a being which reveals its inner constitution," and the Fathers were correct in seeing here an affirmation of the divine nature of Jesus. Their view is substantiated by the use of the present participle *huparchon*, which implies much more than merely "being." Followed, as it is, by verbs which are in the aorist (6b–7), it describes "something which perdures, or goes on as before" when the action of the accompanying verbs takes place. In other words, Christ is and exists *before* the Incarnation, he is God, and continues to be divine even when he takes upon himself the condition of a slave.

One will note that when Paul, along with the ancient Church, spoke of the Person of Jesus Christ, he ascribes to him statements which belong either to his pre-existence, or to his state of humiliation, or to his glorified life. In the God-Man there was but one Person (divine) and two natures; he was God from all eternity, and became man at a definite point in time.

Now this pre-existent Jesus did not consider (= *hegesato*) his treatment as God as a *harpagmon*. This rare word which does not appear in the Greek O.T. and is used only here in the New, has the meaning, in extrabiblical works, of "robbery," clearly unacceptable here, where there is no question of Jesus' usurping or acquiring, by fair means or foul, equality with God. It is not a question of his "ambitioning" to be God. The word must rather mean some good which he already possessed, a good which would ordinarily be clung to, his divinity. Jesus is divine, yet he does not choose to be paid now the divine honors which are rightfully his, and which he will enjoy at the proper time.

These divine honors are described in the phrase: *to einai isa theo*. The word *isa* means "equal," and when used as an adjective indicates an equality of nature; when used adverbially, it signifies an equality of rights and of treatment. That is, to be treated as God's equal (which he is). If Jesus is divine it follows that he has divine rights and privileges. He does not insist upon these, and so, is an admirable example for all of humility and of unselfishness. Let the Philippians take note.

7 *but emptied himself,*
 taking the condition of a slave,
 being made in the likeness of men

The first Adam sought a glory that was not his own; the Second Adam renounced that which was his (Jn 17:5) so as to receive it from the Father as a reward for his sacrifice (8:50,54). That very Jesus who has just been described as divine and pre-existent (= eternal), emptied himself (= *heauton ekenosen*). In other words, by his *divine* will (with which his *human* will, by a choice that was meritorious, concurred from the first moment of his conception [cf *Sum. Theol.*, 3, q.34, a.3]), Jesus provided the supreme example of humility and abnegation. The emptying of self (= *kenosis*) cannot mean that Jesus put off his divinity, for God cannot stop being God; the Incarnation was not a step down for him, but an unheard of step up for human nature. The emptying did not consist in God's becoming man, for in heaven Jesus who is God is still man but is no longer "emptied." The emptying, therefore, must mean a deliberate setting aside of privileges and dignity and bliss for the entire period of his earthly existence. But this lowliness would end forever at his resurrection.

The aorist verb, *emptied*, joined with the aorist participle, *taking* describes a single act which has two aspects: from the very moment of emptying himself, Jesus became incarnate. At a definite moment in space and time, Jesus took upon himself the condition of a slave.

Jesus never actually became a slave (= *doulos*), but the word *slave*, chosen for its overtones reminiscent of the Servant of Yahweh, brings out the contrast between Jesus' heavenly dignity and his humble earthly condition. The Son of God became subject to physical laws, liable to human authority, and subject to moral obligations which are not proper to the Son (cf Gal 4:4).

God's Son could have become man without "abasing" himself, but he did not wish to do so, desiring instead to assume human nature in that condition to which sin had reduced it, thus becoming passible, mortal, corruptible, making himself totally one with sinful man. He was "made" (= *genomenos*) in the likeness of man. Not that his humanity was a mere appearance of humanity. That his humanity was real is asserted in scores of other passages; here the emphasis is on his divinity. In thus describing the incredible humility of his new state, Paul indicates that Jesus is no ordinary man (Rom 6:5,8). The "kenosis" covers only the time of his earthly career, and will end forever at the Resurrection.

8   *and in habit found as a man, he humbled himself,*
     becoming obedient unto death, even to the death of the Cross.

From the heights of divine glory Jesus descended to the very depths of humiliation, not merely taking upon himself our human nature with all its sorry infirmities (save sin), but being willing to be taken as a mere man (literally: "having been found [= *euretheis*] as a man as regards his external comportment" [= *en schemati*]). He humbled himself, putting aside his rightful honors, and retaining his human nature, which was so evidently like that of his contemporaries that his neighbors thought him to be the son of Joseph the carpenter.

Jesus pursued the path of humiliation to the bitter end, to the most painful and degrading kind of death ancient paganism had been able to devise — crucifixion. Not that his death was one of passive endurance or a blind submission to inevitable fate; knowing beforehand what lay before him, he deliberately embraced it, obedient unto death. To obey another at great cost of time and money is one thing, but to obey unto death illustrates obedience to an unheard of degree.

These words, then, describe the climax of Jesus' abasement. His death on the cross was, however, the completion of, and the end of, his "emptying of himself." He died because of sin, of flesh, and of the Law, as St. Paul says; but he also died TO these things; they were so many facets of his "slavery," and fell from him at his death. The astonishing depths of his abasement, considering his divine origin (compare Jn 1:1–14 for a similar contrast), and especially the humiliation of his crucifixion and death on the cross, will have repercussions in glory. The debut of his exaltation coincides with his death on the cross.

CHRIST GLORIFIED

9 *Therefore has God exalted him*
  and given him the name
  which is above every name

The second and final act of the drama of salvation is about to begin, and recompense made for the humiliations described in vv 7–8. St. Gregory of Nyssa put it neatly: "The mystery of the resurrection began on the wood of the Cross" (P.G. 44:365). The ultimate conclusion of the kenosis is thus seen to be the resurrection, or resurgence of the divine condition proper to the Word of God. And not only will God reward his Son by raising him up, but he will ascend to the Father, where he will receive a special name and be invested as judge of all mankind. It is not easy to convey the proper idea of this magnificent reward; the Greek text should rightfully be translated as "God has *super-exalted him* . . ." (cf Lk 14:11; 24:26).

Since Jesus was taken to be a mere man by his fellow countrymen as long as he was on earth, that earthly life of his had not expressed his deepest reality. The Father now reveals it. His new dignity will find expression in "the name which is above every name."

In antiquity names meant much more than they do today. They were considered to be in some way identical with, and representative of, the person named. To this day Arabs in and around Palestine are cautious about giving their names to strangers, particularly if the name is written down; for them the name and the person are the same thing, and to have the one is to have (power over) the other. The name represents the person and is indicative of a person's nature, not of his function; it is, therefore, not a mere tag or label, but describes, identifies, particularizes the person named.

What name was given to Jesus? Surely not "Jesus" (= Savior), for Christ was known by that name before he was exalted by the Father. It was, moreover, a relatively common name (Josue and Jesse are variants of it) and was borne by many other Jews. The new name is not expressed until the climax of the hymn, in verse 11.

HOMAGE PAID TO JESUS

10   *that at the name of Jesus*
     every knee should bow
     in heaven and on earth and under the earth
11   *and that every tongue should confess*
     that Jesus is LORD,
     to the glory of the Father.

That "knee should bend and tongue confess" are festive words borrowed from Isaias 45:23, where the reference is to Yahweh; the homage paid to him is to be paid also to Jesus, an external manifestation of an inward recognition of him as supreme over the universe. It is unlikely that the words in 10c (in heaven, etc.) should be taken as describing a three-level universe; the details would not fit very well (some of the demons are in the "upper air" [Eph 2:2; 6; 12], and hell need not necessarily be under the earth); the three divisions, however, do embrace the entire universe. By his incarnation, death, and resurrection Jesus has become Lord of all (Ap. 5:13). Everything about him is of cosmic significance.

Jesus' new title (v 11) is finally given: "Lord." The entire universe should proclaim (and acclaim) him, saying: "Jesus is LORD!" The term Lord (in Aramaic, Maran[a]; in Greek, Kyrios) is an essentially royal title. Applied to Jesus, the term is as old as Christianity itself, and means much more than a reigning king or sovereign. Paul did not invent the title. In the Old Testament, Kyrios is the proper name of God, and corresponds to the sacred Tetragrammaton (= four-letters, for YHWH or Yahweh), the ineffable name of God (Ex 3:14). In the New, it indicates the divine character of the Savior.

The acclamation, *Jesus is Lord*, is also a profession of faith. It includes something from each phase of Jesus' life. He became the man, Jesus; he was the Messias king (= *Christus*); he is the Lord God. Taken together the terms extend from the Incarnation to the establishment of his messianic kingdom, and, finally, to his exaltation and veneration by all.

The homage which the universe now extends to Jesus-Lord redounds to the glory of God the Father.

HINTS FOR HOMILETICS

1. This magnificent passage, placed by the Church at the beginning of Holy Week, is the true key to Holy Week and its sufferings. It is regrettable that this splendid hymn, of such great doctrinal importance, should be so seldom noticed because of the many other activities of Holy Week. A study-club would be an ideal place to discuss it at length. By it many heresies are, as it were, destroyed in advance: that of Arius (for Jesus is true God, not a superior creature, or demiurge), of Sabellius (for there are three Persons in God, not just one), of Nestorius (for in Jesus there was no human person, but a divine one), of Eutyches (for Jesus possessed two natures, one human, one divine), of the Docetists (for Jesus' body was a true body). Most of these old errors persist today under new labels.

2. In our own humiliations and unimportance we have a shining model, Jesus Christ; in his glorification, we have our encouragement. It is a consolation to know that Jesus, who was delivered up to the cross for our redemption, did not thereby suffer the loss of his excellence, but rather, by and through his trials, became the glorious conqueror. God the Father loves Jesus more than he does the entire created universe — and see how he was treated!

"Service" is the hallmark of Christ's work. There are many kinds of service. One involves prestige, glory, recompense; another type is humble, difficult, servile, persevering; the one is proper to a soldier, the other to a slave. The ideal combination is to have the spirit of the one and the abnegation of the other; to serve as a slave with the soul of a hero. Such was the service of Jesus Christ.

3. The mystery of redemptive humility. Jesus' humility destroyed and

healed our human pride. To see God born of a woman, led to death by mortal men, loaded with abuses, is the supreme remedy and cure for pride. "If you are ashamed to imitate a humble man, perhaps you will not be ashamed to imitate a God who is humble" (Augustine, *In Joannem*, tr. 35, n. 16, P.L. 35: 1604). "I set about finding a way to gain the strength that was necessary for enjoying You. And I could not find it. . . . I was not yet lowly enough to hold the lowly Jesus as my God, nor did I know what lesson His embracing of our weakness was to teach" (Confessions, VII, XVIII).

The New Leaven

INTRODUCTION. Today's Epistle is taken from the heart of a passage in which Paul is decisively settling a shocking case of incest which had occurred in the church at Corinth. Strongly recommending what we would call excommunication, a medicinal punishment, he justifies his stand by quoting an ancient proverb, "a little leaven ferments the whole batch of dough." The idea is a good one, and Paul applies it neatly to the moral order, making it applicable to all sinners everywhere.

THE EPISTLE: 1 COR 5:7–8

7 *Purge out the old leaven that you may be fresh dough,*
   since you are unleavened.

Leaven or yeast appears in the Gospel as an image of corruption and of sin (cf Mk 8:15), although elsewhere (Mt 13:33) the word has a good sense. Paul here indulges in a play on two Greek words, *zumoi* and *azumoi,* = leavened and unleavened, as if he were saying "If you have leaven you aren't living." The incestuous man might contaminate others if left in their midst, so the corruption must be gotten rid of. Paul's words are especially significant if he wrote them about the time of the Passover, which recalls the death of Jesus and the resultant transformation of the Christian's life. In telling the Corinthian converts from paganism to destroy the infectious remains of their past sins, he alludes to a well-known Jewish Passover custom, the "searching out the leaven" (= *bedikath hametz*) prescribed in Exodus 12:15 (cf So 1:12). No leavened bread was to be left in the house when the paschal lamb was being slain in the Temple. Modern Jews celebrate the feast of Azymes or Matzoth (= thin flat loaves of unleavened bread). The search for leaven in the house is carried out by the children on the eve of the Passover (Moore, *Judaism,* II, p. 40), and during the eight days of the holiday only unleavened bread can be eaten.

Paul urges the Corinthians to purge out the old leaven so that they might be a fresh dough, a new creature (2 Cor 5:17). In becoming

Christians, they have become *azumoi*, that is, free from the corruption of the old man which leaven signifies. It is interesting to note that Paul speaks to the Corinthians as if they actually were what he wanted them to be. The confidence he shows in them was surely not misplaced.

7b *And indeed our paschal lamb, Christ, has been immolated.*

Here for the first time the Christian feast of the Pasch is mentioned. One ought not, however, conclude from this text that Easter ought to be celebrated on the day of Christ's death, as the Quartodeciman sect (2nd c.) once held. Christ the true paschal lamb was immolated upon the cross, and by virtue of this death Christians are purified from the leaven of their old selves. The Jews shunned leavened bread during the week of the Passover; the Corinthians ought in their turn to rid their community of all traces of corruption, and to abstain from further sin and wickedness.

8 *Let us therefore celebrate the feast,*
not with the old leaven,
nor with the leaven of malice and wickedness,
but with the unleavened bread of sincerity and truth.

The Corinthians' lack of sincerity and steadfastness draws his attention, and Paul justifies the way he has handled the case of the incestuous man with a profound mystical remark. St. John Chrysostom, who knew his St. Paul very well, declares that for the true Christian, all days are the Pasch, all days Pentecost, all days Christmas (cf *Homil. XV in 1 Cor.*, P.G. 61:125). Such feasting is not for a week but for a lifetime. Christians must have the courage to overcome evil by the performance of goodness and truth.

Hints for Homiletics

1. The Resurrection is the visible proof and sign that the Father has accepted the sacrifice of his Son. Christians, then, must "live the Paschal mystery," that is, be ever conscious of their vital and dynamic union with the victorious risen Lord. "Christ's passion and death are the cause of the forgiveness of guilt, by which forgiveness we die unto sin; but Jesus' resurrection is the cause of newness of life which comes through

grace or justice" (Sum. Theol., 3, q.56, a.2, ad 4m; cf also F. X. Durrwell, *The Resurrection*, p. 39, and C. Davis, *Liturgy and Doctrine*, pp. 25–43).

By his death Jesus has broken down the wall of enmity, the "spite-fence," so to speak, which sin had raised up between God and man. Those who share in his resurrection share in the new peace between God and man.

2. The liturgical revival has, and rightfully, focused attention upon the importance of Easter. The ceremonies of the Easter Vigil graphically bring home to us the ideas of new light and new life. No room now for attachment to the old leaven, our old faults; we are now unleavened, freed by a good confession from our sins.

3. A passerby at Hiroshima after the bomb, like a passerby at Calvary, might well have said: "Something horrible has happened here." Those who pass by the tomb of Christ today, like those who gaze upon the Grand Canyon, might well say: "Something marvellous has happened here." Now we know for certain that we go to the Father in and through the glorified humanity of Christ. Our salvation is now truly accomplished.

The Triumph of Faith

INTRODUCTION. 1 John bears a marked resemblance to the Fourth Gospel. Because of the absence of a greeting, the fact that no names are mentioned in it, and because no particular questions are taken up in it, it is thought to be a kind of encyclical letter written to the churches of Asia which were threatened by the beginnings of what we would call Gnosticism. The recipients are frequently called *little children* and *dearly beloved*; John obviously feels himself to be their spiritual father and leader, and warns them against false teachers (2:18–27; 4:1–6). Familiar Johannine terms appear: God is Light (1:5ff), Justice (2:29ff), Love (4:7ff), and Truth (5:6ff). Love goes hand in hand with observance of the commandments, which, though difficult, are not too burdensome for those who, born again by baptism and strengthened by grace, love God (Mt 11:30). Love does not count any labor as heavy.

THE EPISTLE: 1 JOHN 5:4–10

4 *For whatever is born of God overcomes the world.*
And this is the victory that has overcome the world, our faith.

The emphasis here is on the birth, not on the possessor. What is born of God is something that cannot be born of man, because it belongs to the supernatural order of grace and faith, wherein God alone is supreme. One thus born is strong as God is strong, and can conquer the world which is ruled by different principles: lust of the flesh, lust of the eyes, and pride of life (2:16). The perfect participle (*gegennemenon* = born) indicates the abiding nature of our second birth. In what follows, *victory* stands for "the means to victory," for we conquer by faith. The aorist participle (*nikesasa* = has overcome) denotes an accomplished fact, namely, the victory over sin and death gained once and for all by the incarnate Son of God, and shared in by his members.

5 *Who is it that overcomes the world, but he who believes*
that Jesus is the Son of God?

The source of victory over a world hostile to God is a living, practical

118

faith which accepts Christ, the revelation of God, without hesitation. Faith is the root of justification but is not exclusive of hope and love; it keeps before the believer the image and object of the faith: Jesus Christ, the Incarnate Son of God.

6   *This is he who came by water and blood, Jesus Christ.*
    Not in water alone, but in water and in blood.
    And it is the Spirit that bears witness,
    because the Spirit is the truth.

A very mysterious verse. John probably meant it to be against Cerinthus, a heretic who held that the Man-Jesus was united to God from his baptism to the Passion, at which time Christ, a heavenly being, deserted the man to his sufferings. John states plainly that Jesus Christ is God's envoy, singling out two events in his earthly career in which his transcendence is underscored: (1) the baptism by John, when the Father proclaimed him to be his well-beloved Son; and (2) his death on the cross. Some of the Fathers saw a reference here to the sacraments of baptism and the Eucharist, but these seem to be outside the present context, as does the blood and water which flowed from Jesus' side when pierced with a lance (Jn 19:34).

Speaking on Christ's behalf is the [Holy] Spirit who glorifies him (Jn 16:14), bears witness concerning him (15:26), and instructs the faithful (16:13). The Spirit is the spirit of truth; his testimony, therefore, calls for unconditional belief. (Note the variant reading here, "that Christ is the truth." The reading is, however, poorly attested.)

7   *There are three that bear witness [in heaven:*
    the Father, the Word, and the Holy Spirit;
    and these three are one.
8   *And there are three that bear witness on earth]:*
    The Spirit, the water, and the blood;
    and these three are one.

In brackets here are verses 7b–8a, which constitute the famous *Johannine Comma* (= a clause or short group of words). No Greek manuscript before the fifteenth to sixteenth century contains them, nor do the ancient oriental versions, nor the better copies of the Vulgate. The clause appears for the first time in a work by Priscillian, a bishop of Avila (d. 380), but was completely passed over in the great Trinitarian controversies of the fourth century and by all the Greek and Latin Fathers; it was therefore probably not known to them. Most probably the words originated as a marginal gloss and from there crept into the text. The Church reserves to herself the right to pass finally on the origin of the present reading (cf the decree of the Holy Office, June 2, 1927 [E.B. 121]).

According to the Old Testament (Dt 17:6; 19:15), the testimony of two or three witnesses was conclusive. Jesus has in his favor, then, a convincing number of witnesses — three, all of whom concur in saying the same thing, namely, that he is the Incarnate Son of God. The present participle (= marturountes, bearing witness) implies that these three are still bearing witness to him. The water, now the symbol of the Spirit (cf Jn 4:1), was in the Old Testament a symbol of the life which came from God, especially in messianic times. For future generations the Spirit will play an important role as witness, working powerfully in the souls of believers by his gifts (Jn 7:37–39).

9   *If we receive the testimony of men, the witness of God is greater;*
    for this is the testimony of God, that he has borne witness to
    his son.

All men recognize man's ability to give a trustworthy testimony. All the more so, then, must God's testimony in favor of his Son Jesus be honored. The perfect of the verb means that the Father's testimony has not altered. It can be seen still in those apostolic works by which are propagated the life of the Church and the "true life" unto which all are invited.

10   *He who believes in the Son of God*
     has the testimony in himself.

The man who acknowledges his belief in the divinity of Jesus thereby bears witness to his faith in God's truthfulness. The Gospel becomes a rule of life for a believer. The believer sees things God's way, and the witness is within him.

HINTS FOR HOMILETICS

1. Victory is one of the sweetest of human words. Success in an earthly battle or contest of strength or wits, is far less important than

victory in a struggle against sin and spiritual death. Christ by his death has robbed death of its sting for us, and while we must all face it sooner or later, it does not mean defeat for us. The victory of the children of God (believers) is real, and yet is worked out in this life by hope, faith, and love.

2. Without the faith, what would life be like? Without belief in Christ, God, the Church, life has no center but man himself, and men cannot be long satisfied play-acting as God. Where the faith is gone skepticism, bitterness, despair, superstition, and a total immersion in the senses, follows. Statistics show that Catholics are much less given to suicide than any other religious group.

3. Are the Ten Commandments outmoded, too old, too difficult? Not at all. They cannot change unless human nature is changed. Lasting success in life depends upon doing what is right in the sight of God. Filial fear, which means being afraid that one does not love enough, is a higher form of love. And "where love is, there is no labor, or if there is labor, it is loved" (cf St. Augustine, De Bono Viduitatis, XXI, 26, P.L. 40:448).

The Example of Christ

INTRODUCTION. The Prince of the Apostles wrote two letters (1–2 Peter), the first of which is used five times for Sunday Epistles. 2 Peter is not used at all for this purpose, nor are four of Paul's (1–2 Timothy, Philemon, 2 Thessalonians). Probably because the fisherman in Peter would always find writing difficult, he may have availed himself of the services of Silvanus (= Silas) in writing these letters to the faithful living in what we moderns call Turkey. 1 Peter was written about A.D. 64 from Rome (= Babylon), and besides containing the only New Testament statement of Jesus' descent into hell (3:19f; 4:6), it gives some timely advice about how to suffer with profit. Peter's stirring words about their being a new chosen people, a royal priesthood, a holy nation (2:9), and his urging that they strive after holiness no matter what happened to them, must have been a source of strength to the victims of Nero's persecution. Today's epistle begins at 2:21, and develops the subject of slaves and their behavior, begun some verses earlier (2:18).

THE EPISTLE: 1 PETER 2:21–25

21 *Christ also suffered for you, leaving you an example
that you might follow in his footsteps.*

Although he had done nothing to deserve suffering, Jesus suffered for all men, slaves included (The aorist [*epathen*] signifies that these sufferings were fully accomplished in the past and retain forever a permanent value). Slaves often suffered at the hands of their masters. Patience under such trying circumstances is part of the Christian view of life which Jesus the Redeemer came to teach. He left his followers an example or model by which they could learn this lesson. *Hypogrammos* (= example) refers to the letter or word which a teacher traced in the wax of the tablet, and which the pupils learned, the teacher's hand guiding theirs, by tracing them over and over again. Thus Christians by walking in his footsteps must repeat over and over again the patient suffering of Christ, and with his help. The slaves and little people to whom Peter directed these remarks already resembled the Master in their humble life; let them now learn to suffer as he did (1 Jn 2:6).

22 *He committed no sin,*
    nor was guile found upon his lips.

Peter compares the sinless Christ with the famous Servant of Yahweh (Is 53:9). He who was perfectly innocent of any crime was patient under undeserved suffering (cf Jn 14:30; 2 Cor 5:21; Heb 7:26; 1 Jn 3:5); his followers are to imitate him in this. Slaves in the ancient world had a bad reputation for being deceitful and untruthful. (Not, of course, that they had a monopoly on these faults!). Peter holds up to them the example of the Master, whom they should imitate in suffering and in truthfulness.

23 *When he was reviled, he did not revile in turn,*
    when he suffered, he did not threaten,
    but committed his cause to him who judges justly.

Jesus endured suffering with absolute patience and perfect resignation to the will of his heavenly Father. His enemies called him a Samaritan (Jn 8:48), a glutton and a wine-bibber, a friend of sinners (Lk 7:34), and a wicked man (Jn 18:30), and in the end put him to death. Even then, however, like the Suffering Servant of Isaias (50:7–9) he commended his cause to God. "Father, into thy hands I commend my spirit" (Lk 23:46).

24 *He who, on the Cross, bore our sins in his body,*
    so that dead to sin we may live for justice;
    by his stripes you were healed.

Jesus bore our sins (the verb conveys the picture of one bringing material to the altar of sacrifice) on the wood or tree (a euphemism for cross), thus giving all men an example of the redemptive value of suffering (Is 53:5f), for mankind is healed by the bruises of Christ. How well the slaves among Peter's readers understood this! Jesus' bruises would have stung and hurt as theirs did, and the welts which the ready lash raised upon their bodies were like those which tore the flesh of the God-Man. Suffering, then, was not just a misfortune or calamity; it could be something of great value. It definitely was a means of union between slaves and their suffering Lord.

25 For you were going astray, like sheep,
    but now you have returned to the shepherd and bishop of your
    souls.

A sheep without a shepherd to protect it is a piteous sight; it has
no guide to good pastures, no one to draw water for it from the wells,
and stands in great danger of being devoured by wild beasts. Thanks
to their faith, Peter reminds his readers, they are part of Christ's flock.
What an ordinary shepherd does for his sheep, Jesus does for his followers. Only here is Jesus named shepherd (= pastor) and bishop
(= inspector, overseer); he feeds his sheep with life-giving truth (an
activity which the Church continues through the successors of the Apostles), defends them, brings them to green pastures (cf 5:2–4; Ez 34:1ff).
    One can only guess at the impact made upon slaves by Peter's words,
which assured them that they were of personal and spiritual value, that
Christ had come to save them and to be their "good shepherd." The
unexpected revelation that they were of importance in God's sight, that
Jesus who suffered as they so often did had redeemed the world, may
not have brought them immediate physical freedom, but it assuredly
brought them something of the peace which only Christ can give.

HINTS FOR HOMILETICS
    1. The sick and the suffering, like the poor, we shall always have with
us. Inevitably wherever a man builds a house, a thorn tree grows
beside the door. Despite giant strides made by medicine, physical
pain is a faithful attendant of human living. We must, therefore, learn
to live with some discomfort, headaches, runny noses, etc.; it is not
good for man always to be taking pills, seeking physical comfort, well-
being. Europeans in general do not have our manufactured dependence
on nose drops, aspirin, sleeping tablets, etc., but prefer to let nature
handle most minor disturbances. Of course moderate care of the health
and avoidance of suffering is commendable, and any illness which seriously impairs our efficiency should be attended to promptly. But if
despite our best efforts we are chronically sick, we should pray: "Lord,
I would not have chosen this myself, but since you have sent it my
way, I will accept it for your sake. I may sometimes weep for pain,
but I want you to know, Lord, that I wish to suffer in union with you."

Father Walter Farrell, author of the famous *Companion to the Summa*, was never without a headache. A doctor who examined him in 1943 exclaimed, "This man has surely not been able to work for the past fifteen years!" Yet in that period he had started *The Thomist* (a speculative quarterly review), written four books, given many lectures and retreats, conducted a huge correspondence, and been chaplain during World War II on board the *Yorktown*.

2. Some sufferings come to us from outside, such as acts of violence (sluggings, etc.), injustice (employers sometimes cheat on their help, and sometimes the help does not turn in a good day's work), robbery, etc.; the list is a long one and all too familiar. While becoming more social-minded, and working to remedy such abuses, Christians should not overlook the value of redemptive suffering. If it can be borne with Christian resignation and courage, suffering is a badge of honor. It does not, however, dispense anyone from fulfilling the duties of his state in life, or from reacting actively against the causes of unjust sufferings.

3. Our modern world is impressed by the spectacle of Mahatma Ghandi, the apostle of passive-resistance to injustice. First of all, let us not be scandalized at seeing goodness, possibly holiness, outside the Church. But can Christians be satisfied with the passive enduring of evil? Is *that* hungering and thirsting after justice, the proper way to follow Christ? Jesus deliberately *chose* suffering, welcomed it in a spirit of love. And by his expiatory death he changed, not the outward form of government, but the very heart of man. Chesterton makes the point in *The Everlasting Man* that when set side by side with Confucianism, Islamism, Buddhism, etc., the Church may suffer by comparison under one aspect or another, for they can be superior in one point or another (dogma excepted), but surpasses them all in over-all excellence.

The Apostolate of Good Behavior

INTRODUCTION. See page 122.

THE EPISTLE: 1 PETER 2:11–19

11 *Beloved, I exhort, you, as strangers and travellers,*
  to abstain from the passions of the flesh
  which war against the soul

Peter addresses his readers with affection (beloved), for he wishes them to realize that his austere recommendations are prompted by a desire to do what is best for them. The program he recommends will repay them with eternal well-being. It consists in this, that the Christian shall consider himself as one living outside his home or native land (which is heaven), surrounded by a world that is immersed in the senses and hostile to spiritual demands which would curb those senses. The evil to be opposed is not wholly an external one, however, for there resides in each man the baneful heritage of original sin. This is especially noticeable in the unruliness of the body and its desires. The struggle against lust is part of human living and no one is exempt from the struggle. Victory over the flesh has to be won many times, and every day. The most terrible war of all is the one a man has to wage against himself. But without a war there can be no victory.

12 *Behaving honorably among the Gentiles, so that*
  in that for which they calumniate you as evildoers,
  they may, seeing your good works, glorify God
  on the day of visitation.

A Christian's life should be beyond reproach. That a man can be misjudged and slandered even though he does a good work is nothing new. The pagans among whom the early Christians lived did not look kindly upon those whose lives differed from their own. The Christians were accused of the most atrocious crimes (Peter was not, probably, thinking of Nero's official persecution): incest, cannibalism, treason, boycott, disturbing the peace, etc. (cf Ricciotti, *History* I, p. 191ff).

Jesus had predicted that his followers would have to endure such trials (Mt 5:11,16,44). They would live in a world which would construe their lack of conformity as a criticism of pagan customs and moral laxity. The Christians' best defense, Peter declares, is their innocence, which will eventually make an impression upon those who deride and persecute them. When the pagans will be so convinced is not clear, perhaps only on the day of judgment, but perhaps also at that moment when through grace the pagan "sees the light" and is converted.

13 *For the Lord's sake be subject to every human institution,*
14 *whether to the king as supreme, or to governors as sent through him*
   for vengeance on evildoers and for the praise of the good.

Peter next recommends obedience to all lawfully constituted authority, to the king (even if that king was Nero), to proconsuls, legates, even to procurators. This obedience should be founded upon a supernatural motive, "for the Lord's sake." Men cannot live together without authority, and they need it. By it evildoers receive the proper punishment, and those who lead upright lives contributing to the common good are honored and encouraged. Jesus gave an example of the proper attitude toward those in authority when he said, "Render to Caesar the things that are Caesar's" (Mt. 22:21).

15 *For it is God's will that by doing good*
   you should put to silence the ignorance of foolish men.

Submission to rightful authority is the divinely approved way of silencing (literally: "muzzling," as of dogs or oxen) those who calumniate the followers of Christ. Argument seldom convinces a stupid man, but such can be won over if Christians are seen living irreproachable lives. A good life is more effective than a hundred sermons about goodness.

16 *Live as free men,*
   but do not use your freedom as a cloak for malice.
   Live as servants of God.

Freedom, even spiritual freedom, is a heady wine. Some of the first converts thought that freedom meant liberation from all restraint, and used their new found freedom as an excuse for indulging in licentious conduct (Gal 5:13; Jude 4). This was wrong, of course, for Christian liberty is not moral anarchy, and gives no man the right to do anything he pleases. Paradoxically, even in freedom there is a kind of slavery; the Christian must serve God.

17 Honor all men. Love your brothers.
Fear God. Honor the king.

Four quite telegraphic phrases sum up the social duties of the Christian. The Christian must treat all men, whether converts or pagans, Jews or Gentiles, slaves or master, civilized or uncivilized, with dignity and respect. Those who are of the household of the faith should be objects of special affection (Gal 6:10). The fear of God is not degrading, cowardly; it is rather a loving fear which renders a man apprehensive lest he has not done enough for his loving Father. The emperor should be honored. Thus casually, Peter here makes the all-important distinction between God and the most exalted of kings; the distinction was important, for at this time emperors were being accorded divine honors, and actually believed themselves to be divine.

18 Servants, be submissive to your masters with all respect,
not only to the good and kindly, but also to overbearing ones.

The word used here for servants (= oiketes) refers to house slaves, or domestic servants. These must revere their masters and look upon them as God's instruments (Eph 6:5). However human the tendency to weigh superiors in the balance and to love or hate them on human grounds ("No man is hero to his valet," the English proverb goes), the Christian slave should look upon obedience to his master as an obligation. Like Paul, Peter accepts his world as it was, and instead of abolishing slavery which was an accepted part of the social fabric, counsels both slave and master to fulfill the duties proper to their states in life.

19 For it is a grace to endure pain for God's sake,
while suffering unjustly.

Under the old regime, slaves had absolutely no rights, and often suffered cruelly and unjustly, depending upon the whims and temper of their masters. Peter teaches that obedience is always pleasing in God's sight. Pain or affliction (= lupe) is primarily something touching the mind or spirit. Nothing rankles so much or arouses such resentment as injustice; it has ever been so. Patient endurance of undeserved wrongs, however, is precious in God's sight, if done for him and not out of some unworthy motive such as flattery, cowardice, etc.

HINTS FOR HOMILETICS

1. The first thing a pilgrim must remember is that he is a pilgrim. Taking with him only what he needs for his travels, he should not dally on the way. Often he will see bargains or interesting sights which tempt him to stop. If he keeps his mind fixed on his home, he will not allow himself to become embroiled in affairs which do not really matter. Many forget that they are pilgrims and come to look upon the world as their permanent abode, dedicating themselves to the acquisition of earthly goods. St. Paul reminds us that "We have here no lasting city" (Heb 13:14). Bede Jarrett's *No Abiding City* (Newman, 1949) deserves reading.

2. The Church is often accused of siding with the party in power and with the privileged classes. It is more accurate to say that the Church recognizes the obligations of all men, high or low, and never ceases to remind them of their mutual duties. The Church teaches that just war is possible, that rebellion can be the correct and virtuous course of action. But the Church never loses sight of the principle that one should never embark upon an action which will cause more evil than it will produce good.

3. It has been said: "There would be no bad pagans if there were no bad Christians." In what way does my practice of the faith make me different from those who have no religion at all? Only in matters pertaining to the Sixth Commandment? to divorce or birth control? What interest do I take in matters of justice?

IV SUNDAY AFTER EASTER

Living Faith

INTRODUCTION. The author of this Epistle was not the Apostle James, but James "the servant of God . . ." This makes him James "the brother of the Lord" (Gal 1:19), one of those who are always distinguished in the N.T. from the Apostles (Acts 1:13ff; 1 Cor 9:5). This James then is not the son of Zebedee, put to death by Herod in A.D. 42, nor is he the son of Alpheus (= ? Cleophas), but one who held a leading position in the mother church at Jerusalem. Paul refers to him as "a pillar" (Gal 2:9); in the Council of Jerusalem (Acts 15:13ff) his was the decisive opinion. James was either stoned ca A.D. 62 (so Josephus), or thrown from the pinnacle of the temple ca A.D. 66 (so Hegesippus). The Epistle was written to Jewish Christians, but not in the classic epistolary mode (cf 1:1f). An impersonal letter, it strongly resembles the book of Proverbs, but is far superior to that sapiential work inasmuch as James was deeply imbued with Jesus' moral teachings. Because James in his epistle insisted upon the necessity of works, Luther condemned it as an "epistle of straw." Various dates ranging from the early 40's to as late as A.D. 150 have been assigned to it; most Catholics place it either ca 49 (in which case it would be the earliest writing of the New Testament) or A.D. 58.

THE EPISTLE: JAMES 1:17-21

17 *Every good gift and every perfect present is from above,*
     coming down from the Father of lights
     in whom there is no change, nor shadow resulting from changes.

Having just spoken (v 13ff) about temptation, James makes it clear that from God only goodness comes; no one can reasonably blame God for temptations — a man's own passions explain them perfectly well. God sends his gifts from above, that is, from heaven. He is the Father of Lights (cf 2 Cor 1:3; Eph 1:17; Jn 8:44 for similar expressions), for he is the author and creator of all heavenly bodies, even those which seem to be the sources of our light — the sun, moon, and stars. Although not a professional astronomer, James in an obscure phrase (*parallage he tropes aposkiasma*) alludes to astronomical matters. Unlike the signs of the zodiac or any of the constellations, unlike the sun and moon whose movements through the heavens sometimes terminate in the eclipsing of their light, God does not change; he is immutable. The Father of Lights does not change. He is "clothed with majesty and glory, robed in light as with a cloak" (Ps 103[104]:1–2. The psalm is a magnificent hymn in praise of God the Creator).

18 *Of his own will he has brought us into being by a word of truth, that we might be a kind of first fruits of his creatures.*

As far as we are concerned, God's most perfect gift to us is the gift of spiritual birth, or justification. While the term "to bear, or to bring forth" (= *apekuesen*) is not limited to the female principle, it is oftener used in that sense, and here suggests the tenderness of God's love for us. He willed us into being, *bouletheis* implying a movement of the will following upon a choice. Perfectly happy in himself, God who had no need to create chose to make us and to raise us to the supernatural order, to the life of grace (Dt 32:18). It was inevitable, perhaps, that some (Calvinists) should misinterpret this text and explain it as justifying a denial of human liberty in the matter of salvation. James says no such thing, but merely points to God's freedom in acting "outside the divinity."

The *word of truth* by which we are begotten is not to be understood as referring to the Logos (Jn 1:1), nor to Jesus, but rather as referring to the Gospel (cf Eph 1:13) or the ensemble of God's revelation to men (cf Ps 118[119]:43).

The fruits first ripe were, in olden times, plucked and brought as an offering to the Lord (Ex 23:19; Lv 23:10,17) in recognition of God's rights to the entire harvest, and in gratitude for his bounty. The first fruits were an earnest of the harvest, which was at the disposal of the owner of the fields. In NT times, however, all of the fruit is seen to belong to God. The convert Jews of the fatherland were God's first fruits; they were also a pledge of the harvest of the Gentiles. When in their turn the Gentiles received Christ, they became the first fruits of a still greater harvest to come.

James qualifies the term "first fruits" by "a kind of" (= *tina*), thus reminding his readers that their supernatural rebirth is only expressed by approximation and analogy; this new birth is a spiritual one. In the old dispensation the Chosen People as such was called God's son; in the new, images like regeneration, filiation, and birth apply directly to individuals. By grace, the believer shares in the very life of Christ.

19 *Know this, my beloved brethren.*
   Let every man be quick to listen,
   slow to speak, slow to anger.

James' readers were doubtless already convinced that what he writes is true. What they must realize is that the word of truth imposes obligations upon all; they must be willing to listen (Sir 5:11; Prv 1:5; 10:18ff), must not jump at the chance to tear things apart by empty arguments, and must avoid anger (Prv 14:29). Life can be needlessly complicated by an unwillingness ever to listen to another, or to hear what he says.

20 *For man's anger does not work the justice of God*

An angry man (or woman) is less likely to do what is just and holy in God's sight. It is quite human, however, to identify one's own outbursts of anger with zeal for the cause of God, and to feel that God can well be served by deeds of violence. Not so, says James, at least not always. Generally speaking a man's anger does not serve God's cause.

21 *Therefore laying aside all uncleanness and abundance of evil,*
   receive with docility the implanted word
   which is able to save your souls.

Spiritual growth goes hand in hand with the elimination of bad habits. The moral virtues are in fact good habits designed for the rectification of the passions. If moral uncleanness ($=$ hruparia) becomes a habitual state of mind, it will overflow into outward actions ($=$ perisseia) such as uncharitableness, spite, meanness. One must, however, combat not only an excess of vice, but the vice, the bad habit, itself. A wise man will not only be favorably disposed toward the Gospel, he will welcome it into his life no matter what the cost (3:13). James urges that this saving word be received with docility. The Greek word he uses for docility ($=$ praus) is elsewhere translated as "meek" or "gentle"; it describes a beast that has been tamed, for a gentleness behind and beneath which there is strength firmly held in control. Thus docility does not mean loss of strength or weakness, but *discipline*, as exemplified in the performances of professional actors, golfers, and singers.

The *implanted word* of the Gospel, ingrafted into our very souls, is to be received, not with anger (v 20) but with mildness (see above, *praus*). No obstacle should be allowed to stand in the way of the Gospel, which must sink deep roots into the mind and heart, and to manifest itself in Christian actions (Mt 7:24; Jn 13:17; see Jer 31:33).

HINTS FOR HOMILETICS

1. The fundamental note of the universe is liberality (Bergson). God's lavishness in creating and maintaining the subhuman world is surpassed by his generosity in spiritual matters: he has given us the needed Redeemer, promised us heaven, established a Church, instituted the sacraments. What sort of generosity is reflected in my life toward the giver of all good gifts?

2. An open mind is fine, but not if it is open at both ends, advertising men will say. Who listens any more? pays attention? Why listen or remember? Modern propaganda is largely dedicated to material causes (politics, advertising, etc). The saving word of the Gospel needs spokesmen on every level of life, for faith comes from hearing. One has to cultivate silence in which to listen to and ponder over the word of God; then he is ready to speak. Silence is preparation, not a vacuum.

3. Our anger, petty rages, impatience, and irritability seldom accomplish much good, because they arise from an unworthy cause, our pride. We need to practice patience — God is patient and we can imitate him — and to become God-controlled. Thus masters of ourselves we can serve others. We will not lose our sense of moral indignation, but use it when we ought to become angry (e.g., over social injustices); where it concerns ourselves we ought, generally, to "count to ten"!

V SUNDAY AFTER EASTER

Christianity in Action

INTRODUCTION. See page 130. The connection between the Gospel and the believer's actions is perfectly obvious: the precepts of the Gospel should govern a man's whole life. James develops this theme with the striking but often unappreciated example of a man looking into a mirror.

THE EPISTLE: JAMES 1:22–27

22 *Be doers of the word, and not hearers only, deceiving yourselves.*

The world is divided in every age, it seems, between *doers* and *talkers*. James urges his readers to be doers *of the word*, that is, to carry out the demands of the Gospel. The phrase is semitic in tone, and may be an echo of a saying of Christ which was not incorporated into the Gospels (= agraphon). Paul (Rom 2:13,21 ff) and James seem to have used a common source (Mt 7:24–27; 23:3ff). It is strange how men can deceive themselves into thinking that their word is as good as their deed.

23 *A man who is a hearer of the word and not a doer*
  is like a man who looks at his natural countenance in a mirror;
24 *for he looks at himself and goes away,*
  and immediately forgets what sort of person he was.

The Gospel is a mirror in which a Christian can study his spiritual appearance. One looking into a mirror sees where the dirt is that needs washing, the tousled hair that needs combing, and the tie that needs straightening before one "fits the (social) picture." On a spiritual plane, a man can examine himself to see his good points and the bad ones, to see where his conduct squares with the Gospel, where it needs touching up. As a man looks into a mirror for a definite purpose, it is quite unreasonable for him to notice a stain on his face and do nothing about it; if he is that uninterested he will in time surely forget all about washing up. The man who so acts shows how little he cares whether he fits into the gospel picture or not. He also shows that he does not know himself for what he is.

25 *But he who looks into the perfect law of liberty, and perseveres,*
not becoming a forgetful hearer but rather an active doer,
he shall be blessed in what he does.

A good man will not only look into (literally: bend over [to look])
the "perfect law of liberty," which is the Gospel, the new Law which
fulfills the Old Law and surpasses it by its ability to bestow liberty upon
those who follow it; he will conform his life to what he sees and hears.
God approves of such a man, and this kind of doer will know of Christ's
peace even in the present life. The "yoke" of Christ (Mt 11:29) is
one that frees a man from sin (Jn 8:32–35) and delivers him from the
law of sin and of death (Rom 8:2). Knowledge of the Gospel is good,
but not enough; a man must practice its teachings. This cannot be done
in a single instant or in any one act, but requires an entire, dedicated
lifetime.

26 *If anyone thinks he is religious, not bridling his tongue,*
but deceiving his own heart, that man's religion is vain.

Religion (= *threskeia*) is here used of the exterior manifestations of
belief which come under the heading of "religious practices." Externalism
in religion, coupled with an undisciplined tongue, makes a mockery of
religion. The first demand made of a Christian, then, is that he watch
his language.

27 *This is religion pure and undefiled before God and the Father:*
to visit orphans and widows in their affliction,
and to keep oneself unspotted from the world.

True Christian piety shows its true strength and vitality in the exercise
of fraternal charity. It is not enough not to hurt another; the Christian
must be prepared for positive action, especially in the case of orphans
and widows. Such help was commanded in the Old Law in God's name
(Ex 22:21ff; cf Ps 68:5), and was generously given in the New (Acts 6:1;
1 Tim 5:3f). The widows and orphans represent, of course, all those who
are in sorrow and in need.

James apparently thought his readers were in danger of forgetting the
need to practice charity toward the unfortunate. He also reminds them
of their need to keep themselves unspotted and clean, in a world which

was notoriously given over to sensuality (cf 1 Pt 4:3; Rom 13:13).

The practice of one's religion involves much more than being good to the afflicted and keeping oneself unstained by the prevailing moral corruption, but it is unlikely that James intended to give a complete picture of what is pleasing to God and the Father. He cannot be thought to condemn other actions done in God's honor, such as for example: prayer, fasting, doing penance, receiving the Sacraments.

HINTS FOR HOMILETICS

1. The tongue is a truly amazing thing, capable of producing the loftiest and the lowest of results; it is an instrument of both good and evil. The power of the spoken word is well nigh incalculable (recall how during World War II the leaders of all the warring countries were superlative orators: Churchill, Mussolini, Hitler, F.D.R.), and the pen is mightier than the sword. Bridling the tongue (see St. James's remarks on the tongue in chapter 3) is a necessary but herculean task, if good works begun out of the love of God are not to be spoiled by vicious talk, or other such sins.

2. The mirrors of the ancients were far inferior to ours, and one had to use them longer to see in them what we can perceive instantly in ours. The Gospel is a perfect mirror, and shows back to the one who looks into it exactly what Christ's followers are expected to do. There the ideal of Christian life (love of God, of neighbor, of self-forgetfulness) is clearly pictured. The Little Flower preferred the Gospels to learned spiritual treatises (cf M.M. Philipon, O.P., "The Little Way to Greatness," Cross and Crown 1 [1949], p. 322).

3. Are we doers of the word, or hearers only? Practical piety demands that we join our belief with the practice of that belief in our daily life. Mere knowledge is sterile; knowledge of God's ways plus practice of the faith is a fruitful life. Moreover, we must accept, and put to good use all of the Gospel, not just those parts of it which appeal to us.

SUNDAY AFTER ASCENSION

Readiness

INTRODUCTION. Because of its astonishingly rich doctrinal content, 1 Peter was much commented upon in the early days. It treats in passing of such things as Christ's pre-existence, his redemptive Passion, the resurrection, baptism, the Trinity, the Church (cf also p. 122). Today's section is concerned with the proximity of the Parousia (how the early Christians loved that subject!) and how best to prepare for it — by practicing Christian love.

THE EPISTLE: 1 PETER 4:7–11

7 *The end of all things is at hand.*
   Be therefore wise and sober with a view to your prayers.

The proximity of the second coming of Christ and of the Judgment deeply stirred the early Christians (Phil 4:5; Jas 5:8; 1 Jn 2:18, etc.). In modern times some scholars have tried to make this expectation of the End the central point of Jesus' own teaching, but in this they are certainly following a false lead; Jesus was much more concerned with a positive, present reality, the Kingdom of Heaven which he was establishing. At most, eschatology was on the edge, but not at the center of his preaching. After his death and resurrection his followers were keenly aware that his return from the dead presaged a new age and the end of the present order; in this they were correct. They were conscious of being in the last phase of the world's history, relatively but not absolutely close to the last night of the world. This fact stimulated them to great activity and was reason enough to make them lead good lives. Jesus had urged them to be vigilant and to pray, for no man knew the day nor the hour when the last day would dawn (Mt 24:36). Following this lead, Peter urges his readers to temperance of mind and soberness in matters of drink, and this so that they will be able to say their prayers (note the plural, prayers). The day is near, perhaps not imminent but near; meanwhile they must bear with their crosses and practice Christian virtue.

**8 Above all, maintain a constant love among you,
   for "love covers a multitude of sins."**

Grace helps a man to become master of himself and of his passions, but besides this the Christian has an abiding obligation to love others. Peter gives as his reason for urging this unselfish kind of love that it "covers a multitude of sins" (Prv 10:12). From the context it is clear that Peter is not referring to the love one may have for God (as Lk 7:47), but to love of one's neighbors, a love that prompts a man not to reveal or to harp upon his neighbor's faults (Prv 17:9). Such love is the correct way for a Christian to behave (he loves sinners, but not their sins), and will in time make its beneficiary ashamed of his sinful behavior, or uncomfortable in it, after the fashion of Paul's "coals of fire on his head" (Rom 12:20).

9 Be hospitable toward one another, without murmuring.

Hospitality, given with cheerfulness and without grumbling, proves the reality of one's love for others (Mt 25:35ff). The poorer members of the early Church, and poor itinerant preachers, provided many opportunities for the practice of hospitality; what public accommodations there were in those days were hardly suitable to, or within the reach of, the lowly followers of Jesus. The exhortation to hospitality recurs frequently (Rom 12:13; Heb 13:2; 1 Pt 4:9, etc.). In Islam, hospitality is still the first law of the desert.

**10 Each man, according to the grace he has received,
    put yourselves at one another's service,
    as good stewards of the manifold grace of God.**

Christians should be quick to help one another, sharing this world's goods with them (= hospitality), and exercising the special grace given to them in their behalf. Grace, which sometimes signifies the charismatic gifts, may also refer to very unspectacular grace. God's gifts to man all have certain social obligations attached to them, and the recipient must respect God's intentions in such matters, administering the gifts carefully, mindful always of the inevitable accounting he must make for his administration of them.

11 *If anyone speaks, let it be as the words of God;*
   if anyone ministers, let it be as with the strength
   which God provides.

Peter refers here to the charismatic improvisations which were a common feature of the first Christian meetings (cf 1 Cor 14:2–19; Acts 11:27 f; 2:4ff). Those who were so "favored" were sometimes looked upon as prophets (Acts 11:27f). They must not, because they were so chosen, become proud, or try to please men by showing off their wisdom; let them simply be conscious of the dignity of their calling.

Some members of the community were called upon to serve others by exercising corporal works of mercy (hospitality, care of the sick, of orphans, etc.), and their ministry also included public services carried out in the church (cf 1 Cor 12:28), especially those touching the liturgy itself.

These offices were not to be looked upon as mere natural duties but were to be judged from a supernatural point of view. Such works were possible only because God supplied each man with what he needed to do it well, or well enough for God's purposes. The deacons were soon helped in works of charity by deaconesses (Rom 16:1; 1 Tim 5:9).

11b *So that in all things God may be glorified through Jesus Christ,*
   to whom belong glory and power for ever and ever. Amen.

The Father is glorified by the glorification of the Son. All apostolic works are energized by the desire to glorify God by serving and praising Jesus Christ. Nothing, of course, can add anything to God's glory and power, for he has a right to and actual possession of them both (2 Pt 3:18). Omnipotence and glory (= public recognition with praise) he has had and will have from all eternity (= for *ages of ages, or time without end*).

Amen, a Hebrew word used in almost all languages as a liturgical formula, expresses agreement with what has just been said. In the Old Testament, Amen was uttered aloud by the people at the end of prayers and thanksgiving (1 Par 16:36) and on other occasions (Neh 5:13; 8:6). It also was frequently used as the termination of a doxology. The word means *so let it be, truly, even so.* What Peter is saying here then is, To Jesus Christ let there indeed be glory and power. . . .

HINTS FOR HOMILETICS

1. Time flies, and both the evening of life and the day of judgment advance rapidly upon every man. Death catches many people unprepared (the number of those who die without making wills is unbelievably high); how should one prepare for that moment which ushers in eternity? By leading a good life all the time, not waiting until the last moment to pray or to seek absolution. Cf Vonier, *Collected Works*, I, p. 57ff; and Granada, *Summa of the Christian Life*, III, p. 323ff.

2. Peter urges us to be careful and sober, to use our heads and to pray a lot. He urges us to practice love of neighbor, to practice custody of the tongue, to work actively in pious (parish and social) projects, and cheerfully to practice hospitality according to our means.

3. Talents are given to be used, and Jesus condemned the lazy servant who failed to develop his. To the objection that we have no particular talent we may retort that "the loaves were few until the apostles began to distribute them; then, although the wants of many were satisfied, many baskets were filled with the fragments that were left over. Just as the bread increased in the very act of breaking, so those thoughts which the Lord has granted to me in view of this work will, when I begin to share them with others, be multiplied by his grace. Thus in the very act of distributing I shall, instead of becoming poorer, be made to rejoice in the marvelous increase of wealth" (St. Augustine).

The Coming of the Holy Spirit

INTRODUCTION. The Apostles, together with Mary the mother of Jesus, spent the ten days following the Ascension in prayer. But now the days of quiet recollection were over, and the time had arrived for the fulfillment of Jesus' promise. Luke indicates the time, the place, and the persons involved in this decisive moment in the life of the Church. The "witnesses" are about to receive the "power" they shall need to carry out their important function.

THE EPISTLE: ACTS 2:1–11

1 *When the day of Pentecost had come*
they were all gathered together in one place.

The word *Pentecost* is an adjective, and means "fiftieth." The meaning being so clear, it was not customary to supply the word *day*. Pentecost was one of the three great feasts (the Passover and the feast of Tabernacles were the other two) which every able-bodied Jew was obliged to celebrate in Jerusalem (Ex 23:14–17). *Pentecost* is a Greek word; in Hebrew the feast was called *Weeks*, or the *Harvest feast*, or *Day of first fruits* (Nm 28:26). It was one of the most solemn and joyful occasions in the Jewish liturgical cycle, and the faithful assembled for it in great numbers, some of them coming from a great distance.

It does not seem likely that the "*all*" refers here to the 120 disciples who had assembled for the election of Mathias, but rather to the Twelve (cf Acts 1:14). The place is commonly understood to have been the place of the Last Supper, the Cenacle or upper room. This room is located in the Syrian Quarter of modern Jerusalem, next to the Church of the Dormition (of Mary). The Moslems are in possession of this spot, thinking it to be also the site of David's tomb (which it assuredly is not).

2 *And suddenly a sound came from heaven*
like that of a violent gust of wind
and it filled the whole house where they were sitting.

What actually happened can only be described, and that inadequately, by comparisons drawn from our familiar world. First, without any warning, along about 8 o'clock in the morning (cf 2:15), there was a confused but loud noise which seemed to originate in the heavens. It was not the wind but definitely sounded like it, and the noise filled the whole house, not just the room in which they were sitting. The wind was often a sign of God's presence (cf 2 Sm 5:24; Ps 103[104]:3, "Yahweh rides upon the wings of the wind"), and it is not improbable that the Apostles sensed that this wind announced the fulfillment of Jesus' promise to send the Holy Spirit (cf Jn 7:37–39; Lk 24:49; Acts 1:5–8).

3 *And there appeared to them tongues as of fire dividing,*
   and it sat upon each one of them.

The presence of the Holy Spirit was next announced by something which was not fire, but looked like a fiery globe of fire which, as they gazed upon it, began to part into fiery tongues of unspecified size, which then descended upon each of them. Fire too was often a symbol of God's presence and power (cf Ez 1:4; Ex 3:2; 13:21; Mal 3:2; Dt 4:24). These Pentecostal flames dividing into tongues are related to the gift of tongues, which is now described.

4 *And they were all filled with the Holy Spirit*
   and began to speak in other tongues
   according as the Spirit gave them to speak.

The patriarchs and prophets of old had received help from on high when the *Ruah Yahweh*, or *Breath of the Lord*, descended upon them. But that visitation was for particular occasions and emergencies, in a word, temporary. Now the very source of divine help, the Spirit itself, is being given to the Apostles, and in such a way that they would be able to transmit it to those who would in time replace them and carry on their work. It is believed that at this moment the Apostles were confirmed in grace and never thereafter committed a serious sin; the Spirit resided in them in a stable and lasting manner. Not, of course, that they already possessed the Beatific Vision, for they too had to walk in the obscurity of faith, not understanding everything — but they were thenceforward to be completely loyal to God. The Apostles began to speak in tongues other than their own. What precisely occurred is, because of the brevity of the account, difficult to ascertain. Some have argued that speaking in so many tongues all at once would have sounded like bedlam; they prefer to think that the Apostles spoke *only one tongue*, and that the miracle was simply one of *hearing* — the hearers, whatever their nationality, thought they were hearing their own tongue. And yet the text (v 4) says that *they spoke in other tongues*. It does not appear, however, that the Apostles had this gift permanently, or that they ever spoke all of the languages spoken on earth; the languages they spoke on this occasion can be determined from the list of peoples present in Jerusalem (9–11). The gift of tongues resembles in some respects (4, 11, 13) the charismatic gift of speech (= *glossolaly*) which was so striking a feature of prophecy in Israel (Nb 11:25–29; 1 Sm 10:5f, 10–13; 19:20–24; 3 Kgs 22:10), and of the early Church (10:46; 11:15; 19:6; 1 Cor 12–14; Mk 16:7). The prophecy of Joel (3:1–5) was now realized. The gift of tongues cannot be explained satisfactorily as the natural result of a deep religious and emotional experience; it was completely supernatural and miraculous, enabling Galilean fishermen to speak in the tongues given to them. On the other hand, some of their hearers did not understand any of these tongues. Those who understood were those who were salvation-conscious; the others mocked the disciples and pronounced them drunk (2:13).

5   *Now there were in Jerusalem dwelling there,*
    pious men, Jews, from every nation under heaven.

Allowance must be made here for hyperbole: Jews had come for the feast from all over the Diaspora, and had "settled" in Jerusalem, that is had found lodgings there for the duration of the feast. Religious minded pilgrims were accustomed to remain in the Holy City as long as their piety or circumstances allowed. The term "Jew" is noteworthy. "Juda" and its derivatives (Judas, Jude), means "May God be praised." Thus the very word "Jew," so often used as a contemptuous epithet, actually is eloquent with praise of God. Many children were given this ancient and honorable name.

6   *And when this sound occurred*
    the crowd gathered and was bewildered,
    because each one heard them speaking in his own language.

The sound was so loud and unusual that it was heard in all parts of the city. Many hurried toward the source of the sound (people follow sirens today to see the fire), and thus encountered the Apostles, who had come from the Upper Room and were making their way through the streets to the public squares, or perhaps to the Temple area. But the meeting did little to enlighten them, and they could make little sense out of what was going on.

7 Filled with amazement and wonder they said:
    "Are not all these men who speak Galileans?
8 And how is it that we hear,
    each of us in his native language?"

With the exception of Judas, all of the Apostles were Galileans, and their native tongue was an Aramaic flavored with a Galilean twang (cf Mt 26:73). All the more reason for the newcomers to be surprised and confused. The universal language, lost during the building of the Tower of Babel, has now been restored, in vivid anticipation and symbol of the universal mission entrusted to the Apostles. Note that if the "speaking in other tongues" had not already been mentioned (v 4) one might conclude (v 8) that the miracle was in the hearing of the bystanders.

9 "Parthians, Medes and Elamites,
    inhabitants of Mesopotamia, Judea, Cappadocia, Pontus and Asia,
10 of Phrygia and Pamphylia, of Egypt and of that part of Libya
    belonging to Cyrene, and visitors from Rome,
11 Jews also and proselytes, Cretans and Arabians,
    we hear them speaking in our own tongues
    of the wonderful works of God."

The Parthians, Medes, and Elamites were people from east of the Tigris, whose language was Persian (= Zend). The peoples from Mesopotamia, Judea (= possibly Syria or Armenia is meant, as Judea far to the south interrupts the geographical direction of the description), and Arabians spoke a related Semitic language. The others mentioned all spoke Greek, the "English" of that day. The Romans temporarily residing in the city were sufficiently conversant with Greek to use it in dealing with the people. This "list" of peoples was not composed on the spot by the crowd itself, but is a summation of what various people in the crowd were saying, a Lucan parenthesis, since the second half of verse 11 echoes the end of verse 8. The universality of the Church, a theme dear to Luke, is involved. As he wrote, Luke may have had "the most excellent Theophilus" and other Roman readers in mind; he mentions visitors from Rome and at once distinguishes them from Jews and proselytes. True proselytes were pagans who had accepted Judaism and been circumcised (cf Ricciotti, *History* II, p. 203ff). They are to be distinguished from devout sympathizers (10:2) who obliged themselves to certain of the commandments only (cp Mt 23:15).

The "mighty works of God" means, principally, the words and deeds, life and death, resurrection and ascension of Jesus the Redeemer, the incarnate Son of God, for the Apostles in their ecstatic, Spirit-inspired utterances would surely have spoken of nothing else. From this verse it is clear that there was a religious and moral content to the words of the Apostles. The crowd was obviously deeply stirred, amazed even, at what they saw and heard.

Hints for Homiletics

1. At Bethlehem, angels sang of the glories of God; now the Apostles fearlessly proclaim the Gospel in Jerusalem. At Bethlehem Jesus was born; Sion, the capital city of David, witnesses the birth of the Church. The holy Spirit strengthened the fearful Apostles, made them bold witnesses to Christ, of whose divinity there could not now ever be question. Yet some even today do not know that there is such a thing as the Holy Spirit, or how important a part that Spirit plays in the life of the living Church.

2. The Holy Spirit, sometimes still referred to as the Holy *Ghost*, is not a "haunt" inhabiting the ruins of the Church, but the living Paraclete or Defender promised by Christ. He does for Christians what Jesus did for the Twelve: instructs, encourages, illumines their minds, warms their hearts with divine love. This Spirit is universally present in the Church, guiding and strengthening her as she faces the crises of each new age.

3. The Holy Spirit works mightily in the daily lives of all members of the Church, and is particularly active in the lives of the faithful who are striving for perfection without the help of the rules or Constitutions

which are proper to religious. Distinction must be drawn between eccentrics who have recourse to the Holy Spirit to justify their idiosyncrasies, and genuine believers who react progressively more readily to the promptings of the Holy Spirit rather than to the mere dictates of reason. The Church does not operate as a "Business" (on that basis it would have gone under long ago), nor according to human standards of acting, but, under the guidance of the Spirit, pursues Jesus' work of saving souls in the same way he saved the world: by suffering, death, frustration, and apparent failure.

The Inner Life of God

INTRODUCTION. In today's Epistle we have a kind of hymn similar to the lyrical passage in Rom 8:35ff, but differing from it in that it is as it were the conclusion of the doctrinal exposition. Struggling with the problem of God's providence, especially as it concerned the Chosen People (9-11), Paul was in the end struck with admiration at the way God utilized the temporary blindness of the Jews for the conversion of the Gentiles. He says also that divine mercy has not deserted Israel, but can and will bring it back into God's good graces. Carried away by this dazzling vision of God's mercy, Paul expresses his humble and grateful acknowledgment of the infinite wisdom and goodness of God in a brief lyrical outburst.

THE EPISTLE: ROMANS 11:33-36

33 Oh the depth of the riches, and of the wisdom,
    and of the knowledge of God!
    How unsearchable are his judgments,
    and how incomprehensible his ways.

The Vulgate gives the impression that there are only two divine attributes, but the Greek clearly indicates three of them: riches, wisdom, and knowledge. Paul recognizes the depths, that is, the immensity and profundity of all that is proper to God; God is infinite, and all that is said of him must be understood in this light. It would therefore indicate a definite lack of perception or of tact, as P. Lagrange points out, to try to define what Paul declares to be unfathomable. However, Paul spoke to be understood, and his words convey some knowledge. God's riches are the inexhaustible treasures of his grace, his goodness (10:12), and his mercy (11:32), and although unable to measure the immensity of these admirable qualities, Paul cannot contain his admiration and appreciation for them.

Wisdom and knowledge are not easily differentiated, except that wisdom implies the intelligent use and disposition of all that knowledge

147

has acquired. Here, both terms refer to God's astonishing plan for the salvation of mankind.

It is not only the divine attributes of God which are puzzling to man, but his manner of dealing with man which is based upon divine wisdom. God's judgments are frequently disconcerting, sometimes cause men dismay. It is relatively easy to acknowledge the supreme perfection of the divine nature and of God's attributes, but not so his judgments and ways of acting in the world. We would prefer it if we could discern some pattern in his actions, if we could hit upon the secret which prompts his intervention, and could understand what direction he is taking. In vain, however, for God's ways are not our ways. Whether he decides to show mercy, goodness, or justice, we are at a loss to understand him. All we know is that all his actions are anchored in infinite goodness. Our ways are petty ways; his are infinite; our wisdom and knowledge is limited, his, unlimited; man is within limits fairly predictable, God is always unpredictable, unexpected, and astonishing. It is well for us that he is also merciful.

34 *For who has known the mind of the Lord,*
     or who has been his counsellor?
35 *Or who has first given to him, that he should be repaid?*

To underscore man's utter inability to cope with the depths of God's riches and wisdom and knowledge, Paul dips into the Old Testament. Deeply impressed by God's utter self-sufficiency, he quotes Isaias 40:13 (cf 1 Cor 2:16), and with modifications, Job 41:3 (cf Acts 17:25). The two citations emphasize the fact that God owes nothing to any of his creatures, and needs no one's advice. As he is infinitely rich, he cannot be "given" anything, or cannot be bribed. Infinitely good, he is always the first to give. In this connection St. Thomas has remarked, with his customary acumen, that God's love is not inventive, but creative, that is, he does not love a creature because it is good; he actually bestows upon that creature whatever good it has (cf *Sum. Theol.*, 1, q.20, a.2).

36 *For from him and through him and unto him are all things,*
     To him be glory forever. Amen.

What remains, then, if man cannot penetrate the depths of God's knowledge, help him with advice, or assist him with human resources?

Only this: to recognize that all things depend upon God, and not upon man. God is the Creator of all things. He holds the reins of his creation firmly in his hands, all things have come about through him. Moreover, he is the final goal of all things. Paul's terms are general and cannot be pinned down to any particular historical events, but what he says is true in both the order of nature and that of grace. Why God does what he has done is explainable in terms of divine mercy and goodness alone (cf 11:32). Under such circumstances a wise man will give glory to God, and be faithful in carrying out his will. (Cf 1 Cor 8:6.)

In verses 33–36 there is a threefold rhythm: three divine attributes, three questions, and three relations of things to the Godhead. Reference to the Trinity should not be forced upon the text, but no other truth of the faith is so utterly incomprehensible to man. It was doubtless this aspect of the text which prompted its selection for Trinity Sunday.

HINTS FOR HOMILETICS

1. How the tremendous mystery of the omnipotence and omniscience of God, and man's free will, can be reconciled, is clear only to God. Both ends of the mystery, however, are matters of faith, and intriguing invitations to plumb the depths of theology.

2. The Trinity is a mystery that is as old as God. It is the most ancient of mysteries, for all the others — Creation, the Incarnation, the Redemption, etc., presuppose it. Acceptance of the mystery separates Christians from all other believers (Jews, Moslems, Unitarians, etc.). Far from being mathematical nonsense (Catholics are accused of teaching that $1 + 1 + 1 = 1$, whereas that is NOT the mystery of the Trinity at all), it reveals to us the very life of God: three divine Persons subsisting in one common divine Nature.

The story is told of St. Augustine that, while wrestling with the mystery of the Trinity, he was one day strolling along the seashore. As he went along he espied a small child busily pouring water dipped from the sea into a small hole which he had dug in the sand. The child made many trips to and fro, and Augustine, intrigued and amused, asked him what he was doing. "I am going to empty the ocean into this hole," the child replied. Augustine could hardly believe his ears. "Why, dear boy," he said, "that's impossible." "Yes," replied the child, "and with your human mind,

Augustine, you can never fathom the mystery of the Trinity." And the child disappeared. The point is that this mystery will provide the blessed in heaven with food for thought throughout eternity. Heaven will never be a place of boredom, because the Trinity will there be an unfathomable source of interest and happiness.

3. The faithful leave the church with what the priests give them. They must then be instructed in regard to the truths of the faith, and especially should they be instructed concerning the great mysteries of the faith. Where there is mystery there is certain to be nourishing food for the mind, just as where there is a forest there is certain to be game, and where there is a locked door, there is something valuable hidden. The truth should never be condemned unheard.

II SUNDAY AFTER PENTECOST

The Importance of Love

INTRODUCTION. John's three letters closely resemble the Fourth Gospel in style and outlook. The first letter is the most important of the three, and appears to have been a kind of encyclical addressed to the churches of Asia (Minor). John reveals his inmost thoughts, and the reader is thus introduced to John's favorite themes: light (1:5ff), justice (2:29ff), love (4:7ff), truth (5:6ff). The true follower of Christ will be observant of the great law of Christ: love God, and love your neighbor.

THE EPISTLE: 1 JOHN 3:13-18

13 *Do not be surprised, brethren, if the world hates you.*

Why should the world hate the followers of Jesus? By world (= *kosmos*) John does not mean the earth or the universe or mankind, but rather whatever is opposed to God, depraved, immersed in sin. The pattern of sin, seen first in Adam's fall and in Cain's murder of his brother, has crystallized a basic opposition: those who lead good lives are persecuted in one way or another by those whose paths are evil. Why this should be so is simply explained: a good life is a standing reproach to a bad one; a life led according to God's law cannot be judged dispassionately by those who live on a purely human level, according to fallen nature. Jesus had warned his disciples to expect just this (cf Jn 15:18ff), and Paul had repeated the warning when writing to his favorite disciple (cf 2 Tim 3:12). The lives of all the saints provide ample proof of the accuracy of the prediction. Despite the opposition, however, the faithful should be consoled by the thought that such difficulties cannot upset or truly hinder the plans of divine Providence. St. Teresa of Avila successfully founded her monasteries, the Curé of Ars carried on his mission, and St. John Bosco built orphanages and hospitals and schools. God will have his way, and no amount of opposition can prevent him from doing so.

14   *We know that we have passed from death to life,*
       because we love our brethren.
    He that loves not, abides in death.

John now reminds his readers of their status as adopted children of
God. This they already know and appreciate. They have passed from a
state of spiritual death, in which they were separated from God by sin,
to a state of spiritual life. This blessed transition was accomplished by
their baptism, or was restored to them by penance. The sign that we
have made this transition is our *love for the brethren* (cf Jn 5:24, where
the same idea is connected with *belief* in Jesus Christ). How consoling
it must have been for those first Christians (it is consoling to ourselves
also) to be assured by the disciple whom Jesus loved that the love we
show toward the brethren is a sign of a vigorous spiritual life and of
genuine union with God. John emphasizes his positive statement of fact
by rephrasing it negatively: He that loves not abides in death.

15   *He who hates his brother is a murderer.*
    And you know that no murderer has eternal life abiding in him.

It is relatively simple to acquire the name of Christian, but the title
is an empty one if a man harbors hatred in his heart. By its very nature
hatred tends to the destruction of the hated object; hateful thoughts
may not be translated into action, but the man who hates has already
committed murder in his heart. He may never be accused of this in the
external forum, but God who reads the heart shall accuse such a man.
Echoing the words of Jesus, "Every one who looks lustfully upon a
woman has already committed adultery with her in his heart" (Mt 5:24),
John labels the man who hates, a murderer.

A distinction must necessarily be made between wishing a man evil,
or rejoicing in his misfortune, which is hatred, and instinctive feelings
of dislike or antipathy, which can be controlled and in the end conquered by grace. It is not possible to like all men in the same way, but
it takes all kinds to make a world, and all must learn how to get along
with all types of men.

Eternal life, for John, means the sharing of God's life, even while on
earth. One shares God's life through grace, the seed which after death
blossoms forth into glory. Hatred is not the proper climate for grace

(Mt 5:21–28; Gal 5:19–21). The world may live in hate; the Christian must live in love, so that eternal life may abide in him.

16   *By this we have known Love,*
     that he gave up his life for us;
     and we ought to give up our lives for the brethren.

Jesus has taught us what love means by his voluntary sacrifice on Calvary. John had learned the lesson well, for his is the Gospel of the Good Shepherd, who said: "Greater love than this no man has, than that a man lay down his life for his friends" (Jn 15:13). It is also John who writes "God is love" (1 Jn 4:16). The words he uses are simple ones, but they tell us how deeply impressed John was by the Passion of Jesus. Every Christian must be ready to follow Jesus' example, to die (literally, *to put aside his life*) for the brethren. This is the supreme sign of fraternal love, and by itself alone suffices to identify a martyr as a saint. Such an extreme measure is, in fact, often demanded under special circumstances; every country can boast of heroic Christians who have died while serving the sick and the poor, especially in cases of epidemic and disaster.

17   *If anyone has worldly goods and sees his brother in need,*
     and shuts up his heart against him,
     how does the love of God abide in him?

The follower of Christ is not often called upon to die for others. If, however, he should be ready to give up his life for the brethren and for all men, all the more should he part with his worldly possessions if these can help his needy brother. John says nothing about having a great abundance before helping others; Christ's followers share their goods whatever these may be. To close up one's heart (literally, *bowels*, understood as the seat of the nobler emotions), and not to give, after seeing a brother's need, offends against Jesus' teaching and example (cf also Dt 15:7,11), and recalls the parable of the Good Samaritan (Lk 15).

18   *Little children, let us not love in word or speech,*
     but truly and in deed.

In speaking to his spiritual children, John frequently uses Jesus' familiar, loving address to his disciples; they are his "little children." He exhorts them to be sincere and active in imitating Christ in word and deed. Many love their fellow man in theory but not in practice, but the true love of God prompts men to good works for their brothers and sisters in Christ, not on a global scale, but here and now, to this one and that, in their own particular neighborhood. Fine words are not much help to the poor and helpless. (Cf Mt 5:21–23.)

HINTS FOR HOMILETICS

1. Love and hate are the two basic human passions, and love is the very heart of Christianity. God is love, and his children ought to be like him: unselfish, generous, merciful. And to some extent they are, for the notions of solidarity and brotherhood, so much appreciated today, are Christian in origin, and represent greater achievement of spirit than the most impressive scientific discovery concerning the workings of blind, deterministic atoms. Many problems of social and racial justice provide material for a practical demonstration of belief in the brotherhood of all men under God.

2. The poor you shall always have with you, Jesus promised (Mt 26:11). Love should prompt his followers to help the poor. When on Judgment Day the sheep will be separated from the goats, it will not be done on the basis of what they have done, but on the basis of what they have not done for the poor (Mt 25:31–46). — It is better to lack a few things, St. Augustine wrote in his Rule, than to have too much. Today's poor often have cars and TV sets, play golf and bowl, etc.; often, however, they live in slum areas, mentally at least. And this mental poverty is the worst of all, especially when it involves ignorance of the life-giving truths of the faith.

3. In John's use of the word truth one detects the influence of the Old Testament. For the Hebrews, truth was not an abstraction so much as a person or a thing. It involved the notions of virtue, uprightness. To do the truth, or to walk in it, or to speak the truth, is to be of the truth; these are so many ways of saying that one "is of God." Compounded in the notion of truth are such ideas as stability, continuity, constancy, fidelity, loyalty, integrity, teaching, doctrine. Truth is a solidity offered to man, something or someone on whom he can rely absolutely; the contrary of truth is not error, but deceit, evasion, failure to fulfill one's part in an engagement (cf G. Auzou, The Word of God [St. Louis, Herder, 1960], pp. 159, 209f).

Christian Trials

INTRODUCTION. Toward the end of his first letter, St. Peter exhorts the faithful (they were in the main converted from Judaism) to steadfastness in the faith. He could not have known that Nero was about to unleash the first persecution of the Church, but his advice could not have been more timely or more appropriate. Two verses from today's passage (vv 8–9) form part of the Church's evening prayer and are sung daily at Compline.

THE EPISTLE: 1 PETER 5:6–11

6 *Humble yourselves, therefore, beneath the mighty hand of God, that he may lift you up in due time.*

Since God resists the proud and brings their plans to naught (v 5; Prv 3:34; Jas 4:10), St. Peter urges the practice of humility (= lowliness in the good sense). God gives grace to the humble, and with his all-powerful hand will raise them up *in the time*. The Vulgate adds "of visitation" from 2:12; reference is thus made to the time of the Parousia, or Judgment Day. Until God wills otherwise, Christians should willingly and humbly accept what God permits to happen in their lives. St. Peter himself — so generous-hearted, so impetuous, so often failing, so *human* — could hardly have spoken lightly of humility and trust in God.

7 *Casting all your care upon him because he cares for you.*

The aorist form of the verb "casting" suggests that Christians make up their minds once and for all to trust God in all things. Here is an excellent formula for living. "All your care" (= *merimnan*) means all the anxieties and worries which distract mankind; these cares should be put into God's very capable hands, as a child confidently puts a toy that doesn't work right in the hands of his loving father or mother. After our Lord's Incarnation, Death, and Resurrection, there can be no question about his caring for us; that is the most certain fact in all human living. The abandonment to divine Providence recommended by St. Peter is strongly reminiscent of Jesus' words in the Sermon on the Mount (Mt 6:25–34; cf Phil 4:6; Ps 54[55]:23), and is an effective remedy for the loneliness which desolates the heart of man. If we have care for our own, one can imagine how much more God must care for us.

8 *Be sober. Watch. Your adversary the devil*
   like a roaring lion goes about seeking to devour.

For all his trust in the heavenly Father, the Christian must always be on the alert, because he has enemies, and not all of them are of this world. Confidence in God should not be allowed to induce a false sense of security. The proper use of food and drink are indicated by the most elementary prudence, as is watchfulness. "Eternal vigilance is the price of liberty."

The adversary (*antidikos* = the opponent in a lawsuit, or plaintiff) of every man, and especially of the Christian, is the devil. The very name, Satan, signifies "adversary," the enemy of God and of all who belong to God. St. Peter compares him to a hungry roaring lion, an unforgettable image of the enemy of mankind. Satan is like a lion because of his strength — he is still an angel, although a fallen one — and is said to be roaring because he is hungry for the destruction of all that is good. Truly, the sight of numerous believers practicing virtue, and remaining loyal to Christ under the most distressing circumstances, must infuriate the devil (cf *The Screwtape Letters*, by C. S. Lewis).

There is a striking parallel between this pericope and the parable of the Sower (Mt 13:1ff). In both, there are three obstacles which endanger the kingdom of God in the souls of men: (1) trials, (2) worries over temporal affairs, and (3) Satan. Satan goes about seeking whom he may devour; the birds in the parable devour the seed which did not take root; the devil eats men, and he is never filled.

9 *Resist him, firm in faith,*
   knowing that the same sufferings are being endured
   by the brotherhood in the world.

The most savage onslaughts of Satan cannot penetrate the saving shield of faith (Eph 6:16; 2 Cor 10:4). The devil will try to shake the believer's faith in Christ, but this belief is renewed and strengthened by repeated acts of faith. Faith alone gives the believer something secure and unchanging to hold on to amid the tempestuous trials of life in this valley of tears. It is in fact impossible to live a human life without suffering at all. St. Peter, himself strong in faith, has written (4:12–14) of the value of unsolicited sufferings. St. Paul declares that "through many tribulations we must enter the kingdom of God" (Acts 14:21; cf 2 Tim 3:12). Followers of the Crucified must expect to have to suffer in this world. They should draw comfort from the fact that their sufferings are part of human life, that they do not suffer alone, and that things could always be worse. It is important to bear sufferings cheerfully and in a manly fashion; many will be influenced by our reaction to persecution and suffering.

> Halts by me that footfall:
> Is my gloom, after all,
> Shade of His hand, outstretched caressingly?
> (*Hound of Heaven*)

10 *When you have suffered a little, the God of all grace,*
    who has called you unto his everlasting glory, in Christ,
    shall himself restore, strengthen, fortify, and establish you.

Peter does not say that after a little suffering God will call his followers to glory, but that, after suffering a little while, "he who called them to glory, in Christ, will restore them (Vg has "perfect you") i.e., their depleted natural resources and strength, will invigorate and confirm them in the faith so that they will not be shaken. Faith can do this by reminding Christians who suffer that God is the fountainhead of all good things, and that he has called them as adopted children to the same heritage of glory as Christ. Before granting such a great boon, however, he tests their good will and their faith, by suffering.

11 *He has the power for ever and ever. Amen.*

In conclusion Peter utters his praises of God's irresistible power, strength, and dominion. It is not so much a prayer as an assertion of fact: God has always been the Almighty, and can do all things. In the twinkling of an eye, he can make up for and cause to forget the trials and troubles of a lifetime.

HINTS FOR HOMILETICS

1. It used to be possible, according to an ancient Greek fable, to list all one's trials and sufferings and, once a year, get rid of them by dropping them in a box near the temple of a god. This, however, was the catch. One had to draw from the box a list of troubles deposited there by someone else. Very soon people learned that their own "crosses" suited them better, and were more "comfortable," than another's.

2. The devil, a malignant enemy, never sleeps or grows tired. Knowing our past lapses from goodness, he is sly and crafty and ceaselessly active. He hates God and all of God's friends. But he can harm no one unless he is invited into a soul by deliberate, serious sin. When, however, the devil tried to make the saints commit sin, they vanquished him by prayer and fasting. Many people, even some Catholics, do not believe in the devil, but he is none the less real for their disbelief. The powers of evil are often organized on a world-wide scale that surpasses mere human intelligence or planning.

3. *In the time.* The Parousia lies hidden in the future. It may be delayed a few hundreds or thousands or millions of years, but it *will* come; what is in the womb of time *will* come forth. But a far-distant *eschaton* is not a very impelling motive for leading a Christian life. One must therefore reflect that "the time" will come for each man at death, and that death is not far off for any man. We must all be sober, be vigilant, and watchful in prayer.

The Communists attack the Christian attitude as being one of "pie in the sky," and as encouraging a lack of concern with the problems of this world. A sermon on the true meaning of Christian *hope* would dispel this distorted view. Cf Walter Farrell's vivid explanation of "Religion" in his *Companion to the Summa,* III, 301ff, and Carré *Hope and Prayer* (Kenedy, 1955).

Redeemed Man and the Universe

INTRODUCTION. In speaking of our adoptive sonship and coheirship with Christ (Rom 8:12–17) Paul has penetrated deep into the mysteries of the spiritual life. But he was a supreme realist, and resolutely faces the real problem posed by the existence of pain and suffering in this life. On all sides, one sees unfulfillment, frustration, futility, both in the world of man and of nature. But Paul faces the present suffering, sees beneath the surface, and lays hold of its deeper meaning. This he expresses in a lyrical outburst which has definite eschatological overtones, considering the end and completion of the present order in the providence of God.

THE EPISTLE: ROMANS 8:18–23

18 *For I reckon that the sufferings of the present time*
are not worthy to be compared with the glory
that is to be revealed to us.

Far from being an obstacle to salvation, suffering is, rather, a guarantee of eternal glory. This is proved by the actual state of the universe (19–22), by our present condition (23–25), by the assistance of the Holy Spirit (26–27), and by the workings of divine providence (28–30).

Paul reckons, like a man balancing glory and suffering on a scales (= *logizomai*), that the sufferings (= *pathemata*) proper to this world are a light affliction (2 Cor 4:17) when compared to the glory which awaits those who die in union with Christ. These sufferings of "the present time" are in opposition to the glory of the "world to come"; the two ages are distinguished absolutely. The present with its sufferings passes quickly, and will be followed by the abiding glory of God's presence. Paul stresses the certainty of this glory which shall be revealed to us. That glory already is, for God is in glory; it has only to be revealed, and Paul assures us that it shall be manifested unto us (not in us, as if *in nobis*, but unto us = *eis umas*); it will reach out to and include us in its radiance.

159

19 *For creation awaits with eager longing*
the manifestation of the children of God

In a wholly unusual manner, Paul turns his attention to inanimate nature, and his vision suddenly widens to embrace the universe. In this cosmic view he depicts the whole world as waiting for the manifestation of the glory which is to be bestowed upon man. By creation (= *ktisis*) all irrational creation is meant. Paul's genius fastens upon the tension in the world, and in a daring personification pictures it as impatient for the beginning of the new order (= *apekdechetai*, the eager longing of creation, or, the eagerly awaiting creation looks forward to that day), straining, as it were, at the leash, eyes fixed ahead in eager anticipation of the manifestation of the glory awaiting redeemed man.

20 *For creation was made subject to vanity, not of its own accord,*
but by reason of him who subjected it in hope.

Brought originally into being for man, all creation is graphically pictured as having fallen under a curse because of Adam's sin (Gn 3:17f); Paul, therefore, here affirms the solidarity of all creation with man. Creation was made subject *to vanity*, that is, to that which is without result, which fails to reach its term, to futility (= *mataioteti*). The word is appropriately used of the disappointing character of the present existence, which nowhere attains the perfection of which it is capable (or if so, only momentarily), and which it always seems to promise. Once sin had come the world was made subject to frustration and futility, in the sense that its harmony was and is destroyed; it is as if the world has been forced to detour from its proper end, and compelled to serve a purpose for which it was never made. The laws of change and of death were operative even before the Fall (the carnivora for example always ate meat, which involved both factors), so something more is indicated here than mere physical constraint. It is rather something akin to "topsyturvydom." The world is a prey to purposelessness, and does not seem to hit on all its cylinders!

The violent repression of nature's complete and natural fulfillment was not caused by Adam, who misused a part of that nature, but by God himself, and creation accepts its sentence because of God's authority. The sentence is not a death sentence, for hope remains. Nature's destiny is linked with man's, and there is the prospect of ultimate deliverance.

21 *For creation itself shall be freed from its slavery to corruption and enter into the liberty of the glory of the sons of God.*

The Greek philosophers aimed at liberating the spirit from the bonds of flesh, for they considered the body a prison for the spirit, and matter as something evil; Christianity looks forward to the liberation of matter itself (for a similar extension of salvation to the nonhuman world, cf Col 1:20; Eph 1:10; 2 Pt 3:13; Ap 21:1–5) as part of the eschatological fulfillment, and has never taught that we shall one day be "liberated" from our bodies. The future lot of animals is nowhere described, nor their part, if there is to be any, in the new order to come.

22 *For we know that until now all creation groans in its travail.*

Literally, all creation, in a cosmic symphony of sorrow, groans and writhes as if in the throes of childbirth. The suffering that is in the world is not the pain of agony, but that of parturition (Claudel). What Paul refers to is not so much this or that type of suffering (physical pain, or social or political evils), but the absence of full happiness, a universal lack of glory, a general longing for glorification, or the universal hope and desire for greater things to come. The sources of Paul's ideas are to be sought in Isaias (65:17–25) and the Psalms (113[114]:4), where mention is made of a new heaven and earth. Paul says nothing very definite on this mysterious subject, and attempts no scientific guess as to how the renewal shall take place. Nature itself will not be changed, essentially; nature groans only because it is not free in its functioning. It awaits, therefore, not incorruptibility, but liberty; the change may be restricted to man himself (cf Mt 19:28; Acts 3:19–21; 2 Pt 3:13; Ap 21:1–5; Henoch 45:4f; 51:4f; 4 Esdras 7:75; 13:26–29).

* * *

These few verses (19–22), in which man's solidarity with the rest of creation is affirmed, rank among the most brilliant of Paul's "creations." The idea is startling, for we are not ordinarily accustomed to look upon humanity as forming a unity with or being a part of all created beings. Man is, however, not a self-contained unity; he is like a radio station, sending and receiving messages from the whole universe. The perfect man, Jesus Christ, came to "bring all things to a head" (Eph 1:10), for all things are "through and in him" (Col 1:15f). The Incarnation and Redemption, then, have repercussions throughout the entire universe, rational and irrational.

The grandeurs of astronomy were a closed book to St. Paul, but the discovery of interstellar immensity does not discredit his concept of the solidarity of creation. The mere measurement of distance and mass, the analysis of the elements and orbits of the heavenly bodies, fails to disturb the divine causality which brought them into being, and cannot interfere with the finality which the Creator implanted in his creation. The universe must always be given its religious significance, which cannot change; a sentence has the same meaning whether written in small letters or in capitals. Jesus Christ is the center and dynamic heart of both the material and spiritual world, and guarantees its restoration by the restoration of humanity.

23 *And not only it, but we ourselves,*
    who have the first fruits of the Spirit,
    we ourselves also groan within ourselves,
    while awaiting adoption as sons, the redemption of our body.

It is not only nature that groans, because nature's disquietude is paralleled in Christian experience. We who have received the firstfruits (= the first installment) of the Spirit, and the very Spirit himself (cf v 15), long for complete fulfillment, for an adoption which will extend to our bodies as well as to our souls. It has never been a Christian teaching that we shall one day be redeemed from (= liberated) our body, or that our souls are unwilling prisoners in our bodies. After the resurrection our bodies will not only be reawakened, but glorified, forever delivered from the dominion of perishable elements.

HINTS FOR HOMILETICS

1. Sermons on heaven are few and far between. This is surely a mistake. Men have to know where they are going, or they will make no effort to get there. Heaven may not appeal to them because they think it is a place only for floating on clouds, playing harps, singing hymns. No sane man wants a dull, monotonous, uninteresting, unending existence; such a concept of heaven misses entirely the tremendous dynamism of

the true notion of being with God. When one is interested in something, how the time flies; in heaven a thousand years will seem as but a day, and one day as a thousand years. And no one can imagine the delights God has stored there for those that love him.

2. The restlessness of our age is part of the picture of Original Sin. We are never satisfied, and what we have is never enough. The danger here lies in the possibility that men who are disappointed, disillusioned, and disgusted with the things life on earth has to offer, may in the end conclude that there is nothing else to look for. There is, and it is heaven, the unchanging, perfect, utterly satisfying life with the Supreme Good, God.

3. For a highly poetic, but gripping application of Paul's concept of the solidarity existing between all creation and fallen man, read, in Leon Bloy's The Woman Who Was Poor (pp. 75–81), of the visit to the zoo.

V SUNDAY AFTER PENTECOST

Pattern for Christian Living

INTRODUCTION. It has been sadly observed by many, throughout the ages, that good people are not always kind, gracious, and benign. Paradoxically, goodness is not always attractive. It is possible to be in the state of grace, but quite un-Christlike in one's dealings with others. Yet St. Peter remembers Jesus' words: "a good tree brings forth good fruit," and proceeds to urge his readers to translate their belief into positive action. His words apply to all Christians.

THE EPISTLE: 1 PETER 3:8–15

8 *Finally, be all of you one of mind, compassionate,*
   lovers of the brethren, tender-hearted, humble of mind.

Christians should have an esprit de corps, should be of one mind on the really big issues. This is not a recommendation of the "herd-instinct" but rather a profound perception of the need for all to maintain the common faith; in the life of the spirit, too, there must be "unity-in-diversity." The practice of the faith rests upon the foundation stone of fraternal charity. Besides the unity of spirit, there should be sympathy or compassion for the brethren. Sympathy is not necessarily weakness; it means "to suffer with" another, and St. Thomas has rightly estimated sympathy as one of the causes of joy (cf *Sum. Theol.*, 1–2, q.38, a.3). Christian sympathy is not clinical, but personal and tender. One might translate the Greek word (*eusplangchnoi* = tender-hearted) as mercy; in classical Greek it conveyed the idea of courage, also. Sympathy, mercy, and kindness toward the brethren are the marks of a true follower of Christ, who is unfailingly courteous toward others.

9 *Not rendering evil for evil, nor insults for insults,*
   but on the contrary, blessing. For unto this you were called,
   that you might inherit a blessing.

Jesus had said "Bless those who curse you, pray for those who ill-treat you" (Lk 6:28). The early Christians had much to suffer from their pagan neighbors, and human nature being what it is, had frequently

164

to be reminded to return good for evil (cf Rom 12:14–21). Called to imitate Christ, they should expect to have to suffer, but for the practice of charity there awaited them a special blessing or gift — eternal life. For eternal life awaits the Christian as his lot and his inheritance, if he is faithful to the example Christ has set him.

10   *For he who would love life and see good days,*
        should keep his tongue from evil,
        and his lips from speaking guile;
11   *turn from evil and do good, seek peace and find it.*
12   *For the eyes of the Lord are upon the just,*
        and his ears are open to their prayer,
        but the Lord turns his face against those who do evil.

The quotation is from a psalm (33[34]:13–17), and stresses the fact that holiness of life guarantees the efficacy of prayer and insures the blessing of God. The blessings promised to those who curb their tongues and do good, are, in the psalm, largely of the material order (a peaceful and happy life on earth). They are more strikingly fulfilled in the spiritual order by gifts of grace and a closer union with God.

13   *And who is there to harm you,*
        if you are zealous for the good.

Christians must not do what is evil, but they have to reckon with the powers of evil. Evil cannot be avoided altogether, but experience shows with startling clarity that evil cannot harm the good; if a man suffers for his religion, he is not destroyed by that very fact. If he maintains his integrity under severe trial, a man need not fear either God (at the Judgment) or the devil (at any time). A remarkable instance of this occurred in the early part of 1918, when a band of Spartacans, an extremist Socialist group, broke into the palace of the papal Nuncio in Munich. Eugenio Pacelli calmly and courageously confronted them, and, although their revolvers were pointed at his heart, reminded them that they were on extra-territorial ground, etc. In the end they went away, leaving him unharmed.

14   *But even if you should suffer for justice sake, blessed are you.*
        Do not be afraid of them, and do not be troubled,
15   *but sanctify Christ [the Lord] in your hearts.*

Two things — suffering and blessings — go simultaneously together. If it should happen that a man suffers from men while doing good, he does not thereby lose his reward, for the eyes of the Lord are on the just, and their reward will be great in heaven (Mt 5:10–12). Sometimes their reward begins on this earth. History records the astonishing calm and confidence of the martyrs as they faced their tormentors; their love for God, whom they praised and reverenced (lit., "sanctified") in their hearts, ruled out fear. They were God-centered, not self-centered men.

HINTS FOR HOMILETICS

1. In an age given over to the "realization of one's personality" St. Peter's recommendations may seem strange. But his advice is excellent. He urges his readers to turn their thoughts away from themselves, and unto God. Sound psychology, equally sound theology; a creature is always a creature and not the center of the universe. Putting God in first place makes a man a genuine "eccentric" — his center is outside himself. But he is not oblivious of his fellow Christians, whom he needs in order to live a human life. If God is dominant in man's life, that life will be characterized by a unity and diversity which are productive of beauty and delight. One should recall that only an organ with many different lengths of pipes can produce truly great music.

2. The Church and Christianity are not "negative" but "positive" in showing men how to live. God is the positive in every human life, as the lives of the saints testify. St. Thomas remarks that avoiding evil is one thing, but that it is more perfect to attain to good (Sum. Theol., 2–2, q.157, a.4).

3. Our language is rich in maxims which counsel control over the tongue. Man's ills come from his tongue. Nothing so deserves a long imprisonment. Let not your tongue cut your throat. The tongue is the enemy of the neck. Under the tongue men are crushed to death. One's tongue has often broken one's nose. The mouth: that which is most often "opened by mistake."

ON COURTESY

Of Courtesy, it is much less
Than courage of heart or holiness
Yet in my walks it seems to me
That the grace of God is in Courtesy.
(H. Belloc)

Baptism — Death and Life

INTRODUCTION. The letter to the Romans is not a dogmatic treatise, patiently worked over and rewritten for purposes of clarity, but a letter in which Paul has woven various aspects of Christianity around the theme of faith and justification and salvation. The end result is of an impressive complexity and richness, somewhat too lofty for our usual consumption. However, it well repays patient study.

In Romans 1–4, Paul has much to say about justification and justice. The kind of justice he has in mind is not distributive justice but salvific justice (1:17; 3:21–26), an act of God whereby man is made just (justification = *justum fieri* or "to be made just"), and God shows himself faithful to his promises. Paul has stated that the salvific justice of God comes by faith in Jesus Christ (3:22); here he ascribes the state of justification to baptism. There is no contradiction, nor two different principles of justification or holiness. Faith and baptism are necessary for salvation (Mk 16:16); baptism externalizes and consecrates the interior disposition of faith. That, however, is only the initial step, for justification is to holiness as the first glimmer of dawn is to the noonday sun, or as the bud is to the full-blown flower. "Justification" is a word describing the first instant wherein one becomes, by divine act, justified, or just. "Sanctity" is the development of that same justification. Initial faith is sufficient for justification, but it is obscure, and bound up with hope (Rom 5:2); it must grow in strength (1 Cor 16:13) and loyalty (2 Tim 4:7) until the Beatific Vision renders all faith useless (1 Cor 13:10).

Showing a brilliant insight into the mystery, Paul declares that where sin was multiplied, grace now abounds still more (Rom 5:20). Such words can easily be twisted to mean that evil should be done that good might result (cf 3:8), or that one need not worry about sin, since Jesus had so completely conquered it. Such conclusions were absolutely distasteful to Paul, who never tired of insisting that the struggle against evil was at all times a serious and personal obligation (6:1f). He nowhere hinted that salvation was an automatic affair, as if Christianity were a mere mystery religion. For him the only way to be sure of salvation was to be faithful in leading the new life which faith and baptism confer on the followers of Christ. He will explain, in today's Epistle, the death which was the prelude to this new life.

The Epistle: Romans 6:3–11

3 *Do you not know that all of us who were baptized in Christ Jesus,*
    were baptized in his death?
4 *We were buried with him, through baptism, in death,*
    so that as Christ was raised from the dead
    through the glory of the Father,
    we also should walk in newness of life.

Paul refers to a teaching already given to those who were on the verge of receiving baptism — "Know you not?" The Christian was symbolically associated with the death of Christ in the primitive rite of baptism by immersion. To be plunged beneath the waters of baptism was like being dead and buried; to emerge from the waters was symbolical of resurrection and new life. To be baptized in (lit., *into*) Christ means to be incorporated into him (Gal 3:27), to be associated with him in his death, at the very moment when he became in truth the Savior of mankind. This death is mystically but truly realized for us in baptism. By it we have everything in common with Christ: crucifixion, death, burial, and also, his new life, his glory, his inheritance. This is Paul's way of saying that by baptism we are raised to the supernatural order, to a new being and a new power of action. It has all been brought about by the brilliance and splendor of the all-powerful Father.

The mere accident of Catholic birth is not an automatic assurance of a place in heaven. One ought, however, to be grateful for having received the grace of baptism and to have been made one with the Savior from childhood on. While the "new life" will not be total and final until the resurrection of the body and its restoration to the soul, it is here and now a very real life. Strange as it may seem, it is sometimes possible to tell a baptized from a nonbaptized person just by looking at his face.

5 *For if we have become one with him in a likeness of his death,*
    we shall be so also in a resurrection like his.

As only the dead are buried, baptism indicates a kind of death, i.e., a death to sin. Resurrection is also signified, and to a new life. We become a "new creature" (2 Cor 5:17) and a "new man" (Eph 2:15) as a result of that death which removes the barrier which had for so long separated man from God. These happy results are due to the fact that we have become, in an exceedingly mysterious way, "one with him." The word Paul uses to express this idea (= sumphutoi) refers to a growing together, and was used of plants and trees. It represents here, then, a vital act of incorporation, a real union in being such as exists, say, between members of a body and the head.

6 For this we know, that our old man was crucified with him,
    in order that the body of sin might be brought to naught,
    and we ourselves might no longer be slaves to sin.

The idea of "our old man" in the sense of "ourselves" is a strictly Pauline creation (cf Eph 2:15; 4:22,24; Col 3:9) and is probably original with him. It refers to the carnal man, dominated by sin. This old man was nailed to the cross with Christ (i.e., was con-crucified) and suffered the same painful death as Christ did when he destroyed the dominion of sin (cf Gal 2:19; 5:24; 6:14). Before receiving baptism, the Christian's body was a "body of sin" (i.e., sinful), and as such had to be brought to naught. Not that the body in which and by which we commit sin is to be destroyed, but that it shall no longer be the home of sin, or dominated by sin to the exclusion of Christ. The body shares in our new freedom and is in the very depths of its being freed from sin. But a lifetime of effort lies ahead of all, just the same (cf Col 3:5).

7 For he who has died is freed of sin

To illustrate his point that the mystical death of baptism is a death to sin, Paul appealed to a juridical fact admitted by all: Death closes all lawsuits. Earthly courts have no jurisdiction over the dead. If this is true in the natural order, all the more reason why the mystical death undergone in baptism should close the case of sin. This death is followed by a resurrection to a new life animated by the spirit of Christ; if all goes well, this new life will culminate in a glorious and eternal resurrection (1 Cor 15:12).

8   *Now if we have died with Christ,*
     we believe that we shall also live with him.

It is here that the similarity in death between the Christian and Christ
ends. The Christian is not now like Christ, for Jesus is glorified and
immortal while the Christian still lives out his life here below. The new
life begun at baptism is indeed a new life of grace (Rom 7:6; 2 Cor 5:17;
Col 3:10; Gal 6:15), and one which by its very nature is eternal, but it
will be perfected only in the future and consummated only after death.

9   *Knowing that Christ, raised from the dead, dies no more.*
     Death has no more power over him.

Unlike Lazarus, Jesus rose from the dead once for all, and his rising
was an entering into glory. Only the past, together with its sins, is
forever dead. The personification of Death, here (in the next verse, sin
is personified in the same way), is to be understood as a literary device,
not as a literal statement of fact.

10   *His death, he died to sin, once for all;*
      but his life he lives to God.

The meaning of Jesus' death to sin Paul explains in 2 Cor 5:21 as
something undergone for our sakes; it was for our sakes that God made
him to be sin who knew nothing of sin (cf 1 Pt 2:22). By dying on
the cross Jesus won a decisive victory, and perfectly discharged the obligation he had taken upon himself for our benefit. That same death suffered
once and once only (= ephapax) forever severed the connection between
him and sin, and he now lives glorious and immortal, forever united
to God.

11   *Even so, do you reckon yourselves to be dead to sin*
      but alive to God in Christ Jesus.

Jesus' death has robbed sin (notice the personification, again) of all
claims against the new, redeemed humanity. Sin has lost its slave. Christians should think of themselves as bound to Christ, after baptism, in
the same way that Jesus is forever bound to the Father. Their conduct,
outlook, and manner of thinking ought now to reflect those of Christ,
the Second Adam (1 Cor 15:45), in whom sin has no place whatsoever.

The phrase "in Christ Jesus" sums up all that Paul can think of when he speaks of union with Christ.

HINTS FOR HOMILETICS

1. The symbolism of baptism should be explained. Just as the Chosen People passed from the land of bondage through the waters of the Red Sea into freedom, he who is baptized passes from the darkness and slavery of sin, through the waters of baptism, into the liberty of the sons of God. — At Jesus' baptism there were three things: a dove, the heavens opened, a voice from heaven saying: "This is My well-beloved Son." At every Christian baptism the Holy Spirit descends, heaven is opened, and the Father is well pleased.

2. In La vie chrétienne (see Verités fondamentales), Charles Peguy reveals a remarkable insight into the very heart of reality: He writes: "The sinner is at the heart of Christendom. . . . No one knows so well what sanctity is all about — unless it is the saint." Jesus would not have become man, St. Thomas holds, if Adam had not sinned, but he did come upon earth to save us, being, as one might say, less interested in saints than in sinners. His sacraments are not for saints only, nor are they rewards for being good; the sacraments are for sinners. Wherever there are sinners, Jesus is close by, even at the door. Wherever man is, he is deeply involved in the fearful but titanic struggle between sin and grace. Biographies of notable converts (e.g., Sigrid Undset) stress the importance of this struggle; it is more real than most of the material problems which preoccupy men.

3. The present practice of baptizing by pouring water, instead of by immersion, needs explaining. The root meaning of the word "baptize" is "to dip, to immerse, or to wash." The substance of the rite has then been safeguarded, and the sacrament has undergone only this minor change (pouring), easily justified by circumstances and by the authority of the ancient Church.

Christian Freedom

INTRODUCTION. Christianity teaches that man has been delivered from sin, and some of the first Christians were tempted to think that they were therefore preserved from all sin by their union with Christ, or could not fall into sin because they had died, been buried, and had risen with Christ. Paul attacks this position in a sparkling passage vivid with dialogue, questions and answers. Should we continue in sin that grace may abound? By no means (= me genoito), for our accounts with sin are closed, and we are living a new life under grace (6:1ff). But then, should we sin because we are no longer under the Law, and sin no longer has power over us? Paul answers vehemently in the negative, urging instead that those who had willingly become converts (cf 6:17 — "from the heart") should now be slaves to justice, lest they die a spiritual death.

THE EPISTLE: ROMANS 6:19–23

19 *I speak in human terms because of the infirmity of your flesh ...*

Paul has just used the very familiar image of *slavery* in his graphic appeal to the Romans *not to sin*. He might effectively have used the notion of *liberty*, except for the fact that his readers were still spiritually very weak (1 Cor 3:1); along with their moral weakness there was also a corresponding intellectual feebleness. Their intellectual incapacity to handle the new doctrine of liberty stood clearly revealed by their very questions (6:1,15). Later on, when they are properly disposed for it, Paul will speak to them more openly about love. Now, however, he will talk a language they can understand.

19b *For as you offered your members as slaves to uncleanness*
       and to iniquity unto iniquity,
           so now offer your members as slaves to justice, unto sanctification.

Paul thought it best, for the present, to represent the situation of new converts to the faith under the aspect of *serving God* by those (bodily) members which had been dedicated to sin. A dissolute life (*uncleanness*), like steps, tends steadily downward. "Iniquity unto in-

172

iquity" suggests that each stage was lower and more perverse, than the last. "Sanctification," however (= *hagiasmon* in the accusative), suggests a consecration to and union with God that is increasingly purer and more intense.

Paul had nothing more complicated in mind here than to urge his readers to show a zeal for justice equivalent to that which they had once manifested for evildoing. Their former slavery to sin had inevitably led them away from the ways of holiness. Paul's words resemble those of his Master, who had once declared that "No man can serve two masters."

20 *For when you were slaves of sin,*
     you were free as regards justice.

Now begins a play on the word *free.* The freedom of the sinner is a fugitive thing, fleeting, disappointing, ending in disillusionment and often in despair. His *freedom from justice* is in reality the most degrading kind of *slavery.* One becomes a slave of sin by deliberate acts against one's conscience, each sinful act being an abuse of free choice. Knowing by personal experience how unsatisfactory sin is, these converts should know better than to expose themselves to it again. Better by far to be free from sin and close to God than to be a slave of sin.

21 *What fruit therefore did you have then?*
     You are now ashamed of them!
     For the end of such things is death.

This statement can be variously punctuated. If the question mark is placed after "ashamed," the answer to the question would be: "No fruits at all." But if the sentence is punctuated as above, as if the question read: "What did you get out of your sins?" the answer is extremely dramatic and not at all unlike Paul: "Your sins turned out to be only bitter fruit, of which you are now rightly ashamed." Sin, a principle of disorder and disillusionment, separates man from God. In other words, it terminates in temporal and eternal death.

22 *But now that you are freed from sin and enslaved to God,*
     you have your fruit in sanctification,
     and your end life everlasting.

In being free from sin and submissive to God, Christians will find, not the disappointment of sin, but the truly human satisfaction of virtue, a savory fruit which remains, and sanctifies, and will bring them to everlasting life. Paul declares then that Christians have been emancipated from sin; he does not say that they have already attained to final perfection, but holds up before them the vision of the goal of all their striving: everlasting life.

23   *For the wages of sin is death,*
      but the gift of God, life everlasting,
      in Christ Jesus our Lord.

Now suddenly, in a marvelous metaphor drawn from military life, Paul depicts sin as handing out wages (= *opsonia*) for services rendered. But the wages are deadly. The term *opsonia* referred to a soldier's ration money, or pay in general. Avoid sin, Paul writes, because sin pays its devotees what they deserve, a mortal blow, destroying within them the eternal life of grace given them in baptism. On the other hand, eternal life is not given to men as their rightful due, as their salary justly earned; eternal life is a gift from God, and cannot be either bought or paid for. Paul cannot bring himself to speak of this heavenly gift in, as it were, a commercial way; such a gift transcends all such considerations. And yet he would not have denied, if asked, that man has the power to merit a reward while doing God's work in the state of grace; although he would have said that here too there is more gift involved than merit. Theologians all agree that without grace man can do nothing pleasing in God's sight.

The dominant idea in Paul's mind here is one of *service*, an active service, a notion which runs through all the Old Testament. God's most favored children, Moses, David, etc., were his "servants." Christians entering God's service at baptism might, Paul feared, have been somewhat repelled by the idea that Christianity was simply a new kind of slavery (i.e., degradation), but Paul saves the day with this unexpected metaphor drawn from the military world and suggesting not only active service, but service with pay in a noble profession. Paul was proud to be a "slave" of Jesus, considering such a slavery to be more honorable than any of the titles which men confer upon their fellow men in order to honor them.

The arms of a Christian are the members of his body. These he can and should use in such a way as to sanctify himself and so obtain eternal life. His new life is one of flight from sin, but on the positive side it is a consecration to justice and to the service of God. One becomes holy "in Christ Jesus our Lord." God helps those who serve him.

HINTS FOR HOMILETICS

1. *The gift of God is life everlasting.* For about a month before Christmas, a priest once told me, his mother used to send him to the store almost every day, and, when he brought back the change, told him he could keep it. Thus when Christmas came, the boy had enough money to buy his mother a gift. She was delighted with it and expressed her pleasure at his thoughtfulness (and, to be sure his "good taste!"). Not for some time, however, did that boy appreciate the fact that he had been able to do what he did only because his mother had put the means in his hands. God is like that mother. He gives us our talents, our graces, so that we can use them in his honor, and so gain eternal life.

2. Fire burns, pitch defiles, water seeks its own level. In the same way, sin destroys the life of God within us. One can never really "get away with it" where sin is involved. Penance is required for past sins, and God must be served with good actions, prayer and fasting, a life of virtue.

3. Soloviev once wrote that religion, being a direct revelation of the absolute, cannot be merely a "thing by itself" but must be "all or nothing." In other words, one cannot relegate religion to a corner in life, to one day of the week, for example. To serve God means a total commitment, a giving of one's whole life.

Children of God

INTRODUCTION. The main theme of Romans is, as is well known, man's justification by faith and his growth in that faith by his imitation of Christ. The life of the spirit is characteristic of the Christian, and Paul spends some time extolling its beauty (Rom 5–8); the lives of all the great saints and mystics rested upon the doctrine set forth in these chapters. The intimacy of man's union with God receives here a remarkably felicitous expression.

THE EPISTLE: ROMANS 8:12–17

12 *So then, brethren, we are debtors,*
    not to the flesh, that we should live according to the flesh, —

Having outlined his theme (8:1–11) that Christian living is a life according to the Spirit and not according to the flesh, Paul spells out some practical conclusions which follow. Although the kingdom of sin has been destroyed, and although the Christian has been buried, has died to sin (cf 6:8ff), and has risen to a new life in union with his Savior, sin remains a real possibility for the Christian. Paul warns his readers against sinning after having been baptized, and in so warning them, gives a conclusive answer to the questions raised by his imaginary objector. No, one should not sin that grace may more abound, and one should not sin because he is free of the Law (cf 6:1,15 and p. 172ff).

We owe nothing, Paul declares, to our sinful flesh, which with its ever unsatisfied desires and imperious demands is a ready instrument of sin and of death. Since we are not under obligation to it, we do not have to cater to its unruly desires. The flesh shall continue to clamor for indulgence and satisfaction even after we have entered upon our new life.

Paul seems to have forgotten to finish his sentence, but it would have been something to the effect that we do owe a great deal to the Holy Spirit, and should therefore live according to the dictates of that Spirit.

13 *For if you live according to the flesh, you shall die.*
    But if by the Spirit you put to death the works of the body,
    you shall live.

Here once again Paul reveals himself to be, not a great visionary or dreamer, but a supreme realist. He boldly states an uncomfortable truth: Christians can sin, even after being united with Christ in his death and resurrection. With uncompromising clarity Paul pronounces the fearful penalty for sin — not a physical but a spiritual death. If each Christian follows the promptings of the Spirit, he shall live a deepened spiritual life. Not, however, without a death struggle; the body with its sinful works wars against the mysterious and austere life of the Spirit in us.

Paul uses the word *spirit* (= *pneuma*) repeatedly, and in different senses. At times it refers to the Holy Spirit, who pours forth the love of God in our hearts (Rom 5:5), and at others it is the Holy Spirit as Gift, as an inward principle of the new life which God gives (1 Thes 4:8; Jn 3:34, etc.). The word can also be used of the soul of man, of his spiritual self, of a state or disposition of mind (Rom 8:15f). It is not always easy to determine which sense Paul has in mind but it seems clear in this passage that he means the Holy Spirit.

The works of the body must be put to death in order to live the life of the Spirit. The variation between "flesh" and "body" which occurs in this verse may have been prompted by literary considerations. Still and all it seems more probable that Paul here uses the "body," which shall one day rise from the dead to share the glorified life of the soul, in preference to "flesh" which oftener than not has the undesirable connotation of "frailty," or "sin."

14 *For all who are led by the Spirit of God are sons of God.*

Here is a thumbnail sketch of the Christian life. The Holy Spirit is a principle of action, directing the Christian to perform truly divine acts. This Spirit *leads* the believer in the ways of the spirit. But the manner of leading depends upon what is being led, and men are not led as animals are, but are led freely. Grace does not destroy nature; man remains free under the divine motion. (The old Scholastic axiom holds true in things spiritual — whatever is received, is received according to the mode or manner of that which receives it.) The freedom enjoyed by man is quite other than those instincts which guide animals; they are more led than they are anything else, more acted upon than acting, since their mode of acting is determined and fixed by their natures. But man, while acted upon by God, also acts, since he has freedom of will.

And yet freedom is not enough to make a man a son of God; the Spirit too must be active. The Spirit is not to be identified with sanctifying grace; the Spirit is a Person, a substantial being, whereas grace is an accident, something educed from the potentiality of the soul by the omnipotence of God. One becomes a child of God by grace, and in that same moment the Spirit is given (cf Gal 4:6).

Paul declares that the sons of God are led by the Spirit of God, thus suggesting that docility to the impulses of the Spirit is the supreme law of the spiritual life. To be under the influence of the Spirit is to lead the life of a son of God. The extent to which one human being can influence another (or whole generations) in the purely human order (e.g., the saints: Benedict, Dominic, Francis, Ignatius, Teresa, etc.; the philosophers and theologians: Aristotle, Plato, Thomas Aquinas, Descartes, etc.; and the sociologists: Karl Marx, etc.), gives some faint idea of the marvelous way the Spirit can influence the children of God. The very quintessence of the mystical life is precisely that docility to the promptings of the Holy Spirit which so marked the lives of the saints.

15   *For you have not received the spirit of slavery to fall back into fear,*
     but you have received a spirit of adoption,
     whereby we cry, "Abba! Father!"

This verse and the following are more or less a parenthesis, clarifying the notion of adoptive sonship. One can readily imagine how fear dominated the thinking of slaves — fear of work, fear of the master's displeasure, fear of punishment. The Christian by baptism has received a new spirit, or attitude of mind, a new outlook; by grace he has been given a spirit of adoption, a different inward attitude toward God (gift of piety). The spirit of adoption is not a new tag or label, a mere change of name; he who has received such a grace is no longer what he was (he was a slave, now he is a son), no longer thinks as he did before, nor feels toward God as he did before. Adopted by God he can say, "I am his son, and he is my Father."

In all this there is not the slightest trace of pantheism. Paul would be the last one on earth to suggest that we become part of the Godhead. By grace, however, one does share in the very life of God, while remaining always a creature. The Spirit is something extrinsic to the believer (cf Eph 2:18f; Rom 8:26ff).

"Abba, Pater!" is a combination of Aramaic and Greek, the second word translating the first. Jesus himself spoke in this fashion, prayed rather, in the Garden (Mk 14:36). The two words were possibly made a part of the liturgy and also used in private prayer because of the tender memories they evoked. Christians were not the first to pray to the Father, but it is noteworthy that there are 263 references to the Father in the New Testament.

It will not escape notice that Paul once again, after starting out with "you have . . ." ends the sentence "we cry." Not for anything would he wish to exclude himself from this prayer of filial devotion.

16   *The Spirit himself bears witness with our spirit*
      that we are children of God.

Now the Father has only one *natural* Son, but many children by adoption; of this the Spirit assures us. Our cry of "Abba, Father" is a sign of the inward activity of the Spirit (cf 2 Cor 5:17); residing in us, he has his part in this cry (cf Gal 4:6), and this assures us of its truthfulness, we are God's children. The word *children* (= *tekna*) proves that our filiation is not a purely legal affair; even more than "son" (= *huios*), "children" signifies a natural filiation, due to our supernatural union with Christ through grace.

"We are" refers to the faithful as a whole, and also to individuals who make up that group. All should appreciate the fact, that our present feeling is no guarantee of final salvation (cf Conc. Trid., Sess VI, cap. ix; 1 Cor. 4:4). No Christian should ever be overconfident.

17   *And if children, heirs also,*
      heirs of God and joint-heirs with Christ,
      provided that we suffer with him
      so that we may also be glorified with him.

We are children of God, and therefore heirs also; the sons of a family have a right to an inheritance. This, of course, must be properly understood, for it is we, and not the heavenly Father, who must die in order to gain our inheritance (which is God Himself) and a vital share of his life and glory, joy in the Lord. To gain this inheritance of joy, we must first follow Christ the Way in suffering. God has established an objective bond between suffering with Christ and a share in his glory.

HINTS FOR HOMILETICS

1. It is a commonplace to all who have made the test that passion is never satisfied for long, and in the end is dissatisfying. Man cannot live happily as an animal, because he is only half animal, and has been made in the image and likeness of God. The flesh is not evil, and the spirit good; both are good. However, the flesh is the instrument of the spirit. If we grant the flesh more than we should, we foster an enemy; if we do not give it what is necessary, we kill an ally. We should give it just enough to make it useful (St. Gregory the Great).

2. Without mortification the Christian life cannot prosper. Good habits (another name for "virtue") are acquired only by sustained effort, by struggle, by repeated victories over self. There is a danger in growing weary of being good. The old Roman axiom, *Corruptio optimi pessima*, means that when a talented man or woman trips and stumbles, the result is nothing short of tragic. The destruction of a material piece of great art is a tragedy, but not nearly so great as the destruction of grace, which is priceless, in the soul.

3. New Life in the Spirit, and Sonship with God, are two doctrinal high-lights of great importance in our times, when the individual seems in danger of being lost in the crowd, and so many are filled with a sense of frustration and defeat. The doctrine on grace and what it does for man ought to be preached vigorously, to restore to men a sense of their dignity and value in God's sight.

Temptation and God's Providence

INTRODUCTION. Some of the first converts thought their salvation assured from the mere fact that they had been baptized. Paul does not share this view, and warns the Corinthians that like the Jews of old, they too might incur God's displeasure. Presumption and overconfidence must always be avoided, and Paul writes to deepen the Corinthians' awareness of their responsibilities, and especially to correct their attitude toward paganism and pagan practices.

THE EPISTLE: 1 CORINTHIANS 10:6-13

6 Now these things happened as examples for us
    so that we should not desire evil things, as they did.

The historical incidents described in 10:1-5 have become, for baptized Christians, types (= tupoi) of what might happen to them. The Israelites had received many benefits from God, but had come to a bad end; the new converts at Corinth now had received even greater benefits than the passage through the Red Sea, the manna, the miraculous water in the desert, for they had received baptism and the very Body and Blood of the Savior. The greatest graces can end in utter perversity.

7 Do not become idolators as some of them were,
    as it is written, "The people sat down to eat and drink,
    and rose up to play."

The first of the four examples which Paul will cite from the history of the Chosen People was that of idolatry. He has in mind the affair of the Golden Calf (Ex 32:6). Some of the Corinthians had argued that they could take part in pagan temple banquets without taking part in the worship of false gods (1 Cor 8:7-10; 10:14). Paul was quick to see that in such matters one could be blameless in the interior forum, but also that the danger of actual idolatry was not so imaginary as they supposed.

181

8   *Neither let us commit fornication, as some of them did,*
    and there fell in one day twenty-three thousand.

A second example shows how closely fornication and idolatry were connected (Wis 14:12). When in Moab, intimacy with the women of Moab led the Israelites to worship the Baal of Peor (Nm 25:1–9). Twenty-four thousand were punished by death (Paul, quoting from memory, is a thousand short).

9   *Neither let us tempt the Lord, as some of them did,*
    and were destroyed by the serpents.

Nm 21:5ff tells how the Israelites complained about the fare (or lack of it) provided for them in the desert; this was "tempting" or "testing" the Lord, to see if he had the power to punish. He did. Those who had complained were bitten by fiery serpents (i.e., whose sting was as fire), and were healed only if they looked upon the brazen serpent which Moses held up on a stick. The Corinthians in their turn tempted God (i.e., the *Lord* is not necessarily Christ, for the incident pertains to the Old Testament times) by their inordinate desire for the spectacular charismatic powers (14:1ff).

10 *Nor should you grumble as some of them did,*
    and they were destroyed by the Destroyer.

A final example refers to the vociferous discontent of Korah and his sympathizers (Nm 16:41f) against the monarchical rule of Moses and the priestly privileges of Aaron (Ricciotti, *History* I, p. 218f). Paul switches again to the second person plural, aware as he was of the resentment his firm stand against the schismatic tendencies in the Corinthian Church was almost certain to arouse. By *Destroyer* (= holothreutes) the destroying angel sent by God to execute his punishments (cf Ex 12:23; 2 Sm 24:16; 2 Par 32:21, etc.) is meant. That angel's power, he suggests, is still at full strength.

11 *Now these things happened to them in figure*
    and were written for our instruction,
    upon whom the end of time has come.

The Scriptures are written for our instruction, sometimes directly, sometimes in a more subtle fashion. When the events described have, over and above their historical validity, a spiritual significance, a super-added meaning attached to the historical event itself, then we have to reckon with the typical or spiritual sense. That this is truly a scriptural sense is certain from the use Paul, himself an inspired writer, makes of it. The history recorded in the Old Testament is sometimes shocking to our more refined sensibilities, and yet it instructs us (Paul is back in the picture!) who live in the last, or messianic era. These "last times" are of an undetermined duration.

12   *So then, let him who thinks that he stands*
        take care lest he fall.

The logical conclusion the Corinthians should draw from these allusions to the Old Testament is that they should always beware of complacency, or smugness, or overconfidence in their own powers. It is doubtful that even the "strong" brethren can or will remain true to Christ if they continue to flirt with danger (idolatrous services) and attempt impossible compromises with paganism. The victories that the Corinthians have thus far won have been rather small ones indeed. There is little reason for any man to be overconfident: any man can be a pilot in calm waters.

13   *No temptation has come upon you except human ones.*
        God is faithful, and will not suffer you to be tempted beyond
            your strength,
        but with the temptation he will also make the way of escape,
        so that you may be able to bear it.

Temptation is part of man's lot here below, but God moderates all temptations so that they are only "human" ones (= *anthropinon*). In future temptations (= persecutions) the Corinthians can count on God's care for them. This is typical of Paul; when future prospects look gloomy, he reacts positively and sees the "silver lining" in the clouds. A modern writer (Sterne) states it well when he writes that "God tempers the wind to the shorn lamb," and a proverb has it that "one door never closes but that another opens." Paul declares that along with every temptation God provides a "way out," an "escape hatch" (= *ekbasis*). He never requires the impossible of man, and never loses control over man's trials and problems. The doctrine here is much like that of Ephesians 2:10 — God gives what he demands. He demands that we resist temptation, and provides us both with the means to the victory and the victory itself.

HINTS FOR HOMILETICS

1. An explanation of the "senses" of the Scriptures, i.e., of biblical typology, would be in order. Thus by the waters of the Red Sea baptism is prefigured, and by the manna, the Eucharist. Christian morality goes hand in glove with a sacramental life (Baptism and the Eucharist, and all the others). If the Israelites were punished so severely in the desert, one can imagine how sternly Christians will be punished, if with all their knowledge of Christ and all the helps of the sacraments, they should act like pagans. Live well, then, making frequent use of the sacraments; they are the means to, and the safeguard of a holy life.

2. Sex is glamorized today, and purity and chastity are not always properly esteemed by the multitude. But our Lady at Fatima, echoing the lofty teaching of her Son, stressed the value of chastity. Certain positive suggestions help one lead a chaste life: (a) since chastity does not bloom alone, one should cultivate the other virtues (especially prudence) as well; (b) one should avoid all unnecessary stimulants: drink, bad shows, illicit intimacies, etc.; (c) be alert to the proper fulfillment of one's state in life (prepare sermons, feed the children, keep the house and office in good shape, etc.); finally (d) develop the habit of praying to Jesus and Mary and Joseph *in moments of temptation*, and make liberal use of penance and Holy Communion.

3. In the ancient mystery religions, the adepts thought they were "taken over by" a new spirit, a new personality. This meant in practice that absolutely anything the initiated person then did, was good, because no matter how it looked, it was the new spirit acting in a man. Christianity affords no such escape from personal responsibility for one's own actions.

Spiritual Gifts

INTRODUCTION. The Corinthian Church, being as yet a very young church, was beset with ideas held over from paganism. Foremost among these was a great spirit of individualism or factiousness, a preening of self because of "superior" knowledge; there were also marriage problems, the business of eating foods offered to idols, and worst of all, disorders in regard to the charismatic gifts. All these problems form the subject matter of the first letter to the Corinthians.

The charismatic gifts, which assured the proper functioning of the Church at a time when the hierarchy was as yet loosely organized, have been called Christ's wedding gift to his bride, the Church. They were a phenomenon of rather brief duration, for by the time of St. John Chrysostom the obscurity surrounding them was already considerable; the passage of centuries since then has not notably lessened that obscurity. Although spiritual gifts, the charisms, far from making their possessors better men, at times caused them to swell with pride. Something obviously had to be said about them, and Paul does so (1 Cor 12:14). His insistence upon love as the truly important thing forms as it were the heart of his treatment of the gifts (cf *Sum. Theol.*, 1–2, q.68, and q.111).

THE EPISTLE: 1 CORINTHIANS 12:2–11

2 You know that when you were pagans
    you were carried away to dumb idols
    according as you chanced to be led.

Realizing that some of the disorders of the Corinthian church were due to a pagan background and upbringing, Paul speaks openly and firmly, but gently, as to his brothers (v 1): "I would not have you ignorant about these spiritual gifts, brethren!" In their former pitiable condition as pagans they had been led, either by local custom or by their priests or rulers, to the feet of dumb idols. Paul's words contained a world of meaning for ex-pagans; they would now realize how they had "gone along" without thinking, led as it were by their noses (the verb suggests being led away by force) to the feet of dumb idols. One might say that it was a case of the blind being led to the deaf, or the deaf to the blind.

3   Therefore I give you to understand that no one,
    speaking by the Spirit of God, says, "Let Jesus be cursed!"
    and no one can say "Jesus is Lord," except by the Holy Spirit.

Paul, therefore, instructs these ex-pagans in the matter of discernment: not every spiritual gift was necessarily a good one. In their superstition, the ancients used to believe that a man in a frenzy (or ecstasy) was possessed by a "spirit" (this idea lies at the root of our word *panic*; Pan was a god whose presence inspired a sudden terror). Paul makes it plain that a sudden mad shout such as "Let Jesus be cursed!" (= *anathema*) might indeed be voiced in the midst of a religious gathering, but would by its very content prove that it came not from the Holy Spirit or through his prompting. Undoubtedly such cries were heard in the early days of the Gospel; Paul himself (as Saul) and pagan priests or devotees inspired by the Evil One, may have uttered them.

Equally decisive, but in the opposite direction, is the cry: "Jesus Kyrios — Jesus Lord!" This authentic expression of Christian belief in Christ can come only from God (Jn 15:26; 16:14f). It is comparable to that other cry "Abba, Father" as an expression of tenderness and love.

Paul teaches, then, that the charismatic gifts and all spiritual gifts must be judged by their conformity, or nonconformity, with the faith of the Church (cf Gal 1:8).

4   Now there are varieties of gifts, but the same Spirit.
5   And there are varieties of ministries, but the same Lord.
6   And there are varieties of workings, but the same God,
    who works all things in all.

The pagans thought of their gods in terms of monopolies: Apollo for wisdom, Mars for war, Neptune for navigation, etc. Lest the Christians at Corinth should harbor any such false idea, as if the different gifts came from different gods, Paul traces them all (gifts, ministries, and workings [of miracles]) to the triune Godhead: Spirit, Lord, and God (cf 2 Cor 13:13); all the gifts come from the one God. They have then a common origin in the Trinity.

7 To each, the manifestation of the Spirit is given for the common good.

The gifts were given for the good of the Church, and are properly described as graces *gratis datae*, i.e., freely given. Although the charismatic gifts did not necessarily imply the sanctification of the recipient as does sanctifying grace (= *gratia gratum faciens*, or the grace which makes [a man] pleasing [to God]), an individual who used his powers for the well-being of the Christian community was surely not himself wholly unsanctified by the gift. Paul here is using the present tense of the verb (= *didotai*), for the Corinthian church was being liberally endowed with the gifts. He now spreads before their bedazzled eyes some of the extraordinary riches of the divine Spirit. It is not at all unlikely that he does this deliberately, showing how wide a variety of gifts there were, and possibly thus bringing the Corinthians up short with the realization that there were other gifts than their prized glossolaly, or gift of tongues, which he here lists in the next to last place.

None of Paul's four lists of the gifts is exhaustive, and their content varies. Thus here (vv 8–10) nine charisms are mentioned; four of the eight found in vv 28–30 are new ones; seven are given in Rom 12:6–9, and in Eph 4:11, five. There may have been many more. They are listed here in descending importance, the first two pertaining to teaching, the next three to active gifts.

8 To the one, a word of wisdom is given through the Spirit, to another, a word of knowledge, according to the same Spirit. . . .

1. Wisdom (= *logos sophias*). This gift, given by the direct action (= *dia*) of the Spirit, enables the recipient to penetrate and appreciate the most profound mysteries of God's plans in regard to man. It gives the recipient an insight and understanding of God's life, and the divine life in man. Paul's own letters are a good example of this gift (cf 1 Cor 2:6–16).

2. Knowledge (= *logos gnoseos*). Like Wisdom, knowledge is a gift whose possession leads to speech. The difference is that knowledge is

more the discourse of one whose intelligence is supernaturally directed to grasp the principles of the Gospel, than of one who learns by the direct and exclusive action of the Spirit. The catechists provide a good example of men endowed with the gift of knowledge (cf Heb 6:1) according to the Spirit (here Paul uses the preposition kata).

 9   To another, faith, in the same Spirit,
        to another, the gifts of healing, in the one Spirit
10   to another, the working of miracles; to another, prophecy;
        to another, the discernment of spirits,
        to another, various kinds of tongues,
        to another, the interpretation of tongues.

3. Faith (= pistis). This particular gift of faith is not to be confused with the theological virtue, that is, with man's intellectual assent to divine revelation; it is rather an overpowering supernatural conviction that if, here and now, this person should demand a miracle or some such wonder, it would be instantly granted. Such is the faith that moves mountains (cf 13:2). It is a faith that consists in works rather than words, at the behest of the same Spirit. St. Teresa of Avila affords a remarkable example of this gift in modern times.

4. Gifts of healings (= charismata iamaton).

5. The workings of miracles (= energemata dunameon).

The fourth and fifth gifts are very much alike. Gifts of healing may have been given in such a manner that some people could heal one kind of sickness, others another. The working of miracles was the trump card of the early missionaries of the Gospel, and included all that was not included in the gifts of healing. Paul refers to these two gifts with such complete assurance that we may be certain they were actually operative, although not necessarily all of them in the Corinthian community. The careers of both Peter and Paul amply illustrate these gifts in action, and they have been continued here and there in the Church from that time.

6. Prophecy (= propheteia, cf Acts 11:27). As in the Old Testament, in New Testament times there were certain men who spoke in God's name under the inspiration of the Holy Spirit. These men were certified witnesses, as it were. They did not, despite the name, only foretell the future, but also read hearts (1 Cor 14:24f) and spoke in such a way as

to edify, exhort, and encourage their listeners (Acts 11:23f). The chief function of the prophets was to explain, with God's help, the Scriptures, especially the prophecies (1 Pt 1:10ff; 1 Cor 13:2); they are therefore associated with the Apostles in the foundation of the Church (Eph 2:20). A good example of prophecy in the charismatic sense is the Apocalypse of St. John. Paul will point out that prophecy, being something imperfect and obscure, will disappear (1 Cor 13:8–12) before the vision of God seen face to face.

7. Discernment of spirits (= *diakriseis dunameon*). In 1 Thes 5:19 Paul had counseled his readers "Quench not the Spirit" and "despise not prophecies." In an age when false prophets abounded and boldly spoke up in Christian gatherings, an intuitive gift whereby true prophets could be distinguished from false ones was necessary.

8. Tongues (= *gene glosson*). The gift of uttering, while under the influence of the Spirit, a wide variety of unintelligible sounds (the blissful outlet of blissful but inexpressible emotions), was frequently given from the time of Pentecost on. It should not be confused with the miracle of tongues which occurred on Pentecost, for that was intelligible speech, and this gift was not. Yet the Corinthians were inordinately proud of finding it exercised in their midst. Paul deliberately assigns it a very inferior position in his list.

9. The interpretation of tongues (= *hermeneia glosson*). The gift of tongues was of no advantage to anyone but to the person so speaking, unless there was present one who, by another gift, could interpret the mysterious language of the ecstatic. The opportunities which these gifts afforded to charlatans was quickly taken up, and the gatherings of the faithful were apparently at times regrettably loud, boisterous, and dis-edifying. Paul shows great understanding and firmness in his handling of the gifts in 1 Cor 14:1–40.

11   *But the one and the same Spirit produces all these things,*
    apportioning to each one individually as he wills.

The gifts are not distributed, then, according to demand, or to merit, but only as the Spirit wishes, and in proportion to the need of the Church. As the Spirit is the Spirit of God, Paul does not contradict himself (vv 6 and 10), and the Spirit is clearly a person. It has already been remarked that Paul may have been putting the Corinthians in their place by showing them the scope of the Spirit's activity, since when he comes to make a practical decision in their case, he mentions only the gift of tongues.

HINTS FOR HOMILETICS

1. Why are these gifts not given or why do they not exercise a prominent part in the Church today? Has the Church forgotten Pentecost? One should explain that at different times different things are required. The break-through from paganism to Christianity was effected in this manner but in God's all-wise plan was not to be endlessly repeated, especially as these "demonstrations" were the occasion of much abuse. One might compare this era in the early life of the Church to the various parts of the rockets which thrust the "pay load" out beyond the gravitational pull of the earth; having served their purpose, the first-, and second-, and third-stage engines are disengaged. Much profit awaits the reader of St. Thomas' treatment of the "gifts" (cf Sum. Theol., 1–2, q.68, aa.1–8).

2. Pious ejaculatory prayers are of much value and the practice of saying them should be cultivated. They are the promptings of the Holy Spirit, who deals with men individually, and not en masse. Unless one makes a practice of these "sudden" prayers, to be said many times during the day, his mind will be filled with nonsense and useless daydreams.

3. The Church in all ages manifests to the world a remarkable unity in diversity. Christians now, as then, are not all alike, and do not all have the same gifts; not all, for example, are priests or sisters, or mothers and fathers, etc. One should accept this diversity of gifts (talents and graces) as part of God's plan for men and for the Church, and while striving diligently to capitalize on one's own gifts, should not chafe at seeing others more gifted, or occupying higher places than oneself. Each man should cultivate a spirit of responsibility, using what God has given him. No man has everything, it is said, but every man has something.

XI SUNDAY AFTER PENTECOST

The Resurrection

INTRODUCTION. Having begun this letter with a clear statement concerning the fact of Christ crucified (1 Cor 1:18–25), and having next disposed of various pressing social, moral, religious, and liturgical problems, Paul turned his gaze upon the risen Christ. Up to now he had resolved practical problems, appealing to charity or thoughtfulness for others to regulate the use of Christian liberty; now he takes up a major point of belief, and declares that the perfection of charity on earth is only the first stage of the soul's union with God; the union begun with baptism is destined to be crowned by the resurrection of the body.

The error with which Paul now deals (i.e., the impossibility or at least the improbability of bodily resurrection) was widespread among the Greeks (cf Plato's view that the body was the soul's prison, and Acts 17:32), and, apparently, among certain circles at Corinth. Paul is gentle, firm, persuasive. If such a resurrection is impossible, Christ did not rise from the dead. But if he did rise from the dead, as cannot reasonably be denied in view of the evidence, the faithful also shall in their turn all rise from the dead.

Paul here insists on the fact that what he now calls to their attention is not a new doctrine he has just worked out by himself, but part of the tradition tracing back to the Apostles and to the first days of the Church itself (cf Acts 2:25–36; 13:33–37).

THE EPISTLE: 1 CORINTHIANS 15:1–10

1 *Now I remind you, brethren,*
   of the gospel which I preached to you,
   which you accepted and in which you stand

Here is a gentle reminder that, in their excitement over their charismatic gift of tongues, the Corinthians seem to have forgotten the "good tidings" which Paul has preached to them. The whole Gospel, not just certain parts of it, must be accepted, and once accepted, clung to without wavering.

191

2   *Through which also you are being saved,*
      in what terms I preached it to you,
      if you hold fast. . . .
      Otherwise you have believed in vain.

The "good news" had to do with salvation, or friendship restored
between God and man. Somewhat perturbed at their attitude, as the
disjointed sentence suggests, Paul reminds his readers of his teaching
(= *tini logo*) on this subject, and indicates that they must persevere in
their acceptance of what he has preached to them. If they no longer
accept this Gospel, their first belief was to no purpose, and they did not
understand what they once professed to believe.

3   *For I delivered to you, before all else,*
      what I also had received,
      that Christ died for our sins, according to the Scriptures.

The clarification of his teaching (= *tini logo*) now begins. The words
"before all else" (= *en protois*) refer not to time but to the basic and
most important truth Paul had communicated to them — a capital,
central, indispensable point of belief which he himself had received. He
could not have read of it, as the Gospel was hardly as yet written down
(Paul wrote this letter in 57), so he must have learned of it from
apostolic sources which are now reflected in the Gospels. The point was
that Christ (= the Messias) suffered and died for (= on account of)
the sins of man, as Isaias had predicted (53:4-9). But it was by the
resurrection itself, and not by the Old Testament texts, that the eyes of
the disciples were opened, and they understood the expiatory value of
Jesus' sufferings; by them the sins of mankind were destroyed (cf e.g., Acts
13:34ff). Paul will later more clearly express the profound significance
of the resurrection in a succinct formula: "Jesus was *delivered* up for our
sins and *raised* up for our justification" (Rom 4:25).

4   *And that he was buried,*
      and that he has been raised up on the third day,
      according to the Scriptures

Tradition (and all four of the Gospels) taught that Christ was placed
in the tomb, and that he has been raised up from the dead (the perfect
tense expresses a result which abides — Jesus remains alive as the Risen

One) on the third day. The burial recorded in all four Gospels is of great importance, because the tomb was soon to be found empty. The resurrection proved that Jesus was the Messias given by God to his people. This fact had therefore to be found in the Old Testament, and the Apostles were guided by the Spirit to find the image of Christ in the ancient Scriptures. The texts alleged (Ps 15 [16]:10f; Job 19:25ff; Jon 2:1; Ez 37:10ff; 2 Mc 12:43–46) are seen in their true light only against the background of the resurrection. The novelty of that astounding fact was that it took place, not at the end of time, but in time. It is not necessary that the phrase "on the third day" be considered as pertaining to the (old) Scriptures.

5 and that he appeared to Cephas, then to the Twelve.
6 Then he appeared to more than five-hundred brethren at once,
    most of whom still live, though some have fallen asleep.
7 Then he appeared to James, and then to the Apostles.

Paul proceeds to give a list (it is not exhaustive — cf Lk — nor in strict chronological order) of the official witnesses to the resurrection (5–8), beginning with Cephas (= Peter), the first of the Apostles, and ending with the "least" of them, himself. The list is completely masculine, as the testimony of women was disallowed in oriental circles. After denying his Master, Peter was undoubtedly dejected and had lost face among his fellows; Jesus' special appearance to him (Lk 22:32) restored both his spirits and his prestige, and he was deputed to convince the others of the fact of the resurrection.

The Twelve were at this time an Eleven, or in fact only a Ten, for Thomas was absent when Christ first appeared in the Upper Room. But the term Twelve was an official one, similar to that of the ancient decemviri, and need not always have been at full strength.

The occasion of the appearance of Christ to the five-hundred brethren at once is not known, but was probably the one in Galilee referred to at the end of Matthew (28:17). These "marked men" who saw Jesus on this occasion had not all died by A.D. 57, when Paul wrote, and so could still be questioned about the all-important fact.

James also was favored with a vision of the Risen Christ, and his testimony, along with that of Peter, was indisputable and conclusive. Paul had consulted with these two men within eight or nine years after the resurrection itself (Gal 1:18). By the end of the first Easter week, all of the Apostles had been visited by the Risen Christ.

8 *Last of all, as to one born out of due time,*
   he appeared also to me.

Finally, while Paul was still immature and, in his own eyes at least, comparable to a nonviable foetus (= ektroma), he was violently shaken out of his opposition to the new religion and in a most unusual way suddenly transformed into an Apostle. His humble description of himself shows how deeply he esteemed the singular grace which had been given to him on the road to Damascus (Acts 9:5; 1 Cor 9:1).

9 *For I am the least of the apostles,*
   and not worthy to be called an apostle,
   because I persecuted the church of God.

Thus singled out, and now become the Apostle to the Gentiles, Paul always remembered how he had once persecuted the Church of God (cp Gal 1:12–15; Eph 3:8; 1 Tim 1:15). Despite this phase in his life, Christ had graciously effected his enlightenment, and Paul gratefully adds his testimony to that of the other official witnesses — he nowhere intimates that there was any difference between his vision on the Damascus-road, and those which had been granted to the others between the resurrection and the ascension.

10 *It is by the grace of God that I am what I am,*
   and his grace toward me has not been fruitless.
   On the contrary, I have labored more than any of them,
   yet not I, but the grace of God with me.

The great things Paul accomplished for his Lord, given in some detail in 2 Cor 11 and 12, were due to God's intervention into his life. So powerfully does he feel about this that he declared, with a forthrightness somewhat offensive to modern ears, that he worked harder for Christ than any of the others named, taken either singly or collectively. This is quite oriental in tone, and Paul, his mind fixed upon the wonderful graces and visions which had been accorded him, was surely trying to underscore the marvels of grace, rather than to extol himself. His sufficiency was from God (2 Cor 3:4f).

HINTS FOR HOMILETICS

1. Easter is the principal feast of the ecclesiastical year, but few probably would be able to say why this is so; Christmas is the favorite feast for many. It took nothing less than the resurrection to convince the disciples that Jesus was the Messias and the Son of God in a completely different way, a more remarkable way, than they had suspected during his lifetime. His resurrection is the type and figure of our own (cf *Sum. Theol.*, 3, q.56, a.2, ad 4m). It is efficacious at this very moment in that the power of the spiritual life which is presently at work in Jesus, is also being realized now in our sanctification in time and in space. Christ is our *life* (cf L. Cerfaux, *Christ in the Theology of St. Paul* [New York: Herder & Herder, 1959], pp. 69–91, 316–343).

2. Tradition in religion is very important, and our age is beginning to discover all over again just how important it is. Tradition concerning the resurrection goes back without a break to the Apostles themselves. Anything so venerable as this demands our respect. At the same time, we should realize that tradition is not a dead but a living thing; various elements of it will be developed and understood in different ages. That development will always be in a homogeneous line (truth does not contradict truth); the role of tradition in the interpretation and also in the composition of the books of the Bible cannot be overlooked.

3. Shakespeare once wrote: "In religion, what damned error, but some sober brow will bless it, and approve it with a text, hiding its grossness with fair ornament." It is to spare the faithful such confusion that the Church requires a prolonged theological training for her priests; they are to pass on to the faithful the truth which traces back through the Apostles to the Risen Christ himself. But the laity should also know some theology, which is always useful. One need not always be defending the faith; one can also find time to *enjoy* it, by studying and penetrating more deeply into its astonishing mysteries (cf F. X. Durwell, *The Resurrection* [Sheed and Ward, 1960]).

The Great Antithesis

INTRODUCTION. Paul had been forced to defend himself against charges of fickleness and arrogance, first because a promised visit to Corinth had not come off, and second because he had acted so decisively in the matter of the incestuous man (1 Cor 5:1ff), had held himself up as an example to be imitated (9:11f), and had even declared that he had worked harder, and more faithfully, than had the other Apostles (15:10). He had, moreover, written them a harsh letter (2 Cor 2:3). Criticism against him had apparently been made by some who wanted to combine Judaism with Christianity. In his vigorous rebuttal (2 Cor 1:15ff) Paul strikes upon the great antithesis, that of the letter and of the Spirit; he will use it frequently throughout Romans and Galatians, and it will form the very heart of his letter to the Hebrews. This chapter of 2 Cor, incidentally, would be very obscure for us if we did not have Romans 7 to read along with it.

THE EPISTLE: 2 CORINTHIANS 3:4-9

4 *Such is the confidence we have through Christ toward God.*

Instead of conceding the charges made against him, Paul proceeds to declare (1:23ff) that he acted in their best interests, and then affirms that he has not been trafficking in or adulterating the Word of God (2:16f). One can deduce from this that other preachers had been attempting to attach the Gospel to a now outmoded Mosaism, or had been dabbling in a suspicious kind of "knowledge" (= gnosis). At any rate, Paul feels completely confident that he has been preaching the true doctrine, and on this score has no fear of God's judgment for him; all that he has done in God's name traces back to Christ who called him on the road to Damascus.

5 *Not that we are of ourselves sufficient*
to think anything as from ourselves,
but our sufficiency is from God

With touching humility Paul here speaks in the plural, thus showing

196

how well he realizes that he is but one of many laborers in the Lord's
vineyard. In this and the following verse he plays upon the word *sufficiency* (= *hikanotes*), which has the sense of being authorized, fit, qualified, or worthy.

To think anything (= *logizasthai*, i.e., to appreciate or estimate the
results of his labors) . . . indicates how sensitive Paul was to the possibility that his words might be interpreted as boasting and presumption.
He places the success of his work at Corinth in God's hands, and does
not preen himself over it because he knows that he is feebleness itself
(4:7ff = an earthen vessel), and that what strength he has traces back
to God, who had singled him out for his task. The little phrase "as of
ourselves" safeguards the doctrine of free will. Paul nowhere taught that
God's gifts to him were a substitute for his own thinking and planning;
he merely insisted that God was the principal cause of what he had done.
This text should not be used as proof that God moves the free will of
man freely. From the context it is plain that Paul did not have this
in mind.

6   *who has made us qualified ministers of a new alliance,*
      not of the letter but of the Spirit,
      for the letter kills, but the Spirit gives life.

Paul answers the question he had posed (2:16c), "And for this office
who is sufficient" (2:16c)? He himself is "sufficient" (i.e., capable of it),
along with anyone else whom God selects to collaborate with him in
making known the inward transforming reality of the New Alliance
(cf Jer 31:31). This alliance (= *kaine diatheke*) is said to be new in
the sense of being young, fresh, vigorous, and effective. Letter and Spirit
do not refer to the contrast between what is material and what is spiritual,
but rather to two different authorities: to the Law graven upon stone,
and to the operation of the Holy Spirit which directs the spread of the
Gospel. The ministers of the New Alliance were not to explain the letter
of the Law, but to collaborate in the work of the Holy Spirit.

The Old Law (= the letter) kills because it was an occasion of sin.
In itself it was good and holy, but as man is so constituted that after
the Fall things prohibited become desirable to him, the Law is most
unhelpful. The strength or means to resist such desires, the Law could

not give. The Spirit, however, acting inwardly, justifies a man, gives him life, and helps him recognize the good and to do it.

If the Old Law was inferior to the New, then the ministers of the Old Law (a ministry of death [7–8], of condemnation [9–10], and temporary) were also inferior to those of the New. Having fulfilled its providential role in God's plan, the Old Law now became "deadly" for man (cf Romans 7).

> 7 Now if the ministry of death, graven in letters upon stones,
>   was inaugurated in glory, so that the children of Israel
>   were not able to look steadfastly upon the face of Moses
>   by reason of the passing glory of his face,
> 8 shall not the ministry of the Spirit be still more glorious?

The Old Law was inaugurated in glory, and when Moses came down from the mountain his face shone with light (Ex 34:29–35)! But this law led to death. Its glory is now surpassed and even abolished, by that greater glory which is the New Law. The New Law is the "eternal gospel" (Ap 14:6) which confers justice upon men, liberating them from death and condemnation. It follows that the work of the ministers of this Gospel will be more glorious and more permanent than that of Moses. St. Thomas says (in loc.), "That which was given for a time is nothing in comparison to that which is given to abide forever."

> 9 For if the ministry of condemnation was a glory,
>   much more does the ministry of justification surpass it in glory.

Glory is used eight times in five verses. It is the distinguishing mark of the new order of things, and is proper to it. Paul's accusers might think him to be proud and arrogant, but that simply indicated how radically they misunderstood the excellence of his ministry, which was an object lesson in the power of God. The argument in these verses resembles that of Gal 3, Rom 7, and Hebrews, and is called "a minori ad maius," i.e., goes from what is less to what is greater.

HINTS FOR HOMILETICS

1. Grace does not destroy or provide a substitute for nature. Under grace a man must still exert himself to get his work done. It is wrong

either to put one's entire confidence in oneself, or to expect God to do everything.

Abuse of the phrase "The letter kills" leads some to set law aside whenever it suits them (e.g., Friday abstinence, Sunday Mass).

2. Humility, a much misunderstood virtue, is mistaken for hypocrisy, spinelessness, etc. Paul was a humble man — as indeed all the saints were — but not a Uriah Heep nor a Casper Milquetoast. It takes courage to recognize and admit one's own gifts. This is not pride if one is sincere in ascribing them to God, the giver of all good things.

3. We do not do God a favor by working for him; it is the other way around. Reverence for priests — God's ministers — is indicated. In practice this means: call them "Father," show them respect, listen to them.

XIII SUNDAY AFTER PENTECOST

God's Promises and the Law

INTRODUCTION. At first glance this is a very strange selection for a Sunday Epistle. It seems to be concerned with a purely historical crisis which faced the infant Church, namely, the final break with Judaism. The natives of (north) Galatia (which corresponds to what we know as north-central Turkey) were confused by the challenge of the Judaizers, i.e., those who urged that the true Christian should also be a true Jew and prove it by being circumcised. Paul was quick to react to this challenging of the central fact of Christianity — redemption through Christ on the cross. Inasmuch as Judaism still persists in the Christian west, this challenge and problem are relevant today.

Paul had made the point that justification did not depend upon the Law; Abraham was a just man long before Moses received the Law. Yes, it was argued in rebuttal, but once the Law is given, it has to be followed. Not at all, Paul replied, because God's promises do not change. In human affairs a man's will is not annulled, and for this reason one can say that the promises made to Abraham will always retain their validity.

Like 2 Cor 3, this passage is difficult to understand without reference to Paul's words about the Law in Romans 7.

THE EPISTLE: GALATIANS 3:16–22

16 Now the promises were spoken to Abraham and to his seed.
   It does not say: "and to his seeds" as though to many,
   but as to one, "and to his seed," which is Christ.

This verse is an application of the principle that: "No one annuls or alters a man's last will and testament" (cf v 15). The promises are spoken of as many because they were made many times (cf Gn 13:15; 17:8 and 12:7), but Paul will conclude by (3:29) referring to a singular promise. Abraham was promised a numerous posterity and the possession of Canaan. This land, flowing with milk and honey, signified the spiritual (messianic) goods which were to come. Possession of the land was a symbol of an eternal inheritance with God. Made to Abraham in the first instance, the promises were renewed to Isaac and Jacob (cf 22:17; 24:7; 26:4; 28:13).

The beneficiaries of the promises are *Abraham and his seed*. Seed (*zera*) is a singular collective term which admits of plurality and yet involves the note of unity; it is a biblical metaphor for *posterity*. Abraham had other sons who had children of their own, but the promise concerned only Isaac's posterity and was realized or fulfilled, Paul states, in Christ. The Genesis account of Abraham and of his line was oriented toward Christ who would be born of Abraham's seed. The promises, then, were made to Christ also; promises not of the land, but of all that the land stood for (cf Gal 3:26–29).

The celebrated difficulty here is whether Christ is to be understood as an individual, or as a mystical Christ. Opinions are divided. Elsewhere (Rom 4:13–16 and Gal 3:29) Paul seems to look upon *the Christian* people as Abraham's seed; here, however, it is preferable to look upon the faithful as Abraham's posterity only in so far as they are united to Christ; Jesus had first to appear as an historical individual before others could be counted as descendants — through him — of Abraham. To put it more clearly, it is in Jesus himself that the promise made to Abraham was fully accomplished, but this was chiefly in the spiritual order.

Thus Abraham was the *alpha*, Jesus the *omega*; Abraham the beginning, Jesus the end in whom all are unified under the concept of one God, Father of all (cf 2 Cor 5:19; Col 2:10).

17   *Now this is what I mean:*
       the Law, which came into being four hundred and thirty
            years later,
       does not annul a testament previously ratified by God,
       so as to nullify the promise.

The Mosaic Law came into being on Mt. Sinai, about 1250 B.C. But Abraham who lived about 1850 B.C., had received the promises, vouched for by the changeless God, centuries before there was a Law (Paul's numbers, drawn from Ex 12:40f [cp Gn 15:13 and Acts 7:6–400 years] reflect the received chronology; it was not his intention to settle this controversy, nor does the number of years affect his argument.) Paul here joins the thought of vv 15–16, linking the idea of the last will and testament (*diatheke*) to that of the divine promises. If a man's will cannot be changed by other men, God's express will cannot be changed either (Heb 6:17f).

18   *For if the inheritance is from the Law,*
      it is not then from the promise;
      yet it is by way of a promise that God showed favor to Abraham.

"Law" and "promise" (without the article) are two opposing principles. The Messias and all the messianic blessings do not depend upon human efforts, such as one might consider the Law, but upon the divine will. Law and grace then are mutually exclusive. God has bestowed the inheritance (= kleronomia) as a free gift. The perfect form of the verb indicates the permanence of the giving.

19   *What then is the Law?*
      It was added in view of transgressions,
      until the offspring to whom the promise had been made
         should come;
      it was ordered through angels, by means of a mediator.

In the following verses (19–24) Paul shows the temporary nature of the Law. It was given over and above the promises, in view of (for the sake of, on account of, because of) transgressions. Elsewhere Paul speaks harshly of the Law: it is the worker of divine wrath (Rom 4:15), engenders lapses from positive law, is the occasional cause of sin, is an active force of sin (1 Cor 15:56), and gives a knowledge of sin (Rom 3:20; 7:7–13). God permitted such a situation so that men might become aware both of their misery and of the need for his grace (cf Rom 5:20). The Law was added (= prosetethe), not as a codicil to a will, but as a transitory disposition of affairs which would endure until the promise produced its effect. Once the seed to whom the promise had been made had come (Christ), the function and purpose of the Law was at an end.

Paul next points out another deficiency of the Law, as compared to the promise. The Law was given not directly from God himself but through a mediator, which means that it involved not simply the will of God but the will of man as well, a feeble and unreliable element at best.

According to a Jewish tradition (Dt 33:2), the angels had the glorious ministry of assisting at the giving (by God) of the Law on Mt. Sinai.

The intermediary to whom the Law was given was Moses (Acts 7:38,53; Heb 2:2). The very word *intermediary* suggests a bilateral contract, one which could be ruined by the failure of either of the contracting parties. The Law was such a contract, whereas the promise, depending only upon God who is ever faithful to his word, was unilateral.

The numerous interpretations given to the following verse stem from the initial error of seeing Christ, and not Moses, as the intermediary.

20 *Now there is no intermediary if there is only one party,*
     but God is one.

To the majestic solitude or oneness of God, making an inviolable promise which he will keep at the proper time, Paul contrasts the Law, subject of transgressions, given through the ministering angels, and calling for a mediator. Mediation calls for at least two persons and is therefore contingent and not absolute; the promise depends upon God alone.

21 *Is the Law then opposed to the promises of God?*
     Certainly not.
     If a Law had been given that was able to give life,
     justice would surely have been from the Law.

Since the Law and the promise differ so widely, one might gain the impression that they were mutually antagonistic. Nothing could be further from the truth. The Law served the promise, although it was itself incapable of giving (spiritual) life; it was therefore in no way essential to the promise which implies both justice and life.

22 *But the Scripture has enclosed all under sin,*
     so that the promise,
     by faith in Jesus Christ,
     might be given to them that believe.

By Scripture Paul here means either the whole of the Bible, including the Law, or a particular verse (cf Rom 3:10-18 and Ps 13[14]:2f). Two images are blended here: that of a prison in which one is detained, and that of a regime or servitude (of sin). After Adam's sin all men, whether under the Law or not, were under the universal domination of sin (cf Rom 6:12-16). Why did God permit this state of affairs? To manifest his liberality and his mercy, for from this seemingly inescapable servitude he delivered man (cf Rom 11:32; 3:9–26). But only a believer could obtain the promise, and that not by works of the Law but by faith in Christ.

HINTS FOR HOMILETICS

1. What Paul has in mind here is to show how completely different, and separate, Christianity is from the Law of Moses. The Law was a preparation for Jesus' coming, and having served its purpose, had to disappear. Paul is not here making amends, by his harshness toward the Law, for having been its zealous exponent in his early days (Acts 9:1f), but is intent rather on showing that one cannot be in both camps; after a goal has been safely attained one does not go back and read the signs all over again as if the journey were still to be made. To do so would be equivalent to saying that one had not after all successfully reached the desired goal. For him to go back to the Law was the same as denying that the promise had been realized, sin's regime broken, and salvation extended to all men.

2. God is faithful to his promises. Christ is faithful to his. What are these "promises of Christ" which we hope daily to be more worthy of? The chief of these is *eternal life*, an incredible invitation to share forever in God's kingdom. A reading of the New Testament will reveal the extent of Jesus' promises to those who love and follow Him.

3. We should be grateful for being united, by faith and baptism, to Christ the true seed of Abraham. The blessings promised to the patriarch are ours in full measure, thanks to our union with the Savior, and to the sacramental system which is found in his church alone.

Two Ways of Life

INTRODUCTION. The best commentary on this Sunday's Epistle is the passage in Romans 8:1ff. Man is a battlefield, and in his soul the flesh wages war against the spirit. There is no letup between the flesh — representative of pleasure, egoism, and sin — and the spirit — that is, natural reason unassisted by grace, and unaided by a Law which is external to it. And yet, once union with Christ has been achieved through baptism, every man has within himself the spiritual principle which insures for him victory over his flesh. Obviously it would be utter foolishness to return to that condition of life which resembles slavery.

THE EPISTLE: GALATIANS 5:16–24

16 *I say, then, walk by the spirit*
  and you will not gratify the desires of the flesh.

The term *walk* (= *peripateite*) stands here for moral conduct; one's life should reflect one's beliefs. *Spirit* may here refer to the Holy Spirit, but more probably to man's spirit reborn and spiritualized by baptism. *Flesh* is opposed to the spirit, and signifies man's sensual instincts; it may also refer to man's reason in so far as it is dominated by these now evil instincts. Paul has confidence that his Galatian readers will follow the promptings of their rejuvenated spirit; they will know temptation, but not be overwhelmed and oppressed by it.

17 *For the flesh lusts against the spirit*
  and the spirit against the flesh.
  These are opposed to one another,
  so that what you desire to do, you do not.

The struggle between the spirit and the flesh is a universal fact of human experience; Paul develops the same theme in Romans 8. Spirit and flesh are two opposing principles of activity, operative now in the era and sphere of grace, and not, as in Romans 7:15f, *before* the act of faith. The opponents are more or less of the same (human) order, for it would hardly be likely that human flesh should struggle against the Holy Spirit.

The latter part of this verse is difficult. In the man who has been reborn, revitalized, and liberated by baptism and grace, the two mutually opposed principles of action clash repeatedly and violently. Desires to do good encounter solid and stubborn resistance on the part of the flesh, while tendencies to evildoing arouse instant protest from the spirit. From the beginning to the end of a human action, a good will is challenged by the flesh, and a bad one is restrained and held in check by the spirit. It is a constant battle. Of itself reason (= the spirit) is unable to evoke decisive action on the part of the will; in moments of trial it is not human reason nor even a developed sense of honor which come to man's aid, but rather, supernatural motives based on faith. More is needed than unaided reason, if one is to survive.

18 *But if you are led by the Spirit*
   you are not under the Law.

Paul presumes that the Christian leading a spiritual life is ordinarily victorious in the struggle. One is "led" by another, in this case the Holy Spirit. From the presence of grace and the Spirit in the soul of the just man, one may conclude to the absence of the Law, as grace and the Law do not coexist. There is now no external prohibiting and commanding Law; moreover, one who has within himself a better directive principle has no need of a pedagogue, any more than a philosopher needs anyone to teach him the abc's. In proportion as a man becomes spiritual i.e., is led by the Spirit, he readily discerns as evil the works of the flesh (19–21), and the good which he spontaneously does is done with the help of the Spirit (22f).

19 *Now the works of the flesh are manifest:*
   fornication, impurity, debauchery,
20 *idolatry, magic,*
   enmities, strife, jealousy, anger, intrigues, dissensions, divisions,
21 *[acts of] envy, [murders], drunkenness, carousings, and the like....*

Paul frequently mentions specific sins which are to be avoided. Lists comparable to the one here appear in Rom 1:28–31; 1 Cor 6:9f; 5:10f; 2 Cor 12:20f; Eph 4:31; 5:4; Col 3:5,8; 1 Tim 1:9f; 2 Tim 3:2–5. The sins listed here as following from the flesh (there are also sins of an intellectual nature, and much about discord) fall into the following four classes:

1. Sins against purity:

Fornication (= *porneia*) is intercourse with unmarried women, especially with prostitutes. By impurity (= *akatharsia*) Paul means all sorts of sexual sins, including those against nature and others connected with ritual practices. Debauchery (= *aselgeia*) probably refers to licentiousness, to which there is added a note of public and shameless indulgence in lust.

2. Sins of a religious nature:

Idolatry was the official religious error of Paul's world. Christians were therefore liable to find themselves carried along to celebrations of municipal and imperial feasts where an act of idolatry would be the high point. Magic (= *pharmakeia*) refers to clandestine religions which involved sorcery and magic and all types of superstitious practices. Many laws were enacted in a determined but not always effectual attempt to control or stamp out these religions. Both idolatry and magic were practiced with a pomp and splendor calculated to appeal to the senses, and Paul lists them as works of the flesh.

3. Sins against charity:

Following enmities (= *echthrai*), which are hostile feelings or actions, Paul lists three double vices: discord (= *eris*) and jealousy (= *zelos*); angry outburst (= *thumoi*) and displays of selfishness or intrigue (= *eritheiai*); dissensions (= *dichostasiai*) and divisions (= *haireseis*). This last pair point to the existence of sects or factions.

4. Sins against temperance:

First mentioned among sins against temperance is envy (= *phthonoi*), a grave sin against one's neighbor, whose good fortune is considered to be an affront and injury by the envious man. (The parallel list of sins in Rom 1:29 next lists murders [= *phonoi*] here; envy might lead a man even to that.) Drunkenness (= *methai*) and carousings or orgies (= *komoi*) were familiar vices of the pagan world, and complete this appalling list of sins. In writing to the generous Galatians, Paul makes no mention of avarice.

21 *I warn you, as I warned you before,*
      that those who do such things shall not inherit the kingdom
      of God.

Paul had spoken out against such vices on former occasions, when actually present among the Galatians. In his preaching he set great store on faith, but at the same time he energetically proclaimed the conditions of a good moral life to those who were sons and heirs of the kingdom of God. The kingdom is here spoken of under its double aspect of a present and future (eschatological) reality. A man who indulges in one or several or all of these vices thus shows that he is not "of the kingdom," for such vices close the gates of heaven.

22 *But the fruit of the spirit is:*
      love, joy, peace, steadfastness, kindness, goodness, faithfulness,
23 *gentleness, self-control. Against such there is no law.*

In contrast to the works of the flesh, Paul now describes the fruit of the spirit, meaning by spirit, grace; it is possible that he refers also to the source of that supernatural energy, the Holy Spirit. In using the word *fruit* in the singular he expresses the unity and harmony which prevail among the good dispositions in the soul which has been "reborn." The moral virtues are interconnected. Fortunately for man, vices are not so connected among themselves, and some of them would preclude the practice of others. The fruits mentioned here are nine in number. By translating three words in two different ways, the Vulgate has added three fruits: modesty, continence, and chastity, which round out the number twelve.

The first fruit of the Holy Spirit, love (= *agape*), is to be found in a soul which is in the state of habitual grace. An inner joy (= *chara*) in the Spirit follows upon this initial love. Peace is closely associated with joy, and here probably refers to peace with one's neighbor; this does not, of course, exclude peace with God, and peace within oneself. Love, joy, and peace, the interior dispositions of the soul, are as it were the source of the virtues which now are named.

Steadfastness or endurance (= *makrothumia*) implies that a man's peaceful dispositions have been or will be put to the test. Next on the list is kindness (= *chrestotes*), which is "goodness-shining-forth" as in the case of St. Francis de Sales (cp 1 Cor 13:4). Coupled with this is cordiality or goodness (= agathosune) which readily joins in with all good works.

Faithfulness or faith (= pistis) cannot in the context refer to theological faith, but is rather confidence in others. Next, gentleness (= prautes), or strength under control; the word is elsewhere used to describe an animal which has been tamed but not broken. Gentleness has an especial charm when seen in those who are vigorous and strong-minded. Finally, Paul mentions self-control or continence (= engkrateia), as opposed to voluptuousness and intemperance.

Those who produce such fruit need fear no law, as law is for the transgressor (1 Tim 1:9).

24   And those who belong to Christ Jesus
have crucified the flesh with its passions and desires.

They belong to Christ who have been baptized. Precisely at the moment of baptism does one become one with Christ in death, and at that same moment one is "crucified" with him (the aorist means once and for all). By this genuine mystical union with the Savior, believers have placed their own flesh in a state of death, and are thus free to live a life of the spirit.

As the life of the spirit has been described as a *struggle against* the flesh, it follows that the flesh is not yet dead; what *is truly* dead, however, is *sin* (cf Rom 6:2ff; 8:13). The flesh is dead only in principle. The passions are in general sources of evil desires. Paul had no intention of listing the classical categories of passion for the Galatians — if indeed he had ever heard of them; he was simply being very realistic about the difficulties of living a good Christian life.

Hints for Homiletics

1. All Christians especially must practice daily discipline and mortification, in order to maintain the proper balance between the spirit and the flesh. This cannot be done effectively by legislation, but depends upon the individual. A man need not be a notorious sinner before he does penance; but he must recognize the need to conquer and control, within himself, the results of original sin.

2. No man can serve two masters, we learn from today's Gospel.

The Christian is committed by name and baptism to live a good life, and he will know no peace with himself unless he does. To love one's neighbor is the greatest law of life; Paul here points out the many vices to be avoided in order to prove one's love for God and neighbor.

3. Every normal man condemns the "works of the flesh" as enumerated by Paul. These vices are all antisocial, marking the triumph of individual (personal) pride, carried out to the exclusion of the rights and dignity of others, even of one's own family. These vices destroy the stability of relations between men, and are especially destructive of that goodness of heart which holds the social order together. Imagine what it would be like if one of your friends, or a member of your family, were to indulge in these crimes.

Life of the Spirit

INTRODUCTION. Paul has just finished urging the Galatians to walk in the spirit, since they were now lifted up and animated by grace, and by the Holy Spirit. He now proceeds to draw some practical conclusions from what he has said, and will point out certain faults — the small change of human frailty — which dim the beauty of charity, and should therefore be avoided (cf Gal 2:19f; Rom 6:2–14).

THE EPISTLE: GALATIANS 5:25–6:10

25 *If we live by the Spirit,*
let us also walk according to the spirit.

All who have died to the flesh (5:24) have within them the beginnings of the life of the Spirit. But to have received the divine principle of life is not enough; one must follow it out in practice and be true "pneumatics!" (The first *pneumati* is an instrumental dative, the second, a dative of direction.)

26 *Let us not seek vain glory,*
provoking one another, envying one another.

An echo of 5:15 ("If you bite and devour one another . . .") can be detected here. The "vain-glory" Paul mentions was, one suspects, the deliberate performance of good works which would make the doer stand out. The Galatians were apparently ambitious, and even in spiritual matters were known to jockey for position (= provoking one another), each trying to outdo the other. Competition in spiritual matters is always bound to produce envy. In any case, the seeking of vain glory is a waste of time and of talents, especially when the genuinely rich life of the Spirit beckons the believer to true sanctity.

6:1 *Brethren, if a man should be surprised by some fault,*
you who are spiritual should set him right,
in a spirit of gentleness,
looking to yourself, lest you yourself should be tempted.

The one word *brethren* is a sermon in itself. Paul's friendly appeal

211

was calculated to win over his readers, and this approach contrasts sharply with the explosive beginning of the letter (1:6; 3:1). Paul now proposes a case in which a man has suddenly been overtaken (= prolempthe) by some sin, not through malice so much as through weakness. Paul's advice concerning the incestuous Corinthian had been so promptly and zealously followed that he had made a point of seeking pardon for the guilty one. With this in mind (2 Cor 2:6–8) he now sets before the Galatians an example of gentleness (= prautes). If a good man slips, you who are so "spiritual" must be gentle in correcting or setting him right. The word used here to describe this action (= katartizete) was often employed in reference to a resetting of a bone or joint, or of cleansing or mending, for example, fishing nets. The point is that holy people ought not to be harsh in correcting others. Paul suddenly switches here to the singular, as if addressing his remarks to the one deputed to correct the sinner, and reminds such a man that no one is without weaknesses. Sound advice, for nothing so tempers a reformer's zeal as the realization that, but for the grace of God, he might himself be the sinner. Gentleness is the fruit of the Holy Spirit (5:23), and it is anything but weakness or effeminacy; it is rather strength under control out of the love one bears for God.

2 Bear one another's burdens
and so you shall fulfil the law of Christ.

To correct others is a dangerous and tricky business, so the Apostle suggests a practical plan which applies to everyone. Burden or yoke is a common image understood by all; everyone, even the Christian, has certain duties to perform which are his alone. One can help others meet their obligations; not, of course, in such a way as to remove these wholly from their shoulders, but rather so as to help them face their responsibilities. Paul seems to be referring to moral faults here, for these more than anything else burden and weigh a man down. Possibly also he may have had in mind the temptation which precedes, and the remorse which follows, sin. If the Galatians must have a law, let it not be the Mosaic Law, but the law of Charity, which is Christ's (cf 5:14; Rom 8:2). They can help others bear even their moral lapses by encouraging them, showing them compassion, staying them up with an affection that does not falter. This is to fulfill the law of Christ. It is much more than simply to "fill" it, because it involves charity joined with mercy, and zeal accompanied by gentleness.

**3 For if anyone thinks he is something, although he is nothing,
he deceives himself.**

The man who refuses to bear another's burdens does so, probably, because he feels that he himself will never be in need of a helping hand, and in this he is certainly wrong. He is likewise wrong in thinking that he is so unlike the rest of men; his very vanity is sinful. Like everyone else, he is a sinner (Rom 3:23), and should bear this in mind. Without insight a man can do little good for others, or for himself.

**4 Let each one, however, examine his own work,
and then he shall have a reason for boasting in himself alone,
and not in another.**

One cannot erect a tall building using defective materials, and no one can develop a healthy religious life by concentrating upon the faults of his neighbors. What Paul is recommending here is a good examination of conscience (cf 1 Cor 11:28). If this does not uncover many serious faults, it can nevertheless shed light upon one's good points. This is not a bad thing, for such knowledge dissipates the confusion and doubt in which cowardice and false humility thrive. If a man can glory in his own God-given powers and abilities, he has solid footing under his glorying. But such is not the case when a man judges himself in comparison with others.

The word used for "examine" (= dokimazein) is also used to describe the process of refining gold. When this precious substance is melted, the dross floats on the surface and can be skimmed off, leaving the pure gold in the crucible. There is perhaps some irony here in Paul's words, for he seems to suggest that a good look at one's own self might leave little to boast about. That every man has little to offer to others he soon learns from sad experience; but this knowledge should lead to a sound and wholesome humility.

5 For each man shall have his own load to carry.

The examination of conscience just recommended brings a man back to himself and to his own faults; if he has reason to glory, let it be only in the Lord (1 Cor 1:31). But each man shall bear his own burden. The future verb shows that it shall always be thus. Load (= *phortion*) is a more general term than burden (= *baros*, v 2), and is used of both men and beasts. Paul has more than one way of puncturing the balloon of complacency and smugness.

6 *Moreover, let him who is instructed in the word*
   share with him who teaches, in all good things.

Although Paul preferred to make his own way whenever he could (cf Acts 20:33-35), he often appealed to the principle that a laborer was worthy of his hire, especially those who labored in the Lord's vineyard (cf 1 Cor 9:11; 2 Cor 11:7f; Phil 4:10-20; 1 Tim 5:17f). The instructor was either a resident or a transient missionary, and that which he imparted to his hearers was the word of words, the gospel message. Paul obviously did not mean that the recipients of this teaching should out of gratitude reduce themselves to poverty, but he did mean that they should share with their spiritual fathers the good things they did possess.

7 *Be not deceived, God is not mocked;*
   for what a man sows, that he will reap.
8 *He who sows unto his own flesh,*
   from the flesh shall reap corruption;
   and he who sows unto his spirit,
   from the spirit shall reap eternal life.

St. Jerome interprets the first of these verses as an admonition to those who plead poverty as an excuse for not contributing to the support of their catechists. P. Lagrange, however, interprets these words as referring to the whole of Christian conduct, that is, to those who profess to be followers of Christ, and yet live according to the flesh. These deceive themselves and mock God (*mukterizein* = to turn up one's nose, to treat with contempt). The turn is a bit abrupt, but what comes afterward will clarify Paul's idea. No man can afford to be contemptuous of God, for the day of reckoning lies ahead. And, as a common proverb has it, "What a man sows, he reaps" (cf Job 4:8; Os 8:7; Prv 22:8).

By "flesh" and "spirit" Paul refers to "nongrace" and "grace," or to the two principles of life in one who has been baptized.

One who fails to live by the reality signified by his baptism, sows for, or in view of, his flesh (= eis ten sarken); in other words, he does those works of the flesh (enumerated in 5:19ff) which indicate that he has rejected and lost eternal life, i.e., grace. On the other hand, the man who sows in the spirit (= unto or for the spirit) walks in the newness of life, and what he does is pleasing to God. The new life of grace produces the fruits of the spirit; these are not however the harvest; eternal life is the reward for good works because they are works of grace.

9 Now in doing good, let us not grow weary,
    for in due time we shall reap, if we do not lose courage.

As every farmer knows, unless he has taken the proper preliminary steps, he cannot expect a harvest. It is like that in the spiritual life. The chief difficulty here is: not to give way before the monotony of routine goodness (Lagrange). Between seedtime and harvest many months must pass, and the sower might well wonder at times if he has not labored in vain. But good people should not indulge in the luxury of discouragement, of halting along the way; sinners are diligent in their daily commission of evil, and serve as examples of diligence to the saints. One does good by leading a life of virtue, and of love (5:13); if he turns aside from this manner of living, he will fall victim of the works of the flesh. Let him then continue on in good, and when the master of the harvest judges that the time is ripe, he will be able to gather in an abundant harvest.

10 So then, while we have the opportunity,
    let us do good to all, expecially
    to those who are of the household of the faith.

In conclusion, Paul calls for action, especially the action of charity. His words may reflect here some idea that not much time remains, but he is more concerned with urging that when given the chance we should do good to all, whether fellow Christians, Jews, or pagans (cf Rom 2:10f). No one is impervious to good example. Paul wants all Christians to do good, to love — not an abstraction, such as "humanity" but — all men. There is room, however, for a certain preferential treatment of our companions in God's household. Charity begins at home, but when it does, it has a way of not remaining only in the home.

HINTS FOR HOMILETICS

1. One practical way of bearing another's burdens is simply to avoid being an occasion of sin for him by our speech or behavior. Our manner of dress, our subjects of conversation, our misuse of God's holy Name, may well contribute to our neighbor's difficulties in doing good.

2. Jesus was the most sympathetic of men. So too were Paul and all the saints. Sympathy is the mark of unselfish people, who bear patiently with disagreeable companions and neighbors, restrain their tongues, and concentrate their criticisms upon themselves.

3. In 1953 Pope Pius XII repeated St. Paul's admonition not to grow weary in doing good. The Holy Father referred to this temptation as the great trial of the Christian. Each day we must renew our faith and trust in God, and commit to his efficient and capable hands our seemingly unproductive performances of good deeds.

Paul's Prayer

INTRODUCTION (cf p. 89). Ephesus, situated on the west coast of Asia Minor (modern Turkey) opposite Corinth, was once a port city comparable to New York. With the passage of time, however, a combination of earthquakes and the gradual silting up of the harbor reduced this thriving metropolis to ruin. Today nothing remains of Ephesus except the ruins, which are half a mile inland. H. V. Morton succeeds brilliantly in evoking the glory that once was Ephesus in his book, *In the Footsteps of St. Paul.* One may also consult Acts 18:24–19:40.

The letter to the Ephesians is one of the so-called captivity Epistles, written while Paul was a captive in Rome (A.D. 61–63). In it is the famous "digression" (which extends from 3:2–13); occasioned by the use of the word *Gentiles* in 3:1. Carried away by the wonders of God's mysterious calling of those who were not of the Chosen Race, Paul reaches heights of eloquence. The herald of the calling of the Gentiles, he was enraptured by the dazzling prospect of the abolition of all racial, national, and territorial distinctions, and by the vision of the whole human race unified in and by Christ the Redeemer and it was for preaching precisely this doctrine that Paul was now in prison (cf Col. 1:23; 2:1; Acts 21:28).

THE EPISTLE: EPHESIANS 3:13–21

13 *Therefore I ask you not to lose heart over my tribulations*
    on your account; they are your glory.

Paul concludes his digression by facing squarely the question which had surely puzzled and disturbed his converts, namely, how it was that one who preached God's message could be languishing in jail. But imprisonment was nothing new in Paul's life, and he had long ago come to understand that if Christ's sufferings were not a true cause for scandal, neither should those of his servants be (cf Phil 2:17). He understood that he was filling up what was "lacking" in the sufferings of Christ (Col 1:24). Not, of course, that he could add anything whatsoever to the redemptive work of the cross, for his sufferings were imitative only, and served only to indicate his love for, and union with, the Savior. To suffer for Jesus' sake was and is a great honor. The Church, which is the spouse of Christ, has known and will know this mystery of suffering to the end of time.

14   *For this reason I bend my knees before the Father*
15   *from whom every family in heaven and on earth is named.*

Deeply moved, then, at the spectacle of the great mystery which had been hidden from all previous ages in God (v 9), Paul falls to his knees. One bends the knee only in deference to men of high rank, or, in adoration, to God. As Jews usually stood while praying, this action bespeaks intense emotion. Several other examples of this attitude in prayer will bear this out. Solomon knelt at the dedication of the Temple (3 Kgs 8:54); Daniel did so thrice daily (6:10); Peter, before raising Tabitha to life (Acts 9:40), and Paul many times (Acts 20:36; 21:5 etc).

This is not one of Paul's best sentences. He is not praying for those in heaven and on earth, but to the Father, from whom every being or family receives its name, i.e., owes its origin. This could all have been said more easily, but Paul is playing on the words *pater* (= father) and *patria* (= family). It is not therefore a question of all fatherhood being participated from God the Father — there are no "fathers" among the heavenly beings we call angels — but rather of the fact that everything comes from a God who is the common Father or source of all reasonable beings, whether human or angelic. Of all beings other than himself, he is the creator. It is to the omnipotent God the Father, then, that Paul directs his earnest prayer.

16   **That he may grant you,**
        according to the riches of his glory,
        to be strengthened mightily through his Spirit
        in the inward man.

Paul confidently asks, first of all, that the Ephesians be given the strength of the Holy Spirit, "without Whom there is no courage" (Jerome). Paul was deeply impressed by the riches of God, as is clear from his repeated use of this word: the riches of grace (1:7; 2:7), of mercy (2:4); of glory (1:18; 3:16); a richness shared by Christ (3:8). Prodigal in mercy and goodness, God is magnificently liberal, and Paul can hardly speak of him without talking in superlatives. St. Thomas Aquinas shared St. Paul's appreciation of God's magnificence. In his *Adoro Te*, the Angelic Doctor speaks glowingly of the value of the Savior's Blood:

> "Of which a single drop, for sinners spilt
> Can purge the entire world from all its guilt."

The "inward or inner man" is a Pauline creation. By it he means the man who has been regenerated (= reborn) and revivified by grace, through baptism. The "new creature" must lead a "new life," ever deepening his union with the Savior with the help of the Holy Spirit. The "old man" is the same as the "outward man" who stands for the body and its senses; the outward man must be made to yield to the inward man (cf 2 Cor 4:16).

17 *that Christ may through faith dwell in your hearts;*
  that, rooted and grounded in love,
18 *you may be able to comprehend with all the saints*
  what is the breadth and length and height and depth,

Dwell (= *katoikesai*) signifies not a temporary lodging, but a permanent abode. Christ takes up his abode in men's hearts — the seat of man's thoughts and desires — through a faith which should progressively become more profound and influential, as the divine guest makes his presence more commandingly felt in the depths of the soul. Such faith does not grow in extent, but in depth.

From faith, Paul goes on to speak of love. The double metaphor of roots and foundation stone convey the idea of strength; the perfect participles betoken a charity already well rooted and firmly fixed.

Thus prepared, the Christian shall, in union with all other believers, attain to an understanding or at least to a knowledge of something which, from no matter what angle it is viewed, is surpassingly wonderful. In a striking attempt to plumb the unfathomable riches of Christ, Paul uses all possible quantitative measurements. The four dimensions suggest an immensity or a vastness without limits, of the thing to be comprehended by all Christians. Just what it was Paul had in mind when he wrote this sentence has puzzled the exegetes. Some have seen in his words a reference to the mystery of the cross (Augustine, Jerome), or to heavenly bliss, or to faith, wisdom, and the divine perfections. Others argue from the context that Paul meant the Church. It is even more probable that he thus refers to the mystery which he had touched upon in 3:1-13 and which prompted the very prayer he is now in the process of uttering. One is left with an impression of the magnitude and the universality of the divine plan and of Christ's work. And possibly, of the love of Christ, which is to be understood as surpassing comprehension.

**19 to know also the love of Christ which surpasses knowledge,
        that you may be filled with all the fullness of God.**

The love of Christ is the supreme mystery and defies complete understanding, for like God himself it is infinite, without limits. Paul prays nevertheless that his readers will "know that which surpasses knowing" (cf Phil 4:7); one can recognize and savor the immense love of Christ, within certain limits. More, surely, by a mystical experience than by speculation. This foretaste of Jesus' love is a preparation for and a gauge of future bliss. Paul therefore points out the road at whose end "the fullness of God" (= pleroma) awaits, and prays that all Christians attain to the knowledge which enraptures the saints, and also, that they be filled with the plenitude of the divine perfection in so far as this can be communicated to man here below. The fullness or plenitude of perfection is found in Christ (Col. 2:9f), and without ever hoping to exhaust its depths, Christians can advance toward and into this fullness (= eis to pan pleroma). It is suggested that their knowledge is capable of continued growth. They enter into that mysterious "fullness" which is the total Christ, i.e., the Church and, ultimately, the new universe (cf 4:12f; 1:23; 2:22; Col. 2:10).

**20 Now to him whose power, acting in us,
        can do far more abundantly than all that we ask or think,
21 to him be glory in the Church and in Christ Jesus,
        unto all generations, for ever and ever, Amen.**

Paul now closes the dogmatic section of his letter. He has asked that great gifts of grace be given to the Ephesians, and recognizes that he has only scratched the surface by his prayerful demands. God, he implies, can outthink any of his creatures, and has prepared for them more than they could ever dream of asking ("far more abundantly" represents "hyperekperissou" i.e., super-exceptionally-remarkable). Himself extremely conscious of this, Paul closes with a magnificent doxology (= word of praise). He prays that all glory be given to God. God could not act for any reason which was unconnected with or unrelated to himself. Not that he operates from selfish motives, but simply that he is infinite, the Creator of all things that are. Everything that he does, therefore, must in some way redound to his glory. In the last analysis, that is the only motive which can be ascribed to the divine activity outside of the Trinity.

The two great instruments which insure God's glory are Christ, and the Church which is his continuation upon earth. Paul's "Amen" gives his prayer an added solemnity; it is as if he is saying: that God be praised and forever praised, I most ardently desire.

HINTS FOR HOMILETICS

1. From time to time Catholics ought to be reminded of their need to grow in depth, in the faith. The catechism lessons learned in grammar school are accurate, but they are merely the structural skeleton of the faith, so to speak, and this should be filled in with further knowledge. Reading St. Paul, one realizes something of the wealth and depth of our faith; King Midas and his golden touch, or Rockefeller with his millions were poorer, spiritually speaking, than the least of Christians in the state of grace. No matter to which doctrine of the faith one turns, one is impressed by its depth, its vitality, its implications for all generations. The Holy Spirit was to lead the Apostles unto the whole truth, and this vital process goes on continuously as the Church assimilates the truths uncovered by each generation into the changeless revelation of Jesus Christ.

2. Our knowledge concerning the most common wonders of nature (such as the atom, radiation, weather, even such familiar things as electricity) is very shallow. This does not mean that God is shallow. Our poverty does not lesson his richness. His infinite majesty and greatness, his mercy and power, his love and wisdom, ought always to evoke in us a sense of humble wonder and gratitude at what he has done, and to arouse in us an eager anticipation to receive the spiritual gifts he alone can give.

3. We know that from eternity God has decreed to give us many things without our asking (and even without our knowing), but that some

things have to be asked for before they will be given. Paul teaches us to pray confidently. We are not God's poor relations, but his sons and heirs. St. Teresa of Avila counseled her sisters not to insult God by asking him for insignificant things; instead they should ask for something that would take some giving, e.g., a deeper knowledge of his will, of his love, of his Church.

A Plea for Unity

INTRODUCTION. Everyone who has been called to membership in the Church through the working out of the "mystery hidden from other ages," has incurred certain obligations, and St. Paul now sets some of them before the Ephesians. The mystery of salvation is realized among men through Christ and his Church. Paul foresees three dangers ahead, all of them threats to the unity of the Church: discord (Eph 4:1-3), differences of office (7-11), and variation in doctrine (14-15). To offset these dangers he proposes definite countermeasures (4-6; 12f; 16).

THE EPISTLE: EPHESIANS 4:1-6

1 *I entreat you, then, I a prisoner in the Lord,*
    to lead a life worthy of the calling which you have received

There can be no true morality that is not based upon certain fixed principles or dogmas. Having established the point that all who are baptized are members of Christ, and that the Church is one with Christ, Paul now spells out some of the conclusions which follow from this belief. He earnestly exhorts the Ephesians to *walk worthily,* that is, to live and act as befits members of Christ's body. The very greatness of God's gift of spiritual life demands a fitting response on the part of the recipients. *Noblesse oblige* means: "Nobility imposes obligations." Paul makes his point with authority, but without harshness. He is a *prisoner in the Lord,* a prisoner for Christ's sake, because he has preached the doctrine of Christ. One marvels at Paul's vigorous reaction to the cold reality of prison walls; he actually felt it to be an honor to be a prisoner for the Lord's sake, an honor greater than being a consul or a king.

2 *With all humility and meekness, with patience,*
    putting up with one another in love.

Jesus had once said: "Learn of me, for I am meek and humble of heart" (Mt 11:29), and Paul took him at his word, and never tires of urging these virtues on his converts. Humility (= *tapeinophrosune*) or

223

unpretentiousness, is an essentially Christian virtue. It does not require the Christian to deny the undeniable (e.g., his own evident talents or accomplishments) but to take them in stride, realizing that his gifts must be used in a responsible manner, and without boasting. A humble man may perceive that his talents are definitely greater than those of his fellow man, but will on occasion endure being treated as if they were inferior. Along with this unassuming and unaggressive attitude of mind goes *meekness* or *gentleness* (= *prautes*), that is, strength under the control of reason and will, and *patience* or *longanimity* (= *makrothumia*), that precious ally of magnanimity. Men endowed with such Christian virtues will know how to weather adverse circumstances, to overlook affronts.

It is little short of remarkable to note how smoothly St. Paul will alternate between the most lofty doctrine and the utterly practical realities of human living. He was well acquainted with the real "facts of life," and never tired of urging the faithful to put up with the human weaknesses of their fellows, and this for reasons of family affection. This is another way of saying that they must direct their lives from supernatural motives, and follow the example of Christ (cf Col 3:13; and the *Imitation of Christ*, I, 16).

To put charity thus to work along with these very necessary virtues, does not, of course, mean that one should consider human shortcomings as something too inevitable to worry about, or that one should grow tolerant of them. It means rather an active exercise of love for others, a "wishing them well," taking care the while not to become an unjust burden or trial to others. Plutarch once remarked "Never ask [the gods] for freedom from trouble; ask rather for steadfastness in clemency" (Luc. 32).

3 Eager to keep the unity of the Spirit in the bond of peace

In unity there is strength. It is the duty of every Christian actively to preserve and to promote the unity which binds him to the living Church and to Christ. This calls for a strong and unselfish love, but the delicious fruit of this love is peace. One must then take pains to maintain that unity where it is already existing. St. Thomas remarks that no one works for peace if he is blind to the demands of justice.

4 *[There is] one body and one Spirit,*
just as you were called in one hope of your calling

There *is* must be supplied to bring out the sense of vv 4–6. Paul here gives the first of three reasons why unity should be maintained: the Church is one body whose head is Christ. Like all other bodies, this one is pervaded by one Spirit, the Holy Spirit, the pledge of our inheritance (1:14). Just as there is one body and one Spirit, so too there is one hope common to all who are called; hope belongs to this calling, and the "call" itself induces confidence in the great reward which awaits — heaven.

5 *One Lord, one faith, one baptism*

There now occurs to Paul's mind the *second* (and extrinsic) reason for unity. There should be unity among the faithful because there is only one Lord for all, Jesus Christ. He is recognized by all the faithful in one and the same *faith*, a faith which is not a subjective emotion or feeling, but belief in an objective reality — Christ. Jesus is the Savior who has been "put on" like a garment by one and all, by one and the same baptism, for when one is baptized, believing, he is incorporated into the One Lord.

It is strange that Paul does not here mention the Eucharist, which is par excellence the sacrament of unity. Perhaps the explanation of this omission is that he thought unity to be sufficiently expressed by the unity in diversity of the three divine Persons. One could hardly conclude that he underestimated the unifying power of the Eucharist (1 Cor 10:16f).

6 *One God and Father of all,*
who is above all and through all and in all.

The *third* (and transcendent) reason for safeguarding unity in love among Christians is the shining fact that there is for all men the same unique God and Father. As God is one, his family should be one. He is seated in divine splendor, and above all men. So great is his power that he penetrates into and operates within the very core of man's being, making him an instrument in the carrying out of the divine plan. God is present in all men by grace, as well as by his omnipresence and power.

HINTS FOR HOMILETICS

1. Privileges are never given out entirely without strings. The surpassing gift of grace and the call to the Christian life, are privileges to which grave obligations — notably those of unity and charity — are attached. The marvelous oneness of the Catholic Church should be mirrored in the unity of mind and heart existing among her members. In the practical order this same unity should prevail in all parish activities: committees, societies, etc.

2. The humble man is not forever asserting his rights or sounding off about his own particular qualifications for this or that job. Humility is a quiet, unassuming state of mind, rendering a man ready and willing to help in whatever way he can without calling attention to himself. Like the earth from which humility derives its name, this virtue is solid, productive, fruitful. Jesus Christ, the incarnate Son of God, continues to surprise the world by his humility (in life, and in the Blessed Sacrament, in his priests and in his followers). Yet see what humble men have done, and still do, following him.

3. Unity among men is difficult of attainment, as anyone who reads newspaper accounts of international summit meetings (or the UN) is well aware. But there is unity where it most counts: unity in the Church, in the one Christ who is the object of our faith, and in the one omnipotent and omnipresent God. Our strength, then, lies in our close adherence to the Church, to the Savior, and to God. This we can do by faithfulness to our calling, by frequent attendance at Mass, and by the frequent reception of the sacraments.

The founder of our National Academy of Sciences, S. S. Haldeman, was led to become a Catholic because of his studies in entomology (= insects). He reasoned that if God took such care in creating tiny insects endowed with such an astonishing unity of head and members, he must have given that same unity to his Church.

XVIII SUNDAY AFTER PENTECOST

Paul's Thanks and Hopes

INTRODUCTION. Following the literary manners of the day, Paul opens his first letter to the Corinthians first by identifying himself (as an Apostle), and then adding a word of thanksgiving. He follows this custom in all but two Epistles, the fiery Galatians, in which he at once launches into his theme after identifying himself, and in Hebrews. Paul's thanks in today's letter are an acknowledgment of the healthy spiritual condition of his readers notably manifested in such matters as the word, knowledge, and charismata. His words of appreciation shrewdly prepare the way for a candid treatment, in the body of the letter, of certain shortcomings.

THE EPISTLE: 1 CORINTHIANS 1:4–8

4 *I give God thanks at all time for you,*
   because of the grace of God bestowed on you in Christ Jesus

Speaking now in his own name alone (Sosthenes was mentioned in the first verse) Paul thanks God for the special graces bestowed so generously upon the Corinthians. His thanks were continual. It was, of course, impossible that Paul was always *actually* thanking God, for he had many very human and ungraceful things which rightfully demanded his attention, but he has deliberately and consciously thanked God for them, and has in no way ever retracted his thanks; his gratitude was virtually present in all that he did.

These graces were given *in Christ Jesus*. By this brief often used phrase Paul conveyed his belief that Jesus is the perfect mediator of all of God's gifts to man. All who are incorporated by baptism into the mystical Body have their life *in Christ Jesus*, as branches have their life in the vine. The striking graces of the Corinthian church are due to the Savior who has deigned to use Paul as his instrument in producing them.

227

**5 For in him you have been enriched in everything,
    in all utterance and all knowledge**

Because they are now united to Jesus Christ, the Corinthians have
been made spiritually rich beyond imagining, for in Christ are contained all the riches and blessings of God (2 Cor 8:9). From among
these riches Paul singles out two which were bestowed upon them at
the moment of their baptism: *utterance* (*logos*) and *knowledge* (*gnosis*).
Thanks to such gifts, they were able both to know and to express what
they knew. The church at Corinth, despite a few bad members, was indeed
a favored one.

**6 Thus the witness of Christ
    has taken such a firm hold on you**

Thus (= *kathos*, i.e., because, or in proportion as) by the testimony
which Paul had himself borne to Christ by his preaching (= the witness
of Christ), they are firm in their belief, and have been rewarded for it
by many unusual graces.

**7 That in no gift are you lacking
    while eagerly awaiting the revelation
    of our Lord, Jesus Christ.**

That (= *hoste* with the infinitive) indicates an expected result. Paul
hopes that the Corinthians will lack no gift of grace (= *charisma*)
whether charismatic or sanctifying, which comes from God's liberal hand.
They themselves must ardently desire this (= *apekdechomenous*) until,
with the revelation of Christ in glory at the end of time (= the Parousia),
God's plans shall be made known to all.

**8 It is he who will confirm you to the end,
    so that you may be blameless
    on the Day of our Lord Jesus Christ.**

The Lord will himself strengthen the faithful in their new spiritual
life by a vital but mysterious action proper to himself. The life of grace
is that of adoptive sonship (Gal 4:4-7; Rom 8:14-17). Actually the
Corinthians are far from being perfect, but by his grace, Jesus will con-

firm (= bebaiosei) or strengthen them. He who has called them to faith and adoptive sonship will not fail to confer on them also the helps necessary for their perseverance and progress.

Paul cannot always be taken (indeed, who can?) in the strict sense. He does not mean that the Corinthians are confirmed in grace to such an extent that they are no longer capable of sinning; rather, his words are expressive of a hope that they will be blameless (= anegkletoi, irreproachable), that is, will have no grave charge hanging over them on that day. When an ordaining bishop asked (in Greek) whether there was any fault or crime among the candidates for ordination, he used the word angekletoi in much the same sense as Paul does here. He did not intend to imply that they were or were expected to be absolutely beyond reproach (cf Phil 1:20; 2:15–17; Eph 1:4; Col 1:22; 1 Thess 3:10).

Paul refers to the day of our Lord Jesus Christ. Otherwise identified as the day, that day, the Day of God, of the Son of Man, of the visitation, etc., it refers to the accomplishment, in the eschatological era inaugurated by Christ, of the Day of Yahweh foretold by the prophets (cf Am 5:18f). It has already been partially realized by the coming of Christ (Lk 17:20–24) and by the destruction of Jerusalem (Mt 24), but will be consummated by the glorious return (1 Cor 1:7) of the Sovereign Judge (Rom 2:6f). As the date is uncertain (1 Thes 5:1), one must hold himself in readiness at all times. In a sense, for every man death is a Parousia.

HINTS FOR HOMILETICS

1. Few things are more pleasing to men — and, surely, to God — than gratitude for benefits received. We are like the Corinthians in that "no grace is lacking to us." Laudable as an habitual state of gratitude may be, it is a good thing occasionally to actualize — and to put into words — that gratitude.

2. One might profitably develop the idea that the acquisition of the state of grace is the acquisition of life, implying activity and not stagnation. Grace-full activity is perhaps too often presented in a negative fashion — don't do this, don't do that — whereas it is in fact a most positive kind of living, alert, directed by reason, guided by the Holy

Spirit. Awareness of God, acknowledgment of God's sovereignty and majesty and goodness, can be made subjects of everyone's inner conversation with God. And nothing could be more personal.

3. The New Testament is filled with so many references to "the Day" of the Lord, and that subject has been given much attention by authors who hold that Jesus and Paul were both mistaken about "the Day," thinking that it would arrive very shortly. But Jesus declared that no man knew the hour (it was not part of his mission to reveal it), and Paul explained the signs which must precede it, e.g., the coming of Antichrist, and the conversion of the Jews (1–2 Thes and Rom 9–11). But every man will see Christ as his judge at the moment of death, as well as at the end of time.

XIX SUNDAY AFTER PENTECOST

Two Sides of the Coin

INTRODUCTION. In the moral section of Ephesians which begins with 4:1, Paul has a word of advice for both the community and the individuals who make it up. He here draws a sharp contrast between his converts' old life and their new life of grace. Their old life was characterized by futility, dullness of mind, and a depressing fixation on immoral pleasures (4:17–19), but that is not the way of Christ, Paul tells them. They have been taught to put off the old man, to be renewed in spirit, and to put on the new man (20–24).

THE EPISTLE: EPHESIANS 4:23–28

23 *But be renewed in the spirit of your mind*

Renewed (= ananeousthai) is a present infinitive, which means that this particular renewal is something progressive and continuous; the putting on and off of the new and old man (22,24), however, was done once and for all, and is consequently expressed by aorists.

The Christian's mystical death and resurrection are quickly effected through baptism, but the complete transformation or renewal of the inner man takes much more. The "new life" (kaine, or new, suggests a new quality, not newness of age = neo) must be a day by day affair. It is not a static but a dynamic and vital condition. As a man is raised to ever greater heights of grace, his horizons grow ever wider, and in the greater light he sees his defects more clearly, and also how much he needs God's help for further purification, progress, and renewal.

The spirit of your mind cannot mean the Holy Spirit, which is never so named, but the inmost part of a man (cf 1 Cor 2:11), the mind subjected to God by grace (in contrast to the futility of the Gentiles' mind, Eph 4:17). Be renewed, Paul says, by constantly opening your thoughts and desires to the supernatural order. . . . The new state in which the baptized Christian lives is not one that has to be *recreated*

231

at each moment, but it must be faithfully looked after, inspected, and renewed, like the permanent roadbed of a railroad.

24 *And put on the new man*
     who is created in accordance with God's will
     in true justice and holiness.

Put on is a positive expression, balancing the *put off* of v 22. The *new man* is made according to God (= *kata theon*), and has been raised to a new state, that is, has now been restored by grace and made obedient to the Holy Spirit. This creation of the new man is obviously something strictly within God's competence. *Justice* linked with *holiness* appears in one who is made according to God's plan; the combination of the two suggests a genuine perfection in which nothing is lacking. The fruits of virtuous living are soon manifest.

25 *Therefore putting aside lying,*
     let everyone speak the truth with his neighbor,
     because we are members of one another.

The first of the vices to which the old man was addicted was *lying.* The new man has put lying aside, and must now devote himself to the truth. Paul advances an excellent reason for this — we are all united in Christ as member to member (Rom 12:5); the tongue tasting what is bitter does not deceive the stomach. The telling of lies is subversive of social harmony (Mt 5:37); each member belongs to the others. Anything that hurts charity threatens the existing unity.

26 *Be angry but do not sin.*
     Let not the sun go down upon your anger.

A *second* vice to which the pagans were much addicted was that of anger. Adapting a verse from a psalm (4:5) in his typically Semitic way, Paul trims off the conditional phrase "if you should . . ." He does not counsel men to become angry, but in case they do, they ought to take care not to sin. Man's instinctive anger is designed to prevent him from sudden harm; quick and violent reactions are sometimes necessary. Deliberate anger however should follow the perception of injustice. Anger is sinful when there is no cause for it, when it is out of proportion to the situation, or when it is the mere expression of cruelty. Jesus, and all the saints, were justifiably angry on occasion (Mk 3:5).

"Let not the sun go down upon your anger" is a graphic way of saying that one should calm his anger with all possible speed. St. Jerome's "Slay the enemy while he is small," spoken concerning temptations against purity, applies very well to feelings of anger.

27 Do not give place to the devil.

The devil is the arch enemy of mankind. To give place to the devil is to give him free rein or room to act. He is ever quick to press his advantage whenever a man commits sin, especially the sin of anger, which can so easily develop into hatred and eventually into base deeds. Paul recommends the closed-door policy toward anger and toward the devil. Given any opportunity at all, the devil will wreak havoc in souls which should live the new life of grace.

28 Let one given to stealing steal no more, but rather let him labor with his hands at what is good, so that he may have something to share with those in need.

Paul mentions a third vice to be put off by the new man — that of theft. Stealing is the secret and unlawful taking of things which belong to another in justice. There are other ways of obtaining this world's goods. Paul recommends honest work, even manual labor. To work with one's hands, after the example of the Savior himself, is by no means a disgrace, but rather something ennobling. Most men work to provide themselves with the necessities of living and a certain amount of comfort and pleasure. Paul proposes a revolutionary concept — that a man should work with an eye to being able to share of his superfluity with others. His formula for the new life is, work honorably and give generously to the less fortunate.

HINTS FOR HOMILETICS

1. As any confessor knows, the Ephesians had no monopoly on such vices as lying, anger, and stealing. Explanations of each of these are extremely practical. To say "Daddy is not at home" (when he is) may not always be a lie; getting angry may sometimes be a virtuous act, and

234 THE SUNDAY EPISTLES

failure to become angry a sin; and there are (can be) times when "stealing" is not stealing (in case of extreme necessity) but justice (occult compensation).

2. Work is more than punishment for Adam's sin; it is a duty. Everyone dislikes the goldbricker, the shirker, the one who does not carry his share of the load. Moreover, Jesus clearly condemned the lazy servant, and those who do not use the talents which God gave them. One talent well used can do more good than three or five that are not used to capacity. Far better to light a single candle than to bemoan the darkness!

3. Employers often complain that they seldom get a full day's work out of their employees. Sometimes Catholics are more honest in this than others; they should always be honest, whether in paying their bills or in doing work for which they get paid. And let the Christian be generous in sharing what he has with others. He can do this most effectively by contributing generously to his church.

XX SUNDAY AFTER PENTECOST

True Christian Wisdom

INTRODUCTION. Paul continues his exposition of the "new life" (cf p. 231). Besides the avoidance of many specific sins (cf 4:25ff), he now recommends the practice of many virtues, especially those of gratitude, prudence, sobriety, and obedience. The good life is not a gloomy life, and Paul pictures it as being lived against a background of sacred song (v 19).

THE EPISTLE: EPHESIANS 5:15–21

15 *Look carefully then how you walk*

The word *carefully* (= *akribos*) should be joined to *look*, and not to the following word, *walk*. The Ephesians ought to pay careful attention to their behavior (= the moral aspect of *walk*). God nowhere promised to give men graces which would dispense them from watchful care. You have the light, Paul says, so that you may live in light; its possession does not dispense you from tending the lamp. Even the children of the light must keep their eyes open and their minds alert, for spiritual aimlessness leads infallibly to catastrophe.

15b *Not as unwise, but as wise,*
16 *Ransoming the time, for the days are evil.*

The *unwise* are those whose lives fail to conform to their beliefs; the *wise* live by the Gospel (1:8,17). It is ridiculous for a man to attempt to out-mastermind God, to live a sinful life and still think to gain heaven. The Ephesians must renounce their evil ways, and live according to the teaching they have received from Paul.

Ransoming the time has become a famous Pauline quotation. The general idea is that before or in view of the Parousia, men ought to make the most of their opportunities to do good (cf Col 4:5; Gal 6:10), sparing neither time nor effort to buy up for themselves (= *exagorazomenoi*) each passing moment. This can be done by doing good. One need not ask from whom the time is purchased, for Paul's intention was to stress the pains and efforts, not the seller.

Paul declares that the Ephesians (and himself) are living in evil times. By this he did not refer to any physical calamity or disaster (earthquake, plague, etc.) but means that the days are morally evil; they are still under the power of evildoers, and therefore dangerous for the newly born Christian. Each day provides the Christian with many occasions of sin and spiritual ruin; everything seemingly inclines toward evil. All the more reason why one should fill this time doing good, especially as the only thing necessary for the triumph of evil is that good men should do nothing, in which case evil is left free to dominate the world.

17 *Therefore do not be foolish*
    but understand what the will of the Lord is.

The foolish or senseless man (= *aphrones*) lacks common ordinary good sense in matters of conduct. The Christian must keep always before him the ideal: to do in every circumstance what appears to him to be the will of God; *that* is the best guide for life, and bespeaks true wisdom. To know (= *suniete*) the will of God one must scrutinize it carefully in order to learn, not what one can get out of it, but what it demands of him. Christ is the Way, the Truth, the Life. To have the *mind of Christ* (1 Cor 2:16) enables the Christian to live in the midst of a perverse and depraved environment without coming to serious harm.

18 *And do not be drunk with wine, wherein is debauchery,*
    but be filled with the Spirit.

Paul now goes from the general to the particular, from abstract to concrete. The contrast between drunkenness of wine and of the Spirit is striking. True wisdom manifests itself in daily life by temperance in matters of drink. Paul has spoken of purity (3f) and prudence (15); now he turns his attention to the archenemy of both — wine or any strong drink. If he were writing today he might also have mentioned barbiturates and the like. When used without caution or restraint these things deprive a man of his most precious, and most human possession, his reason.

Debauchery (= *asotia*) is also translated as profligacy, licentiousness, riotousness. Paul does not condemn wine or alcoholic drink as such, for it is the abuse, not the use, that is sinful. (There is a description of a "lost week end" in Prv 23:29–35; 20:1.) Strong drink tends to encourage a dissolute life. The pagans observed certain religious feasts with drunkenness and debauchery, thinking thereby to render homage to Dionysius and Aphrodite, Bacchus and Venus. Some of the early Christian assemblies (cf the agapes, 1 Cor 11:20–22) left something to be desired also. But Christian joy should come from serving God, not from drink.

Strong drink is forbidden by law to minors. Long experience has shown that alcohol is for the young like so much gasoline upon the flame. Ovid wrote that "Wine prepares the mind for Venus" and on this Jerome has a purple passage: "For young men and girls, food is an incentive to sensuality. Neither Etna's fire nor Vulcan's isle, nor Vesuvius and Olympus, seethe with such burning heat as does the youthful marrow when flushed with wine and inflamed by feasting" (Ep 54:9). He also quotes his old favorite, Terence, to the effect that "Venus grows cold if Ceres be not there, with Bacchus." And this applies to the old as well as the young.

But there is another kind of drunkenness, one which comes from the Holy Spirit, and not from wine. *Be filled with the Spirit*, he urges the Ephesians. They can be raised to dizzying spiritual heights by the abiding presence and activity of the Spirit of God within them. This is something much more ennobling and satisfying than the passing physical exaltation produced by drink.

19 *Speak to one another in psalms and hymns and spiritual songs, sing and make melody to the Lord in your heart.*

Several features of spiritual fullness are now singled out. In their religious gatherings, the first Christians quite naturally used Old Testament songs, psalms, and hymns, but these they quickly blended with their own (see v 14; 1 Tim 3:16). It is interesting that Paul should think of the Christian life, not as something dour and gloomy, but as tuneful and melodious. This is all the more remarkable because at the time he was a prisoner in chains. But Paul was never dominated by external circumstances. Mentally he was always alert, and he taught his readers a valuable lesson — the song that does not come from the heart is a sorry song. The song on a man's lips should simply be the expression of inward music first heard in the soul.

20 *Give thanks always for all things*
    in the name of our Lord, Jesus Christ, to God the Father;

It is meet and just, always and under every circumstance, to give thanks to God, whether for the trials he permits, or for the blessings he so generously showers upon his children. In a word, whether life brings good things or bad, one should thank him. One should pray as Jesus' disciples, as men wholly dependent upon him. The thanks which the Ephesians will thus offer to God the Father will be a continuation of Jesus' frequent "giving of thanks." One who prays in Jesus' name not only makes reference to Jesus in his prayers, but prays with his authority. And the Father cannot but be well pleased with such prayer.

21 *Be subject to one another in the fear of Christ.*

Mutual subjection is a new idea, preparing the way for what Paul treats in the following passage (5:22–6:9). To be subordinate to others (equals, superiors, or inferiors) is another way of being "filled with the Spirit," in the sense that being subject to others means a willingness to accept and discharge lowly duties in the conviction that these others *may hold God's place.* This attitude was particularly pertinent in the conducting of Christian assemblies, for these too had to be conducted by someone in authority, which even the charismatics were bound to recognize (1 Cor 14:26–40). Over and above this, a certain courtesy and deference to others is always the mark of a true Christian, because such behavior rests upon the belief that all are God's children, that Christ truly dwells in these others and should be reverenced there.

The fear of Christ has a place even in religious ceremonies. It is, however, a loving and reverential fear. Jesus is the guiding star and reason for all that the Christian does.

HINTS FOR HOMILETICS

1. *Time* is defined as the "Now That Flows" and *Eternity* as the "Now That Stands." What has happened in the past is past. The future is not yet. We cannot live either in the past or the future, but only in the fleeting moment we call "now." One's eternity is worked out in this "now." It is *the present moment* that is supremely important.

The souls condemned to hell forever now realize the value of time.

It is worth eternal life, or eternal damnation. We should use it well, being always mindful of discovering, and then acting in accordance with, the will of God. What would God want me to do here and now? One should learn to ask advice in important matters. Our good deeds are the price by which "time" is ours in eternity. We buy time, said St. Jerome, when we use it up doing good.

2. Are we not also living in evil times? The times are indeed evil, but as Pius XI once remarked, every age loves to think itself the most wicked the world has ever known. One should not overlook the tremendous power of good which is also operating in the world. One Sisters' Community distributed more than *four million* hosts during Lent. The number of Masses said at the request of the ordinary folk is an indication of the mysterious but powerful working of the leaven (= the Gospel) in the mass of the world.

3. Parents and grandparents, friends and benefactors, all know the chilling effect of ingratitude. Many never think to say a *thank you* for favors received from men. Will these remember to be grateful to God, as they should be?

A Call to Arms

INTRODUCTION. Physical, material wars can be avoided, sometimes, by effort and prayer, but spiritual war is something that no human can hope to avoid. Paul exhorts the Ephesians to live as true Christians, ready and able to fight for their spiritual welfare.

THE EPISTLE: EPHESIANS 6:10-17

10 For the rest, be strong in the Lord
    and in the might of his power.

Hastening to the end of his letter, Paul addresses his concluding words to all. For the rest is a kind of general conclusion. Be strong is a kind of battle cry, a shout whereby one soldier encourages another in the midst of the fray. The true source of spiritual courage is to be found in the Lord and in his omnipotent power.

11 Put on the full armor of God,
    that you may be able to stand
    against the wiles of the devil.

Courage is essential to any soldier, but even the bravest cannot fight without arms. Here St. Paul specifies what he shall put on, namely the arms which God has forged for Christian soldiers. It is a full armor (= panoplia), the complete armament of the fighting man. A Christian stands to put on this armor, and he must be able to stand erect, ready to face the enemy who is none other than the devil. Stand is another of Paul's favorite expressions (cf 6:14; Rom 5:2; 11:20; 1 Cor 10:12).

12 For our wrestling is not against flesh and blood,
    but against the principalities, against the powers,
    against the world rulers of this present darkness,
    against the spirits of wickedness in heavenly places.

The idea of wrestling with one's armor on is somewhat incongruous. But pa-le describes a kind of combat, including spiritual combat, which

ends only when one of the contestants stands victorious over his prostrate foe. Our enemy is no weak being of flesh and blood, as the Bible describes corruptible man in contrast to the world of spirits (cf Ecclus 14:18; Mt 16:17; 1 Cor 15:50; Gal 1:16), but the devil, who has a personal interest in our spiritual defeat. Satan leads his armies of fallen angels to the combat; they are demoniacal principalities and powers, rulers over the material universe, purveyors of sin and ignorance (= darkness). Their chief characteristic is their wickedness, their malice toward men. The heavenly places wherein they operate are the heavens (1:21f; 3:10; Phil 2:10) or the air (2:2), midway between the earth and God's throne.

13   Therefore take up the full armor of God,
        that you may be able to resist in the evil day,
        and after you have done everything, to stand.

No man could hope to emerge victorious from a struggle with an angel, especially a fallen angel. But God has provided us with a full armor (in the Old Testament he is described as arming himself [Is 59:16ff; Sir 5:17–23]) to use on an evil day of temptation. Paul's experience has taught him to look to the end of the struggle. This will not be obtained by one victory, but by continuous resistance and repetition of victories. The latter part of this verse is difficult to translate. "After you have done everything" (= apanta katergasomenoi) may refer to the putting on of the individual pieces of armor named in the following verse, or may mean: "after you have proved victorious over everything, stand your ground."

14   Stand then, having girded your loins with truth,
        and having put on the breastplate of justice;
15   and having shod your feet with zeal to spread the gospel
        of peace;
16   in all things taking up the shield of faith
        with which you can quench all the flaming arrows
        of the Evil One;
17   and take the helmet of salvation and the sword of
        the Spirit, which is the word of God.

A look at the Roman soldier guarding him was enough to start Paul the prisoner thinking of the armor of the Christian. He enumerates seven items commonly worn by the warriors of his day, but transposes them into arms of light. The aorist middle participles suggest that the Christian must arm *himself*, taking up and putting on with the help of grace the divine armor provided for him and as near to him as his own decision to use them.

DEFENSIVE WEAPONS

1. CINCTURE — TRUTH. The cincture of Paul's day was usually of linen, and served as a belt to hold the robe together about the waist. On setting out on a journey, a man would first tighten the cincture and then pull up his ankle-length robe or tunic so as to give his feet complete freedom of movement. Soldiers used the cincture as a kind of carry-all, and also slipped their swords through it as a kind of scabbard. The Christian soldier must from the start see to it that he lives the truth. Purity of intention and sincerity should guide his every act.

2. BREASTPLATE — JUSTICE. This piece of armor covered the entire upper part of the body, front and back, from shoulders to hips. It was made of heavy linen cloth something like a heavy canvas, and protected the heart. For the Christian, justice or sanctifying grace, which includes all the virtues, gives complete protection for the soul (1 Thes 5:8).

3. SHOES — ZEAL FOR THE GOSPEL. A well-equipped soldier must be well shod, so that he can march quickly and for long hours. Roman soldiers wore strong, heavy sandals which enabled them to march upon any kind of terrain. Paul considers zeal for the spread of the gospel as a kind of strong, well-laced shoe (cf Is 5:27). Zeal, a consequence of love, lightens the step, quickens the movement. The Christian soldier will fight for peace, and sure of his ground will preach the gospel of peace — or be ever prepared to do so if he can — to his adversaries.

4. SHIELD — FAITH. The shield (= *thureos*) of the Roman soldier measured 4 by 2½ feet. It was made by stretching a leather hide over a wooden frame; carried on the left forearm, it covered a man from the tip of his nose down to his knees. The hardened leather deflected missiles and blows that would otherwise have seriously injured or killed the warrior. But where there is a weapon there is a new defense, and where there is a defense there is a new weapon. The answer to the ancient

shield was flaming arrows, which when embedded in the shield quickly rendered it worthless and exposed the soldier to direct attack.

There is one shield, St. Paul writes, that never fails to ward off blows, and fends off even the fiercest onslaughts of the devil. This shield is faith in God. In all temptations, faith serves — better than all argument of reason — to protect the Christian soldier. The eternal truths of the faith cannot be destroyed by the malicious attacks of the enemy.

5. HELMET — SALVATION.   A soldier's helmet is designed to protect his head, which is the principal target of the enemy. Modern helmets have proved their usefulness in countless engagements; no fighting man can afford to be without one. The Christian soldier has at his disposal the helmet of salvation-already-begun and almost as good as acquired; in an earlier letter Paul had made reference to the hope of salvation, as a helmet (1 Thes 5:8). The knowledge that the Redeemer has come and has inaugurated the era of salvation fills the soldier with confidence and hope.

OFFENSIVE WEAPONS

6. SWORD OF THE SPIRIT — THE WORD OF GOD.   It is not a soldier's business merely to parry the blows rained upon him by his enemy; he has also to fight back. For this purpose he was armed with the short two-edged sword (= machaira). The Christian soldier likewise was possessed of a powerful weapon, the Scriptures or Word of God. Like the sword of the cherubim who guarded the entrance into Paradise, this sword puts to naught the powers of sin and of error. Jesus himself, by his use of the Scriptures against the devil (Mt 4:4,7,10 etc.), proved how powerful a weapon the word of God is.

7. PRAYER (v 18).   To these arms of light there must be added another, the weapon par excellence of prayer (= proseuche). With this weapon the Christian warrior can strike anywhere and anytime, from close or from afar, with greater rapidity and precision than any offensive weapon yet devised. The Roman legions had the most advanced material weapons of their day, but the Apostles, armed only with the power of their prayers, conquered Rome itself. Paul recommends prayer in all its forms, whether adoration, petition, thanksgiving, vocal, or silent.

HINTS FOR HOMILETICS

1. An occasional sermon on the fallen angels, their power and sleeplessness, their malice toward mankind, will be very useful. A false sense of security on our part plays into their hands. Compared to these creatures man is hopelessly outclassed, intellectually and by nature. We must make humble use of the weapons God provides for us in this struggle.

2. For a spiritual war, spiritual weapons are required. And these are the ones we have: truth, justice, zeal, faith, hope, the Scriptures, and prayer. What shall we say of a soldier who does not use the weapons he has? Or of their leaders who never explain to them what their weapons are, or how they should be used?

3. In an age so impressed by the material advances of science as is our own, a sermon on faith is particularly to be recommended. The early Americans must have appreciated Paul's description of this shield, and perhaps have wished that their covered wagons were as fire-resistant to the flaming arrows of the Indians. Faith protects us from something much more dangerous than an attack on a wagon train.

XXII SUNDAY AFTER PENTECOST

Paul at Prayer

INTRODUCTION. Philippi was the first European city Paul had visited and he had founded the first European church there. How he happened to go westward at all is related in Acts 16:12–40. His affection for the Philippians was something special. When in Thessalonica (4:16) and at Corinth (2 Cor 11:9) he had received financial help from them, and when in Rome (4:18) he had been gladdened by the arrival of Epaphroditus bearing gifts from them. This emissary had, however, fallen ill in Rome and Paul writes to assure those who had sent him that Epaphroditus was recovering nicely. This epistle is the most relaxed, personal, joyful, and affectionate of Paul's writings. He refers to the state of his own health, warns about abuses, and finally, in a passage of singular beauty and tenderness, he thanks them for their sympathy and help in his time of need.

THE EPISTLE: PHILIPPIANS 1:6–11

6 *For of this I am convinced,*
that he who began a good work in you
will bring it to completion up to the day of Jesus Christ.

Their past generosity and faith make Paul confident (= pepoithos) that they will in the future continue in their faith and good works. They had shown their devotion to the Gospel by financial support of the work of preaching it, and also by their willingness to suffer for it (1:29f). God by his grace (2:13) began a good work (= the life of grace, the gift of justification) in them, and will surely carry it through. Thus unobtrusively Paul reminds his good readers that they can always increase in perfection and in the love of God until the day of Jesus Christ; if they do not grow spiritually more mature, they will inevitably become spiritual cretins. Paul keeps his gaze fixed steadily upon the Parousia (= the day of Jesus Christ). The work begun by Christ and propagated by Paul cannot die out until (eis = up to) the day of general judgment.

246

7   It is right for me to be so minded about you all,
       for I hold you in my heart
       both when I am in bonds
       and when defending and confirming the gospel,
       you who all shared with me in grace

Paul feels it only proper to express his sentiments in their regard. When he thinks of Philippi and its people he feels both gratitude and satisfaction, for they share with him in the grace of the apostolate, unimpressed like himself by the fact that their herald was sometimes in jail. Whether he was defending (= apologia) or establishing (= bebaiosei) the Gospel, they were quick to help in whatever way they could.

8   For God is my witness, how I yearn for you all
       in the heart of Christ Jesus.

Confirming his remarks with an oath, Paul calls upon God himself to bear witness to the purity and loftiness of his love for the Philippians (epipotho = a tender longing). His ardent love was primarily super-natural, and universal — he yearns for all of them, not just for a few chosen friends among them.

In the heart of Christ Jesus is a powerful metaphor descriptive of the perfect spiritual union Paul had in mind. The heart (= splanknois) refers to the nobler viscera, lungs, liver, and especially the heart, as all these react to all the emotions — love, anger, envy, jealousy. It is note-worthy that even Paul's love is associated with the Lord; he loves his friends in Christ Jesus, and desires nothing apart from him.

9   And this is my prayer,
       that your love may more and more abound
       in knowledge and discernment,

Knowledge (= epignosis) refers to a deep intellectual understanding of all revealed Christian truths, and along with it, discernment (= aisthesis) or insight. Man's love for God and neighbor goes hand in hand with his knowledge of God. By all means, then, let that knowledge be constantly augmented. Love gives insight into all things. The heart has reasons the head knows not of.

10 *So that you may approve the important things,*
    and that thus you may be innocent and without offense
    unto the day of Christ,

The text is difficult to translate; the Vulgate has *ut probetis potiora.* One must weigh (*ta diapheronta*) the things that make a difference, that really matter in and for their spiritual life. The church at Philippi was made up of young converts, with as yet no traditions; as a result, each day brought with it new problems concerning the application of the newly learned Christian principles to practical living. Paul prays that they may be given a sound judgment and right instinct (supernatural prudence), so that in all circumstances the primacy of the spiritual might be preserved.

Paul prays that they may be *innocent* and *without offense.* The word *innocent* (= *eilikrineis*) may derive from a Greek word which means "to sieve out" so as to leave only the pure substance; or from the words for "sun" and "to judge," which would suggest looking at something and judging it in the clear light of the sun. In this latter case it would mean that Paul wants the Philippians to be so genuinely Christian that they could stand up under even the scrutiny of God himself. *Without offense* (= *aproskopoi*) means "not to offend by bumping against or striking." Perhaps Paul intended to remind his readers, in a delicate way, that while it was good of them to have provided him with financial assistance and sympathy, it is nevertheless extremely important that they busy themselves in the apostolate of good example, in view of Judgment Day.

11 *Filled with that fruit of justice*
    which comes through Jesus Christ
    unto the glory and praise of God.

All the more reason why the Philippians should be innocent and blameless, because they have been filled (note the perfect tense) with the fruit of justice, i.e., with good works done while in the state of grace (cf Eph 2:10). Justice or righteousness, Paul's equivalent for our familiar "state of grace," is given to men as a gratuitous gift through Jesus Christ. In this last phrase (through Jesus Christ) one becomes increasingly aware of the absolute importance of Christ. If any man is filled with goodness, it is through Jesus, the Man-God, now risen from the dead and seated at the right hand of God. United to man by his sacred humanity, he now joins man to God, i.e., sanctifies him, through that humanity which is, and for all eternity shall ever be, the conjoined instrument of his divinity. He is lavish in his giving, yet man's co-operation is always required. Thus will the tree of justice bear fruits of justice through Jesus Christ; man's dependence upon the Savior is now and always absolute, from one moment to the next (2:13; 3:9).

To fill men with the fruit of justice is no small matter; so marvelous an action shall redound unto God's glory and, once men have perceived it, unto his praise. Why does God so act? Surely not because of any need on his part. From all eternity and before the creation of the world, he was absolutely and blissfully happy in himself. If he chose to operate outside of the Godhead by creating the world and sanctifying man, it is because he is intrinsically good in himself, and he intends only to communicate his goodness, his perfection. Whatsoever he does create, however, will redound to his extrinsic honor and glory. We are touching lightly here on a tremendous and profound mystery, one thanks to which we are all the richer. (Cf Sum. Theol., 1, q.44, a.4 and ad 1m, 4m; and Denz 1783: In order to manifest his perfection through the benefits which he bestows on creatures — not to intensify his happiness nor to acquire any perfection — this one and only true God, by his goodness and "almighty power" and by a completely free decision, "from the very beginning of time has created . . . [the universe].")

HINTS FOR HOMILETICS

1. Priests should be lavish in their praise of the generosity of the faithful. The countless works of charity and the apostolate depend upon that generosity. Yet the giving of money to a good cause is not enough — the Church needs the apostolate of good example. Lay apostles and saints in workshops, on buses, trains, planes, in stores, offices, and homes, are an essential part of the apostolate.

2. How can one grow in love, or in any of the virtues? By exercising those virtues to one's greatest capacity, by multiplying what the theologians call "more intense acts" of the virtue sought after. One cannot lift oneself by the bootstraps, but on the other hand, God will not give the increase unless there is the proper pre-disposition for the increase (Sum. Theol., 2–2, q.24, aa.1–4). Drifting is no good; one must make the effort.

3. Like the Philippians we must all try in our own little way to spread the love and peace of Christ throughout the world, and be ready to suffer bravely and perseveringly for the faith. The faith is strengthened, not by concentrating upon the difficulties it brings to mind and into a life, but by repeated and more intense acts of faith. One cannot do better than to make daily acts of faith, hope, and love, and, before bedtime, to say an act of contrition.

Citizens of Heaven

INTRODUCTION. All was not ideal at Philippi, despite Paul's glowing words of praise. He found it necessary to issue words of warning against false teachers (3:2ff). Then he launches forth on one of his most moving passages (3:7–16), the high light of which is his unforgettable "Forgetting what is behind, I strain forward. . . . I press on towards the goal. . . ." Paul has outdone himself again!

THE EPISTLE: PHILIPPIANS 3:17–4:3

17 *Brethren, join in following my example,*
   and mark well those who walk
   after the pattern you have in us.

Speaking to those who are mature of mind (vv 15,17), Paul almost gives the impression that he is an insufferably conceited individual, not hesitating to hold himself up as an example for them to follow (4:9; 1 Thes 1:6; 2 Thes 3:7–9; 1 Cor 4:16). If he does so, however, it is because he honestly feels that he is an imitator of Jesus Christ (1 Cor 11:1). And hardly has he spoken of himself as a model than he includes others in his class; the "us" probably refers to Timothy, Luke, and Silas (cf Acts 16:11–40). It is as if he said: take a saint for your model, and now that you have attained to a certain degree of the truth (16, cf 12ff) push vigorously onward, not alone, but in company with the "people of God."

18 *For there are many, of whom I have often spoken to you,*
   and now again I say it to you with tears,
   who live as enemies of the cross of Christ.

With his long life as a missionary behind him, Paul could speak from bitter experience of those who were enemies of the cross of Jesus. They had caused him much sorrow throughout his career, these men of pleasure who wanted to hear nothing about crucifying the flesh and its passions (Gal 5:24). He could have been thinking of the Philippians, but also

251

of the Romans (16:17), or Corinthians (1 Cor 5), or of those who denied not the historical fact of Jesus' crucifixion, but its efficacy and value. Apparently the evil has grown since Paul first spoke to the Philippians, for now again he brings the matter up.

19   *Their end is destruction, their God is the belly,*
       and their glory is in their shame,
       their minds are set on earthly things.

Final perdition (= *apoleia*) awaits enemies of the cross of Jesus when time is no more. They glory in things which other men rightfully consider shameful; like beasts they plod along with eyes fixed upon the ground, content to consider only what concerns a material existence. This description of a self-indulgent class of people hardly seems to apply to the Philippians.

20   *But our citizenship is even now in the heavens,*
       whence we eagerly await a savior, the Lord Jesus Christ

Citizenship (= *politeuma*; Vg: *conversatio!*). Paul pictures all Christians as colonials, living far from their fatherland and yet maintaining an organization fashioned upon that of the fatherland, and thus assuring themselves of such civic advantages as order, security, dignity, comfort, and strength. It is as if he had written "Our true homeland is in heaven; here on earth, where we have no lasting city (Heb 13:14), we are exiles from heaven."

Life away from home is sometimes barely tolerable. Paul depicts the eager longing (= *apekdechometha*) which should be theirs for the Savior's coming, for on that day all the infirmities and vexations of corruptible and mortal flesh shall be replaced forever by glory.

21   *Who will transform our lowly body*
       that it may be like his glorious body,
       according to the power whereby he is able
       to subject all things to himself.

One of the things — Paul does not say it will be the *only* thing — which Jesus shall do when he comes will be to change the *quality*, not the *quantity* of our lowly body. Wings, therefore, will not be added, but the body will share in the glory and blessedness of the soul. Even in this life our body is not a vile but a lowly thing. It may be a burden and a drag and be susceptible to all kinds of passion and to sufferings and indignities, but it is also destined to share in God's glory.

4:1 *Therefore, my brethren beloved and longed for,*
my joy and my crown, stand fast so, in the Lord, beloved.

Explosive character that he is, Paul can also be surprisingly gentle and human. Now he multiplies expressions of tenderness which betray his capacity for love. The Philippians must have been moved to hear themselves addressed as the Apostle's joy and crown, but he has won them, and sweet are his memories of success. He exhorts them to stand firmly and perseveringly (1 Thes 3:8) *in the Lord*, maintaining their intimate union with Christ in the mystical body.

2 *I entreat Evodia and I entreat Syntyche,*
to be of one mind in the Lord.

Even in the early days there were divisions of interests. Paul here addresses two ladies whose differences were reverberating throughout the church at Philippi. Diplomatically and with admirable impartiality (he uses the same verb for both — *entreat*) he urges them to bury the hatchet. Evodia and Syntyche are unknown in our literature outside of this passage and there is no way of determining the precise point of their quarrel. They were probably women of some means and rank who had helped Paul when he had visited Philippi.

3 *Yes and I ask you, loyal comrade, to assist these women,*
who have toiled along with me in the gospel,
together with Clement and the rest of my fellow-workers,
whose names are in the book of life.

Whether *suzuge* should be translated as a proper name, or as "loyal comrade, companion, or colleague," has never been definitely decided. Even in ancient times there was much speculation about the term and about the person to whom it referred; Barnabas, Luke, Silas, Timothy, Epaphroditus, and the Bishop of Philippi, have all been suggested. The term does not occur as a name in the papyri. Whoever this man was, Paul urged him to intervene and to help settle the difference between the two women.

It is generally held that *Clement* is not Clement of Rome. The name is a very common one, and the liturgy uses this passage for the lesson of the feast of St. Clement (November 23).

The names written in the *book of life* were those of Paul's fellow workers, and not just the warring women. The expression, *book of life*, appears in both testaments (Ex 32:32f; Ps 69 [68]:29; Is 4:3; Dn 12:1; Lk 10:20; cf *Sum. Theol.*, 1, q.24, aa.1–3), and traces back to the custom of entering the names of citizens or members of a family in a register. God has entered the name of his faithful followers in a book (that is, they are all known to him, for the book is the divine mind) and all these are called to eternal life. It is, however, possible (cf Ap 3:5) that names be erased from the book of life and inscribed, presumably, in a book of spiritual death. Paul cannot have meant to assure his readers of their eternal predestination in the sense that they could no longer sin.

HINTS FOR HOMILETICS

1. Everyone can understand and appreciate good example. Most efficacious when seen in priests and religious, it is best seen in the lives of good layfolk everywhere. It is said of Christ that he began first *to do*, and then to teach; the ordering of the two verbs is very instructive. Let parents and priests both take note.

2. With all the recurring talk about public spirit and civic-mindedness, it is good to reflect that there is such a thing as spiritual-mindedness. We are all called to be citizens of heaven, and are prepared for this by baptism and the other sacraments. By keeping before our eyes the goal toward which we are striving, we shall live with the dignity and tranquillity and responsibility of citizens of heaven.

3. Browning once wrote in *Andrea del Sarto*, "A man's reach should always exceed his grasp, else what's a heaven for." Paul also, and long before the poet, realized the necessity of having high ideals. The highest of all ideals is to imitate Christ (cf 3:13).

Intercession

INTRODUCTION. The city of Colossae, situated about a hundred miles east of Ephesus, once lay on the Lycus, a tributary of the Meander River. The church there, founded by Epaphras (1:7) while Paul was at Ephesus preaching the Gospel to all who cared to attend the school he conducted at Tyrannus' house, was probably the least important ever to receive a letter from Paul. Paul's letter was prompted by the troubles which beset the young church. He insists here as elsewhere that we have been redeemed and reconciled to God through Jesus Christ alone.

THE EPISTLE: COLOSSIANS 1:9–14

9 Therefore, from the day we heard of it,
    we also have not ceased to pray for you,
    asking that you be filled with the knowledge of his [God's] will
    in all wisdom and spiritual insight,

Paul was gratified to hear of the faith (4), hope (5), and charity (8) of the Colossians, and expresses his satisfaction and gratitude for them to the Father, Son, and Holy Spirit. He prays for these believers without ceasing, that is, virtually always. What he asks for in their behalf he tells them in a long sentence (9–20). First, he prays that they be filled with knowledge (= epignosis), a full understanding of the will of God. In Ephesians 1:5–12 God's will is seen to be centered about his plan for saving mankind; in Colossians, however, it concerns each man's duty. Wisdom and spiritual insight are gifts of the Holy Spirit; wisdom looks deeply into the divine mysteries and relates all things to God; spiritual insight and understanding help sort out the good from the bad, no matter what it is. (A missionary, once condemned to solitary confinement, preserved his sanity by saying countless Rosaries, and thus came to appreciate the mysteries of the faith as never before.)

The idea of "fullness" has now been broached. It will appear throughout the remainder of the Epistle, especially in 2:9f.

10   to lead a life worthy of the Lord,
      pleasing [him] in all respects,
      bearing fruit in every good work
      and growing in the knowledge of God,

In view of the supernatural aids given to them by God, Paul feels
that the Colossians should, normally, lead lives quite different from those
of the pagans. He spells out a few of the differences.

They are to walk (= live) in such a manner that in all things they
may please God (= eis pasan areskian). Areskia means human conduct
by which one gains another's favor; not obsequiousness, but a zealous
desire to please God.

1. *Good works* are the fruits of a good life. Just as fruit sustains physical life in us, the fruits of good works nourish us in the spiritual order.
A Christian without good works is as unhealthy as a life led without
fruit. Spiritual knowledge should lead to good works, and in some mysterious way these contribute to a greater comprehension of the ways
of God.

11   strengthened with all power
      through the might of his glory,
      unto all patience and longsuffering;

2. *Spiritual strength,* limited only by the power of God himself, will
enable them to face life's trials and persecutions with *patience* (=
hupomone) and *longsuffering* (= makrothumia). God is particularly
triumphant in those who uncomplainingly endure trials which cannot be
averted, and who without rancor endure wrongs or insults which by
their very nature incline a man to revenge. Constancy and endurance
show the depth of a man's love for God.

12   [with joy] rendering thanks to the Father,
      who has fitted us for our portion
      of the inheritance of the saints in light;

3. A distinguishing mark of a Christian is his joyful thanksgiving for
salvation through Christ (note once again Paul switches from *you* to *us*).
Paul seems to have been outstanding in this, never giving way to self-pity
or fits of depression. Perhaps this was because he saw so clearly the
reasons why a Christian should be humbly grateful:

a) The heavenly Father has made us capable (*hikanosas* = to render a man qualified) of sharing for our own portion (= *meris*) the heritage or lot (= *kleros*) of the saints. The lot of the blessed is nothing short of God himself. In possessing the very source of all supernatural blessings, the saints on earth and in heaven live with God in light. God is light and in him there is no darkness (1 Jn 1:5); those who share in him are consequently bathed in his light. Paul must surely have gone back in memory, as he spoke of being bathed in light, to his own dramatic conversion while on the road to Damascus (Acts 9:13).

13 *He has delivered us from the power of darkness,*
** *and has transferred us to the kingdom of his beloved son,***

b) We who were once enslaved to the powers of darkness have been rescued (delivered) from the arbitrary tyranny (= *exousia*) of the devil (cf 2 Cor 4:4) and transferred into the well-ordered kingdom of God's well-beloved Son, the Church. Through baptism Jesus has broken the ties that held us far from God.

14 *in whom we have redemption,*
** *the forgiveness of our sins.***

c) We can thank the Most High God for redeeming us. Redemption (= *apolutrosis*) formerly meant the release of a slave on payment of a certain sum; Christ's redeeming of mankind meant man's being forgiven for his sins. The price of this deliverance was the blood of Christ. The word *redemption* contains many important ideas, such as the fact that a sinner is really a slave to his sins (and so, free to God) and of himself helpless. It implies also that Jesus gave himself for sinners, died a sacrificial and expiatory death on the cross, and through the infinite value of his sacrifice (cf Eph 1:7) obtained for us all freedom from the past and all its guilt.

HINTS FOR HOMILETICS

1. St. Leo the Great urged Christians to realize their dignity (cf P.L. 54:192f) as brothers of Christ and sons of God. Our knowledge of these luminous truths can always grow. What we learn in our youth is good, but not perfect; one should grow in the faith, for a man's best thoughts

on such weighty matters are not, ordinarily, those of his youth.

2. Thanksgiving Day is not far distant from this Sunday. We should not wait for that one day to thank God. We all too easily overlook the wonderful things God has done for us, or take them for granted as if to say: "Yes, you have been kind, but what have you done for me recently?"

3. An analysis of the cardinal virtue of fortitude (or courage) shows that patience is one of its chief characteristics. Patience may not be the greatest of virtues, but it proves them all to be genuine virtues! In other words, an instinctive reaction of patience in a trying situation is not necessarily a virtuous reaction; constancy under trial is, however (cf Sum. Theol., 2–2, q.136).

Appendix I

THE LIFE OF ST. PAUL

Paul was born in Tarsus, in the province of Cilicia directly north of the eastern tip of the island of Cyprus. A date between A.D. 5–10 is commonly assigned for his birth. He was of Hebrew parentage and of the tribe of Benjamin; his parents were Roman citizens. Named Saul-Paul, he later dropped the honorable name of Saul, which in Hebrew means "Desired One," possibly because the Greek connotations of the name "Saul" suggested one who was staggering (from too much drink?). Tarsus was a famous university city, a rival of Athens and Alexandria in its zeal for knowledge. Quick and intelligent, Paul learned both Aramaic and Greek. His Greek was not that of Homer or Demosthenes, but the more common variety spoken by the merchants and men of the market place; it was called the Koiné, or common Greek. It was very flexible, even colorful, and Paul felt perfectly at home in it, so much so in fact, that at times he coined new words in it, in his attempt to express with greater accuracy what he wanted to say about Christianity.

Between the ages of 13 to 16, Paul studied the Law and the Prophets, along with the current interpretations of the sacred writings. This was normal for Jewish lads of that age. When about 18 or 20 years old, he studied in Jerusalem at the feet of the famous Rabbi Gamaliel, and there learned that he should not seek to grow rich by dispensing the treasures of the Law, but should learn a trade, so as to be able to support himself while so doing. Paul learned how to make tents, and thus was never a burden upon those to whom he preached.

As a young Pharisee Paul became an active persecutor of the Christians. His dramatic conversion on the road to Damascus marked the turning point in his life (ca A.D. 34–37). In the Acts, three accounts of this conversion appear, the last two being those of Paul himself (cf 9:3–18; 22:6–16; and 26:12–18).

After his conversion Paul spent some time in the desert before returning to Damascus, where he proceeded to preach in the synagogues. He then spent fifteen days in Jerusalem with Peter, James, and Barnabas

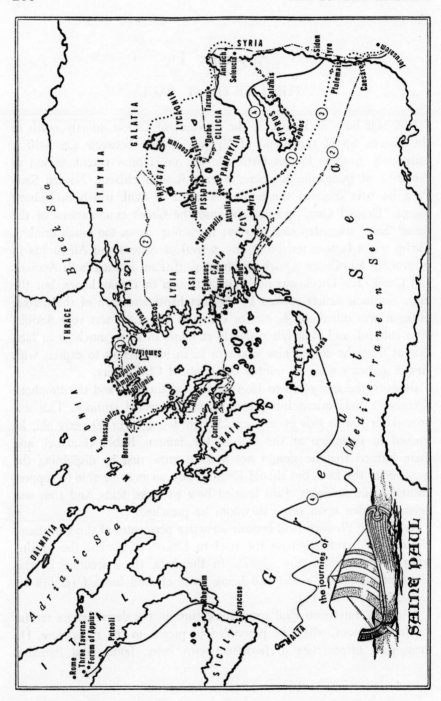

(Gal 1:18f), and then returned to Tarsus, where he remained quietly until Barnabas came to fetch him to Antioch. After a year (43–44) in that city, he was ready to begin the first of his missionary journeys for the cause of Christ.

It is deserving of note that it took some time for Paul to fit into the new order of things; the Lord was apparently in no hurry to use him. Between his conversion and his first missionary journey, not less than eight years elapsed — a long novitiate. But from then on for almost a quarter of a century, he was a man wholly and energetically devoted to the preaching of the Gospel.

The story of the famous Apostle of the Gentiles is recorded in the Acts; other details can be gleaned from passing remarks he makes in his letters. The first missionary journey lasted from A.D. 45–49, and was undertaken with Barnabas and Mark as companions. No letters were written during this voyage. After the Council of Jerusalem (49), Paul set out on a second journey, with Silas for a companion. He had originally planned to go with Barnabas, but when that Apostle had suggested taking Mark along again, Paul had simply put his foot down, recalling to Barnabas how Mark had deserted them on the first trip. Tempers flared and in the end Barnabas refused to accompany Paul! (The quarrel was in time patched up, and Paul will later refer affectionately to Mark.) Luke joined Paul and Silas at Troas, as the sudden switch from "they" to "we" seems to indicate (cf 16:11). The trip lasted from 49–53 and is recorded in Acts 15:36–18:22. The two letters to the Thessalonians were written in this period, probably from Corinth around A.D. 51.

During the third journey (54–58; cf Acts 18:23–21:16), Ephesus became, for two years, Paul's headquarters. But he was eventually forced to flee that city, and did so in company with Sopater, Aristarchus, Secundus, Gaius and Timothy, Tychicus and Trophimus (20:4). Several very important letters date to this period. Philippians (? 56), 1 Corinthians, Galatians, 2 Corinthians (57), and Romans (58).

Paul was arrested in Jerusalem shortly after his arrival there for the feast of Pentecost, A.D. 58. The next two years he spent in a prison at Caesarea, where the governor Antonius Felix resided. This captivity was followed by another in Rome (61–63), during which time the letters to the Colossians, Ephesians, and Philemon were composed. Paul was then released. Unfortunately our sources of information concerning his activities thereafter are practically nonexistent. It seems that he may then have realized his lifelong ambition to visit far-off Spain; he also revisited Ephesus. He was arrested again, and after having written 1 Timothy, Titus, Hebrews, and 2 Timothy, was put to death ca A.D. 65–67. His death took place at what is now called Tre Fontane (= Three Fountains) outside the walls of Rome and not far from where he was buried.

Appendix II

THE LETTERS

From the more than 14,000 letters which have come down to us from ancient times it is possible to reconstruct with accuracy the letter pattern then widely used. Letters began with an address (= praescriptio): Cicero (= the writer identifies himself at once), Attico (= the person to whom the message is sent), salutem (= salutations, e.g., Health!). As there was no need to sign such a letter, it terminated often with the Greek word Erroso (= roughly, farewell, good-by), or, if in Latin, with Vale or Salve.

Up to a certain point, St. Paul followed the ancient style. But he was a man of vigorous personality, and his letters bear the stamp of his strong temperament. With one exception (= Hebrews) his letters usually begin thus: Paul, Apostle (or Servant) of Jesus Christ, to the church (or to the saints) who are at, e.g., Corinth, grace and peace be to you in Christ Jesus.

Following this beginning, Paul would thank God (except in Galatians, an angry letter) for the faith of his correspondents. Next would come the body of the letter, invariably composed of a dogmatic and a moral section. Then he would discuss such personal matters as, e.g., his plans, and always closed his letters with prayers and blessings.

That Paul employed the skills of others in the actual writing of his letters is perfectly clear. At the end of Romans the scribe, Tertius, joins his greetings to those of Paul. At the conclusion of 2 Thes Paul signs his letter in his own hand, making quite a point of doing so. The epistle to the Hebrews, so different in style and treatment from the other thirteen letters, may have been done by a scribe who developed in it some of Paul's favorite ideas.

It is difficult for us to appreciate the difficulties involved in the writing of the simplest letter, two thousand years ago. Writing materials were rather difficult to procure, or at least rather expensive, and those who could write must have been few indeed. Papyrus or parchment served as paper, and the best papyrus would not have been nearly as smooth as our paper. On this material it was impossible to write very rapidly. Modern scholars have taken the pains to reconstruct the whole process of such ancient writing. They have made papyrus, and reed pens, and ink, and have timed their efforts to write. For their pains they have been rewarded with the knowledge that a good scribe could average about three syllables per minute, which would mean about 72 words per hour. The average sheet of papyrus was about the size of a sheet of typewriting paper, and on the average contained about 150 words. Thus Paul's letter to the Romans, which is about 7100 words long, would have required some 50 sheets of papyrus, and about 98 hours of work! As Paul used the daylight hours working at his trade, he must have had to dictate (or write) his letters at night, after work. Two hours per night would mean that Romans took 49 days to write; three hours per night, 32 days! A man of Paul's natural vehemence must have found the slow pace of dictation extremely trying. His customary greeting, *Paulos doulos tou Jesou Christou*, would take Tertius nine minutes to write. Small wonder that Paul's sentences grew more and more complicated. In the introductory section of Romans, verses 2–6 are a parenthesis. In Ephesians 3, a vivid parenthesis develops between verses 1 and 14.

STYLE

Paul is admittedly difficult to read. He was the first to adapt the language of pagan Greece to the service of the profound truths proposed by Christianity. He was a subtle genius, skilled in rabbinical modes of arguing; his powerful mind moved easily in the realm of the abstract. Unlike many prophets, indeed unlike his Master, he was quite deaf to the voice of nature; his writings are quite lacking in charming references to the lilies of the field or birds of the air.

Paul was first and always a city man, and his figures of speech were drawn from such human activities as the games, boxing, soldiery. His images are those of the stadium, of the army, even of the theater, of human anatomy, of psychology. But even such images and references are startling precisely because they seem so much in contrast with what is his usual manner of writing.

As a speaker, Paul must have been dramatic, dynamic. The people of

Lystra (Acts 14:11) were so moved by his natural eloquence that they took him to be Mercury, and were only restrained by his violent reaction from offering sacrifice to him. His letters retain some of his power to stir the blood, as St. John Chrysostom remarks. Few can read such passages as Romans 8:35–39, for example, without being deeply moved.

However, no man has everything. For all the visions and revelations that were lavished upon him, for all his gifts of intellect and of energy, Paul was not endowed with the gift of clear expression. One cannot help wondering at times how much of his letters the first recipients really understood. One may suppose that they understood him better than ourselves, as most of them had heard him speak, and he was not, it would seem, given to brevity. They were therefore more familiar with his ideas, personality, and his pattern than we are; also, they knew the problems which they submitted to him for solution (cf 1 Cor). His long stay in Ephesus and his custom of revisiting his churches when possible must have helped considerably to clarify their ideas and his. Undoubtedly there must have been those who visited him by day and by night; while others found it more profitable to ask Timothy or Luke, his companions, what he was driving at.

All due concessions made, Paul remains difficult to read. It is difficult to reconstruct a man's outlook on life from a few stray letters of his which have somehow survived the corrosion of time. These letters cannot be looked upon as a complete presentation of Christian doctrine, nor of all of Paul's doctrine. They constitute a complementary source of Christian doctrine, but they are themselves echoes of that teaching. Then too Paul did not begin to write until two years after the resurrection, by which time the Church had already formulated her teachings, the primitive catechesis or kerygma.

THE PAULINE LETTERS

1. and 2.   *1 and 2 THESSALONIANS:*

Written *ca* 51 from Corinth. Paul's Thessalonian converts had become worried about the *Parousia*, or Second Coming of Christ, and Paul wrote to instruct them. Especially note 2 Thessalonians 2:1–11 for his teaching on Antichrist and the signs that will precede the last days.

3. PHILIPPIANS:

Written ca 56 (?), from Macedonia. The first European Church was that of Philippi (cf Acts 16:11–40), and it was very dear to Paul. Upon hearing that he was in prison, the Philippians had sent Epaphroditus to him with money and instructions to stay with Paul as a companion and servant. He tells them in this Epistle about his life in prison. They must imitate Christ in a spirit of self-abnegation. Bishops and deacons are mentioned for the first time in this letter.

4. 1 CORINTHIANS:

Written ca 57 from Ephesus. Party factions had raised their ugly head in Corinth, and the Christian community was troubled by Jewish intrigues and various disorders. In this letter Paul answers questions on marriage, paganism, idolatry, women and their emancipation (it does not extend to unveiled heads in church), the Agape, the Holy Eucharist, the charismata of the early Church, and especially, love.

5. GALATIANS:

Written ca 57 from Ephesus. Galatians is, after 2 Corinthians, the most personal and self-revealing of Paul's letters. Judaizing elements had disturbed Paul's beloved Galatians, and, impugning his authority, were urging a return to the Old Law. In his letter Paul pays homage to the Old Law while maintaining that it was but our "pedagogue in Christ." Justification comes through Christ, not through the Old Law. The other Apostles fully approved Paul's position as is indicated here (1–2), and in Acts 15.

6. 2 CORINTHIANS:

Written ca 57 from Macedonia. Paul has to defend himself against the charge of inconstancy (failure to make a promised visit). The most personal of all his writing, it contains his spirited defense of his apostolate 3–6. It is the most impassioned section of the New Testament.

7. ROMANS:

Written ca 57–58 from Corinth. Paul had never been to Rome but foresaw its future greatness for the Church of Christ. There being no particular abuses to correct there, and because this was not a church of his own founding, he penned this doctrinal digest of his teaching. He develops the theme that Christianity is the only way of salvation, for the Mosaic Law is powerless either to sanctify or to save, an elaboration of the theme of Galatians. Romans is the mightiest of his Epistles, and one of the longest.

THE CAPTIVITY WRITINGS

The following letters were written while Paul was a captive in Rome 61–63 (cf Acts 28:30–31). On reading them one gains the impression that he was not terribly worried about the outcome of his trial. He was, it seems, released some time after writing these letters.

8. *COLOSSIANS:*

Written ca 63 in Rome. The Colossians seemed inclined to speculation concerning the angels and semi-Gnostic theories; judaizers were also at work among them. Paul's theme is the *pre-eminence of Christ* as the head of the Church; we approach him directly and not through the angels. "Go straight to Christ" is the motto of the Christian.

9. *EPHESIANS:*

Written ca 63, in Rome, Ephesians may have originally been a circular letter. There is a great similarity between this Epistle and Colossians, except that here it is Christ's *Mystical Body, the Church,* which is the theme. The moral section reminds Christians of their unity in Christ. By reason of their unity in Christ, husband and wife are to practice mutual love and submission, and in like manner children and parents, masters and slaves.

10. *PHILEMON:*

Written ca 63 from Rome concerning a runaway slave, Onesimus. Paul, a prisoner himself, entreats Philemon by the charity of Christ to deal kindly with Onesimus, who is returning to him.

THE PASTORAL EPISTLES

11. *1 TIMOTHY:*

Written after his release from the Roman imprisonment, from Macedonia, ca 65. It is possible that Paul then went to Spain, and from there to Crete, where he left Titus, then to Jerusalem, then to Asia Minor (cf 1 Tim 1:3; 2 Tim 4:13–30; Ti 3:12). Paul tells Timothy that his duty as bishop in Ephesus is to speak out against false teachers (syncretism, Gnosticism, Judaism), and to be faithful to his vocation. Timothy is mentioned in all of St. Paul's Epistles except Galatians and Ephesians (cf Phil 2:20ff).

12. *TITUS:*

Written ca 65. Still in Macedonia, Paul urges Titus to put order in the church in Crete and to ordain only worthy ministers.

13. *2 TIMOTHY:*

From the Epistle we gather that Paul is again in Rome and in prison (4:6–18); the date is about 67. He warns Timothy against a relapse, urging him to follow his own example and to be faithful to his pastoral charge. In a personal and touching way Paul speaks of approaching death, writes of his loneliness, and beseeches Timothy to hasten to him.

14. *HEBREWS:*

Written ca 67 from Rome to the brethren in Palestine who suffer persecution and are thus in danger of falling back into Judaism. There were some doubts concerning this Epistle until the fourth century, but never such doubts as to outweigh the constant tradition that Paul was its author. Possibly he may have employed Apollos or Luke to write it. Theme: superiority of New Dispensation over the Old, for (1) Christ is superior to the angels through whose mediation God gave the Old Law; (2) he is superior to Moses; (3) he is superior by reason of his priesthood; (4) he established a superior sacrifice. The Christians are urged to persevere in faith, to constancy, peace, and holiness, to brotherly love and to purity, to loyalty to Christ and to superiors.

Appendix III

THE SUNDAY EPISTLES

ROMANS

6:3–11	6 Pentecost
6:19–23	7 Pentecost
8:12–17	8 Pentecost
8:18–23	4 Pentecost
11:33–36	Trinity
12:6–16	2 Epiphany
12:16–21	3 Epiphany
13:8–10	4 Epiphany
12:11–14	1 Advent
15:4–13	2 Advent

GALATIANS

3:16–22	13 Pentecost
4:1–7	Christmas Sunday
5:16–24	14 Pentecost
5:25–6:10	15 Pentecost
4:22–31	4 Lent

EPHESIANS

3:13–21	16 Pentecost
4:1–6	17 Pentecost
4:23–28	19 Pentecost
5:1–9	3 Lent
5:15–21	20 Pentecost
6:10–17	21 Pentecost

TITUS

2:11–15	Christmas, 1.
3:4–8	Christmas, 2.

I CORINTHIANS

1:4–8	18 Pentecost
4:1–5	4 Advent
5:7–8	Easter
9:24–10:5	Septuagesima
10:6–13:9	Pentecost
12:2–11	10 Pentecost
13:1–13	Quinquagesima
15:1–10	11 Pentecost

II CORINTHIANS

3:4–9	12 Pentecost
6:1–10	1 Lent
11:19–12:9	Sexagesima

PHILIPPIANS

1:6–11	22 Pentecost
2:5–11	Palm Sunday
3:17–4:3	23 Pentecost
4:4–7	3 Advent

HEBREWS

1:1–12	Christmas, 3.
9:11–15	Passion

I JOHN

5:4–10	Low Sunday
3:13–18	Corpus Christi

COLOSSIANS

1:9–14	24 Pentecost
3:12–17	5 Epiphany

I PETER

2:11–19	3 Easter
2:21–25	2 Easter
3:8–15	5 Pentecost
4:7–11	Ascension Sunday
5:6–11	3 Pentecost

I THESSALONIANS

1:2–10	6 Epiphany
4:1–8	2 Lent

JAMES

1:17–21	4 Easter
1:22–27	5 Easter

ACTS

2:1–11	Pentecost

Index

271